weird dance

weird dance

 *Curious and Bizarre Dancing Trivia*

TIM RAYBORN & ABIGAIL KEYES

Skyhorse Publishing

Skyhorse Publishing books may be purchased in bulk at special discounts for sales promotion, corporate gifts, fund-raising, or educational purposes. Special editions can also be created to specifications. For details, contact the Special Sales Department, Skyhorse Publishing, 307 West 36th Street, 11th Floor, New York, NY 10018 or info@skyhorsepublishing.com.

Skyhorse® and Skyhorse Publishing® are registered trademarks of Skyhorse Publishing, Inc.®, a Delaware corporation.

Visit our website at www.skyhorsepublishing.com.

10 9 8 7 6 5 4 3 2 1

Library of Congress Cataloging-in-Publication Data is available on file.

Cover design by Rain Saukas

Print ISBN: 978-1-5107-3104-2
Ebook ISBN: 978-1-5107-3105-9

Printed in the United States of America

contents

intermission / 125

act II
A Dark and Weird Dance Miscellany

introduction

The Grim and the Unusual in the History of Western Dance

dance like nobody's watching . . . except that when no one is watching, some pretty terrible things can happen. Honestly, even when people *are* watching, awfulness can ensue. And the more awful, the more we are entertained. Everyone loves to hear about a shocking story, a lurid account of misfortune, betrayal, murder, and/or scandal. And as this book reveals, quite a few of these kinds of stories can be found in the world of dance.

We're all familiar with some kinds of dancing. Almost everyone has danced, or tried to dance, at some point in their lives. Some are very good at it; some would be better off taking up another hobby. Some love it, others are too self-conscious to give it much of a go, especially in front of others (back to that "nobody's watching" thing again). Dance has long been a controversial form of artistic expression, both condoned and condemned (sometimes simultaneously) at various points in history. The very act of dancing is liberating to some and threatening to others. Moralists throughout time have decried movement to music, expressing horror that this might lead to other more forbidden—and even more enjoyable—pleasures. That there is an inherently sexual aspect to many dances is beyond doubt, which has led to countless efforts to control or ban them altogether, almost always without success. One might think that would-be censors would have learned after all this time and given up, but no, each new generation seems to bring with it a new crop of folks eager to define art in their own narrow terms. Happily, each new generation of artists has a tendency to resist being told what to do and flips off said establishment. Artists are kind of scrappy that way, and that's a good thing.

Despite such objections from the narrow-minded, dancing has always been popular with both participants and those who prefer not to indulge (or maybe not to embarrass themselves), but would rather watch. Much of the "artistic" dance of the last several centuries falls into this latter category, with genres such as ballet, modern, and jazz being performed by highly trained specialists for the entertainment of spectators, much like symphony orchestras and plays. Many also enjoy learning these styles for their own betterment, and that's a wonderful thing. However, with that wonder comes a huge array of the odd, the unexpected, the dangerous, and the flat-out horrific.

In this book we will explore the strange, the unusual, the disturbing, and the appalling in Western dance, from the view of both dancers and those who watch them. This art form, which can be so compelling and beautiful, has a surprising number of shocking stories behind the scenes. Part I is a caper through history, looking at everything from prehistoric possibilities to Egyptian dwarfs, from Greco-Roman Bacchanals to the very conflicted medieval period. We see dance come into its own in Renaissance royal courts and witness the birth of ballet during the reign of the Sun King in the seventeenth-century. Other forms of dance (such as the scandalous waltz) caused a lot of controversy during the nineteenth century, and the twentieth century witnessed revolutions in style and form that changed the way we think about dancing.

Part II is a delightfully deranged miscellany of dance stories and snippets. We look at the bizarre (and still unexplained) dancing plagues that flared up periodically in the Middle Ages and Renaissance, the use of dance as a medical treatment, and the ominous Dance of Death that haunted the minds of people during the later medieval period. From there, the book peers into the awful and bloody world of ballet to show the grim behind the grace, peruses the pages of some long-winded (and frequently unintentionally funny) anti-dance books, and examines the buffet of superstitions that dancers indulge in to ensure stellar performances and other favorable outcomes. We'll see that dancing in folklore takes a deadly turn, and speaking of deadly, what would a book like this be without some good ghost stories? A few random oddities and the whole Salome craze complete the picture and leave the reader with an altered (and maybe warped) view of this fascinating art.

The names of many of this cast of characters might be unfamiliar to you. You've probably heard of the infamous Mata Hari (and what a story she had!), but beyond that, you may be dancing in the dark. You've undoubtedly seen *The Nutcracker*, but are you aware of its more sinister origins? You loved the story of Snow White as a child, but in the original, dancing played a decidedly deadly and awful role in the story's finale.

Herein you will meet Will Kempe, the famous clown in Shakespeare's acting company, who once Morris-danced all the way from London to Norwich (over one hundred miles) in only nine days, undoubtedly on sore feet. A few decades later, in seventeenth-century Spain, there were dance-offs to settle disputes. Now there's a new TV reality show idea! Speaking of reality shows, modern dancer Isadora Duncan's whole life was one eccentric performance and tragedy after another, right up to her horrible and rather ridiculous death. Then there is poor Emma Livry, a promising young nineteenth-century ballerina whose career went up in smoke, literally. And if you've had the misfortune to be bitten by a venomous spider in old-world Italy, the only way to save yourself is to engage in a frenzied dance to work the toxin out of your system; musicians are standing by to help.

This book presents you with a waltz of the weird, a galliard of the gruesome, a pas de bourrée of the peculiar. Here are tales of dancers, choreographers, audiences, and patrons, ballets, dancing styles and schools, controversies, fights, riots, deaths, and much more, from the frightening to the funny, from the awful to the amazing. You don't need to have a background in dance or dance history to delve in to these accounts, just pick a topic anywhere and immerse yourself for a few minutes or an hour in this strange and unsettling world.

Dancing is an activity that can be enjoyed by all, whether for personal pleasure when partaking, or in thrilling to the astonishing skills of the world's top performers. Perhaps even more so than classical music, ballet and its sisters are dismissed as snooty preserves of a small elite; pretentious entertainments that are not relevant to anyone else. This is unfortunate and simply not true; even if you just prefer free-dancing at a nightclub, you can have much enjoyment from learning about the larger world of dance in all of its fascinating forms.

Whether you've seen dozens of ballets or none, whether you've enjoyed the waltz or the watusi, there is something here to pique your interest, probably tickle your fancy, maybe gross you out, or simply entertain you. You'll soon see that when it comes to dance, the dark and the darkly funny sit side-by-side very well, indeed. Constanze Mozart (wife of a certain famous composer) allegedly once said that "dancing is like dreaming with your feet," but sometimes those dreams can become nightmares. So have a seat, serve up a refreshment of your choice, and enjoy!

weird dance

act I

The Strange Lives and Odd Fates of Dancers,
Companies, Choreographers, and More

1

Ancient and Primal Dancing

dance is found in almost every culture, everywhere in the world that there are human beings. Like music, it seems that there are no groups of people on earth—probably past or present—who don't have some kind of dance, whether for religious or entertainment reasons, or for both. But if that's the case, how long have we actually been dancing? That's a tricky question, and there are no definitive answers, but there are some intriguing clues. This chapter will look at a few of those tantalizing hints from our deep history, and then move on to some examples of dance among the great civilizations of the ancient world.

Did pre-humans start dancing almost as soon as they started walking? Did complex body movements help the Neanderthals survive the Ice Age? What are those human-animal hybrids on cave walls doing, and why are there some stick figures with enormous phalluses prancing about (other than to parade the fact that they have said enormous phalluses, of course)? Even more importantly, why were dwarf dancers necessary in ancient Egypt to send the soul of the deceased on its way? Let's two-step way back to distant times to answer some of the questions you never knew you had . . .

SINGING AND DANCING PRE-HUMANS
⟋ *Just how long have we been booty-shaking?* ⟋

We tend to think of dance as an exclusively human activity; we don't see gorillas waltzing in the mist or komodo dragons twerking in the tropics, and that's probably just as well. Of course, birds and other species do what scientists call "mating dances," using rhythmic movements to attract mates, a practice that's probably not all that far-removed from what young people do at nightclubs every weekend.

But where might the desire to move in rhythm actually have come from? Looking back into our distant history gives some intriguing, if unprovable, clues. Our very ability and desire to dance may well be tied to our ability to stand up straight, and that seemingly simple task didn't just happen overnight. There are various theories about why we do it, rather than lumbering about on our knuckles like our ape cousins. Some have suggested that it might have occurred as ape-like creatures moved from forests to savannahs, to afford them the ability to see over tall grass (and so spot the hungry predators), but this idea is countered by the fact that Australopithecines (such as the famous "Lucy") still lived among the trees and were already partially bipedal.

Another more interesting theory suggests that bipedalism came about in two different stages. The first was with Lucy and her kin, who may have stood up because of . . . fruit? Well, the need to pick fruit, really. Using both hands was a time and energy saving exercise: two hands could carry more goodies, and not having to go back down on all fours reduced the amount of energy needed to get from tree to tree.

When later descendants did move into the rapidly advancing savannahs, their inclination to bipedalism became permanent. This second stage may have happened because remaining upright on two legs reduced the heat that hit their bodies; the hot African sun would shine mainly on their heads and shoulders, but not on their backs and butts. Also, standing up allowed any cooling breezes to hit them more directly, so upright it was. This also affected the shape of the vocal cords, which would one day lead to language, singing, jokes, and political speeches . . . maybe we should have quit while we were ahead.

In any case, with this major development, the rest of the body could—over a very long time of developing—be used more expressively. Over the millennia, these hominids' legs and feet grew stronger, allowing for jumping, running, and generally using their legs for many other things beyond just getting them from one place to another. They may not have been dancing a savannah ballet, but their anatomy was more and more ready for it!

So what might have prompted rhythmic movements? Well, mating, of course. But it's also possible that moving in specialized ways formed a kind of early non-spoken language. Humans dance to express emotions and meaning through movement, so maybe said ancestors slowly developed gestures and steps to indicate things such as "yes" and "no," or to express anger or approval, and perhaps to warn of danger. This body sign language, possibly combined with vocal sounds, grunts, and humming, would have been primitive but effective, an important step on the road to full-blown language, music, and dance.

Dancing around the world is so often communal, and some suggest that this may have come from these very types of activities, which would have increased group bonding, helping to protect a given band of hominids or early humans from the endless dangers of their wild world. Sexual selection and mating rituals can't be ruled out, of course, and seem almost obvious; the male willing to make a fool of himself on the dance floor in order to impress a potential mate is a joke as old as humanity, and was probably just as funny a million and a half years ago.

By the time of the Neanderthals, the Ice Age was in full swing over the northern regions of the planet. This harsh environment would have been deadly to the weak and unprotected, but we know that these hardy cousins of modern humans thrived in it for tens of thousands of years. For such groups, cooperation and bonding were completely essential for survival. Communications through movement and sound would have been an ideal way of forming that bond, expressing emotions, warning of dangers, telling of possible food sources, and whatever else they might need. Even activities like making tools and butchering carcasses might have used stylized movement and specific vocalizations; work songs and dances are very typical in many cultures and may have very ancient origins. Some researchers believe that Neanderthals had quite a sophisticated set of sounds and movements to communicate their needs. So, song and dance may have helped them survive for millennia.

But what about for entertainment? Did these people dance and sing for fun? Some specialists think so. In looking at a number of the caves known to be inhabited by Neanderthals, an interesting pattern emerges: when there are a series of caverns, the materials of their daily lives that remain are usually only found in one area, as if the other places were kept deliberately clean. These may have been sleeping rooms, or the Neanderthal groups may have been small and not needed to spread out. But Steven Mithen (author of the splendidly titled *The Singing Neanderthals*) suggests that these areas may have been set aside for some kinds of primitive performance. They "could have been gesturing, miming, singing or dancing, while other individuals squatted by the cave walls engaged in their tool-making or other activities." Interestingly, the walls in these caves are completely bare, with no signs of art, unlike those of their Cro-Magnon cousins (we'll look at them next). This may have been a skill they simply did not possess, or a concept (painting) that their minds couldn't yet grasp. However, recent discoveries have suggested that Neanderthals may well have also painted on cave walls, with scientific dating on calcium carbonate covering some art in Spanish caves showing it to be over sixty thousand years old. In any case, Mithen offers that the rocky chambers he refers to may have held a similar significance for Neanderthals that their painted counterparts had for early modern humans, but one that was expressed in sound and movement, rather than visual art. If so, what went on in there, presumably by firelight? Singing and dancing? Simple percussion by handclaps or hitting rocks or bones? We may never know.

All of this is speculation, of course, but it seems reasonable to suggest that our very deep ancestors were using music and movement to communicate a whole range of feelings and other information before they could even speak, and that those movements helped to keep them alive in a very harsh world.

RITUAL DANCES IN PREHISTORIC CAVE PAINTINGS?
᧞ *Rock around the clock* ᧞

The famed cave paintings of the Neolithic age have captured the imagination of art historians and aficionados, as well as the general public. These amazing works of literal underground art, dating from tens of thousands of years ago, dot the landscape of France, Spain, and many other countries, both in Europe and beyond. Visible only by fire or artificial light, they depict a staggering number of activities and scenes, particularly those associated with animals and hunting. It's natural to assume that many of these are ritualistic in some form, but there is also the old joke that naming unknown activities from the distant past as "rituals" is a convenient way of saying "we don't know," while sounding very authoritative while saying it.

Still, it seems probable that some of the paintings include scenes of religious or cultic significance, and many scholars assume that hunting and dancing were sometimes interwoven with these. One of the more interesting examples is found in the Magura Cave in northwest Bulgaria. As galleries of cave paintings go, it's a relative newcomer, being at most maybe ten thousand years old. As you can see from the illustration in this book, one drawing seems to depict a hunter and animals on the bottom row, while the upper row may show women (?) in dress-like clothing, dancing and being approached by extremely (ridiculously, in fact) well-endowed males, who undoubtedly want to join in the fun. Is this a picture of some kind of fertility dance? It's possible. If so, it's significant that it was thought to be important enough to immortalize on a cave wall. Or maybe it's just prehistoric porn.

Less certain, but equally compelling, are the images from the famed Cave of the Trois-Frères in southwestern France, not far from the border with Spain. Discovered accidentally in 1914, these underground passages revealed a bewildering assortment of prehistoric cave wall art, generally dated between 13,000 and 12,000 BCE. The most famous of these images is the so-called "Sorcerer," which resembles a curious hybrid of a man and a deer. It is upright on two legs as a human would be, but the upper body is more animal-like and, based on the drawings made of it by researchers, it appears to have antlers and a deer's ears.

The drawing may imply a shamanic figure, perhaps dressed in a deer skin and performing some unknown ritual. Indeed, the figure has been nicknamed "the dancing sorcerer," since many assumed that he was depicted performing some kind of ritualistic dance. Others suggest that he might be a god, possibly one of the earliest attempts to portray a deity that survives, and have noted the similarity between him and other, much later depictions of horned or antlered deities. Whether god or shaman, is this one of the earliest drawings of some sort of religious dance?

The simple (and unfortunate) answer is: we just don't know. It's possible, but it might be something else entirely. Some have even questioned whether the figure has antlers at all, suggesting that Henri Breuil (1877–1961), the French priest and archeologist who made the original drawings from viewing the cave images, may have erroneously seen antlers which were actually just cracks and deformities in the rock. Others have come to his defense and said that the antlers are indeed there, but are engraved (rather than painted) into the rock and so are more difficult to see in photographs.

Another figure in the same cave complex seems to represent more clearly a dancing human/animal hybrid. The drawing is of the profile of a figure with human legs and a bison-like upper body with the near leg raised, almost as if marching. He holds an object which could be a hunting bow, or maybe a musical bow (the first stringed instrument), a bow drill for fire-making, or maybe even some kind of primitive flute. If it really is an instrument, then that would support the idea that "bison man" is dancing to his own music. Of course, he would have been playing—wait for it—"rock music." Sorry, not sorry.

Anyway, the fact that he is surrounded by actual bison and other animals that could trample him to death at any moment doesn't seem to faze him. Maybe this is some kind of ritual music and dance to commune with the bison, or to charm them and make them easier to hunt? Either way, it would have taken far more bravery than most moderns have!

While we may never uncover the details of these daring dance drawings, they may well indicate some kind of ritualized movement that would prove just how long humans have actually felt the need to get down for reasons other than just necessities.

THE BLOODY DANCE OF INANNA
ᒉᐤᐤ *Sowing heads like seeds* ᐣᐤ

The Sumerian goddess Inanna—associated with the later Mesopotamian goddess Ishtar—embodied sex and warfare, creation and destruction, often at the same time. In this way, she has much in common with the lioness-headed ancient Egyptian goddess Sekhmet, who the other gods once had to put to sleep with beer, because her bloody rampage was getting out of hand. These goddesses could, perhaps, be considered the original *femme fatales*, even before the Greek Hera or Biblical Salome (more about her later). Indeed, Inanna was a prostitute herself, and would gather together courtesans and other sex workers. She was sometimes called "the harlot of heaven." The apocryphal "dance of the seven veils," popularized by Oscar Wilde in his play *Salomé*, is often attributed to the myth of Inanna's descent into the Underworld, but ancient texts don't connect the shedding of her seven garments with a dance of seduction.

In her time, Inanna was worshipped as a war deity, and was said not to love the strategy of warfare, but the deep emotions and horrors it invoked.

Because of her propensity for being hot-headed, she was quite dangerous. The ancient Sumerians believed that she fought alongside their soldiers, reveling in the bloodshed, egging on the warriors to attack and kill enemy forces, and punishing those who fled the battlefield out of fear. A hymn written in her honor says:

> She stirs confusion and chaos against those who are disobedient to her, speeding carnage and inciting the devastating flood, clothed in terrifying radiance. It is her game to speed conflict and battle, untiring, strapping on her sandals.

One ancient text says that battle "is a feast for her." It continues, "She washes the tools in the blood of battle . . . Inanna, you pile heads like dust, you sow heads like seeds." What a lovely individual! Because ancient soldiers often marched in time to a drum, warfare became known as "the dance of Inanna."

In some ancient poems, Inanna says that she chases enemies with her "rope dance," braiding the rope into slings to capture the enemy. The "holy jump rope of Inanna" (never had that one in P.E.!) is thought to be a part of a dance performed at festivals in her honor; perhaps Wonder Woman's origin story begins in ancient Sumeria, not Themyscira? In one ancient text, Inanna complains to the god Ea that he has created a terrible monster; it exhibits all her worst and most destructive features. Ea says that the monster will disappear when Inanna starts behaving less violently, and, as a bonus for her continued good behavior, he promises her that one day a year, the people will celebrate her pugnaciousness by dancing in the streets with abandon.

Her dual nature afforded her the ability to don the clothing of both women and men, changing her gender as quickly as her mercurial moods. Because of this, androgyny and gender play also became associated with her. Members of her cult would gather together to mock and challenge social norms, and these gatherings could become quite wild. One of her cultic celebrations was connected to the sacred ritual of marriage, with revelers engaging in orgies and even castration (hopefully not at the same time!). Male prostitutes often attended, their hair adorned with ribbons. These guys would also dance with ropes in her honor. An ancient poem says:

> They gird themselves with the sword belt, the 'arm of battle' . . .
> Their right side they adorn with women's clothing . . .
> Their left side they cover with men's clothing . . .
> With jump ropes and colored cord they compete before her . . .
> The young men, carrying hoops, sing to her . . .
> The ascending *kurgarra* priests grasped the sword . . .
> The one who covered the sword with blood, he sprinkles blood . . .
> He pours out blood on the dais of the throne room.

Well, that sounds like fun! Worshippers of all genders often carried swords, spears, and daggers, sprinkling blood off the ends of the weapons. Scholars are unsure how the blood got there in the first place, but we've taken a guess that the castration might have had something to do with it. Ouch.

Inanna's legendary brutality has survived into modern pop culture. She makes an appearance in Neil Gaiman's comic book series, *The Sandman*, as a washed-up stripper in a seedy nightclub. There, she performs her last dance, first telling the owner that he has never really seen her *dance*. When she does, she destroys the club, herself, and the lustful patrons. Only her friend—also a nude dancer—survives, while the men literally die of pleasure, something her ancient worshippers might well have appreciated.

ANCIENT EGYPTIAN FUNERAL DANCES
ᏇᏬ *Gods, bulls, and dwarfs, oh my!* ᏇᏬ

In a collection of macabre stories about dance, we couldn't forgo including a bit about the ancient Egyptians, who were practically obsessed with death.

Wealthy Egyptians spent their whole lives preparing for the afterlife, ensuring that they had elaborate tombs filled with food, clothes, furniture, and magic texts to help them on their journey. But before their bodies were laid to rest, they would, of course, be embalmed and mummified. And nothing says dance party like an embalming ceremony. Embalming shops had dancers on staff to perform ritual dances in each room where the bodies were preserved and wrapped with linen. Professional dancers today can only dream of that kind of job security. Imagine if funeral homes started employing dancers to liven things up!

Once the body was prepared, the family would hold a funeral procession to bring it to the tomb. Dancers and acrobats followed the body and other ritual accoutrements to help the spirit of the deceased make the journey to the hereafter. Sometimes these dancers worked for specific funerary estates and cemeteries, and from what archaeologists can tell, they performed elaborately choreographed routines. The family of the dead person also hired professional mourners, who would cry, wail, and even tear out their hair in grief. The movements performed by professional funeral dancers likely came from similar gestures of grieving, but the performances were also thought to make the soul of the deceased happy.

Sometimes funeral dances were given to honor specific deities, particularly Hathor and Sekhmet (who were often considered to be different aspects of the same goddess). Sometimes just after the mummification was completed, a specific kind of dance company known as the Acacia House would perform to appease Sekhmet, the lioness-headed goddess of war, pestilence, and healing. The Acacia House not only mourned the dead, but also performed an "offering table" dance to entice the recently deceased to their first meal in the land beyond, kind of like a commercial for an otherworldly restaurant.

At funerals, dancers sometimes performed for Hathor, the cow-headed goddess of motherhood and love who welcomed the dead to the afterlife. This dance involved skipping and leaping in celebration that the goddess was on her way to receive the deceased. In the temple of Hathor in Dendera, a verse reads:

> We beat the drum to her spirit,
> We dance to her grace
> We raise her image up to the heavenly skies;
> She is the lady of sistrum [a kind of rattle],
> Mistress of jingling necklaces.

Recently passed humans weren't the only ones to be honored with funeral dancers. Apis bulls, considered sacred in ancient Egypt, also received their own special performances when they passed on to the afterlife; "bullroom" dancing, perhaps? These animals were selected from herds for bearing special markings associated with the god Ptah, who was believed to have thought the world into existence. They were brought to the temple, and given a harem of cows, because of course they were. The bull's breath was thought to be able to cure illness, and he was brought out into public on certain holidays, adorned with flowers and jewelry. Not a bad life if you can get it. Their funerals and burials were often just as extravagant as those for the pharaoh himself.

On the other end of the size spectrum, human dwarfs frequently appear as professional dancers on ancient Egyptian artifacts, likely because they were thought to embody the dwarf god Bes, who protected the home and mothers during childbirth. Bes, often shown as having the mane of a lion, is usually seen dancing and playing a frame drum. The Egyptians believed that his dancing and drumming would ward off evil spirits and protect the family under his care. Dwarfs were also considered to represent the eternal youth of the sun; because of their small stature, they were seen as being akin to children who never grew up. Some Middle Kingdom texts say that they would perform farewell dances for the sun as it made its nightly descent through the underworld. Djeho, a dwarf dancer who lived around 350 BCE, danced at the burial of an Apis bull, and on a festival day in honor of Osiris, the god of the underworld and eternal life.

Dancing dwarfs were rare and highly valued, sought after to perform "god's dances" for the pharaoh. Scholars aren't in total agreement over what those dances were, but they were certainly pretty important. When six-year-old Pharaoh Pepi II (Seriously? Six years old?) received word that one of his officials had secured a dancing dwarf during an expedition in Sudan, he wrote back that he wanted the dwarf brought alive and well to dance at the royal court at Memphis (that would be the court of the King of Egypt, not the King of Rock and Roll).

Dwarfs or not, in the early days of ancient Egypt, funeral dancers and their managers were almost always women. But by around 2100 BCE, they were depicted as being men, and stayed that way until Queen Cleopatra met that famous asp and ancient Egypt was no more.

These male dancers performed to summon the Muu, supernatural spirits who would ferry the dead across the waters that lead to the afterlife. Without the dancers (whom archaeologists sometimes call the "Muu dancers") or the Muu spirits, the deceased would never reach their final destination, which was considered to be the worst fate that a recently departed soul could face. Wearing tall papyrus headdresses and short linen kilts, they danced side-by-side or facing one another, executing low forward kicks, like a less-flexible version of the Rockettes. They are also shown with their hands stretched out in front of them towards the water, perhaps to ward off dangerous aquatic beasts, such as hippopotamuses and crocodiles. Because offering up your hands and feet to hungry animals is a sure-fire way of getting them to back off.

All of these dances stressed the importance (obsession, really) of proper death rituals in Egyptian culture. Probably no other civilization was so focused on preparing for the afterlife, going to such extreme lengths to help a departed soul on its way. Dancing was only one of countless parts of the whole spectacle as the soul waltzed its way into the beyond.

2

Greece and Rome

the Greeks and Romans seemed to both love and hate dance in equal measure. As in other ages and cultures, there were dances that were approved by the establishment, that promoted cultural norms, and instilled love of the gods and land, and then there were the fun dances that people actually enjoyed. Okay, that might be a bit harsh, but this was the time when the ecstatic dancing of Asia Minor came into its own, with wild, drunken revelries in honor of Dionysus and Bacchus happening often enough that the authorities took notice and tried to clamp down on them.

Beyond such moving drunken orgies, there were dances for almost every occasion: war dances, dances before comedies and tragedies, religious processions, and a host of other excuses to get bodies moving. Many of these might not seem much like what we would call "dancing" today. Other movements, such tumbling and acrobatics, as well as complex hand gestures and body postures were also thought of as forms of dancing, and sometimes these were combined with movements more closely resembling dancing as we know it.

Dancing was undoubtedly invented by the gods, and several Greek myths allude to this, but one of the more striking uses of dance in a mythological account is that of the trials and travails of the infant Zeus.

THE MYTH OF ZEUS AND THE DANCING KOURITES
∽ *Likes babies, but couldn't eat a whole one . . .*
well, yes he could ∽

For the Greeks, things were pretty rough at the beginning of time. It wasn't just a simple "create the world and we're done" sort of thing. The Titans—the precursors to the Olympian gods—had very pointed ideas about who should rule and how. Cronus (identified later by the Romans as Saturn), son of Gaia (the earth) and Uranus (the sky, and stop the juvenile giggling), didn't like how his father was managing things, and so castrated him and deposed him. Imagine if that were the procedure in modern governments. Depending on which version of the myth you read, what followed was either a golden age, or a time of despotism. Some things never change.

In any case, he went on to have several children, but he had heard a prophecy that they would overthrow him, just as he had overthrown his father. So he did what any sensible parent would do—he ate them just after they were born. All except for the youngest, a certain son named Zeus. Cronus' wife Rhea devised a plan to save the newborn godling, apparently getting sick and tired of seeing her children being eaten. After the baby's birth, she gave Cronus a stone wrapped in swaddling clothes, which we can assume tasted exactly like a baby wrapped in swaddling clothes. For whatever reason, the old cannibal didn't notice the difference and mom spirited the young one away to a cave in Mount Ida on the island of Crete.

But little Zeus was not yet out of danger, so Rhea devised a plan: she appointed the Kourites (rustic spirits of the land) to guard her son. She had previously taught them how to dance, and now this skill would come in quite handy. In order to drown out the baby's cries so that Cronus couldn't hear them, the Kourites danced a wild war dance around him at all times. They didn't just dance; they shouted and banged their shields with their spears, carrying out this duty, well, dutifully, and keeping the infant safe. Never mind that this much noise would probably just make any baby cry that much louder, their work did the trick and he was spared becoming a Titanic snack. Zeus grew up, became the god we know and love (or not), and overthrew his father, forcing him to vomit up all of his previously devoured brothers and sisters, who miraculously hadn't been digested, but had rather spent their youth inside his stomach. That's one way to afford daycare. These gods included Hades, Poseidon, Hera, Demeter, and Hesta, who had all had about enough of dad's BS by that point.

Various myths have Cronus being imprisoned somewhere unpleasant (though he was later released), and the Kourites who had danced around Zeus became his first priests. Later worshippers of Zeus on Crete incorporated ecstatic dance into their rituals and rites of initiation, especially those for boys becoming men. Thankfully, the ceremonial eating of infants was not needed to re-enact the myth.

THE ANCIENT GREEK ORPHEOTELESTAE
ᦉ᧞ *Bring out your nearly-dead* ᧞᧞

The orpheotelestae ("OR-fay-oh-TEH-leh-stie" . . . say that three times fast!) were controversial figures, even in the curious goulash of ancient Greek spiritual beliefs. Allegedly followers of the mythic poet and musician Orpheus, they promised to reveal to their initiates the secrets of the universe, if said novices followed certain procedures. The details of this "Orphism" vary (and no one school of thought developed that everyone had to follow), but it often included a belief in reincarnation (an involuntary cycle of death and rebirth), like Hinduism. Understanding this, and following a certain purified way of life, could grant the seeker a final release from this pattern and true freedom after death. There seem to have been genuine "Orphic brotherhoods" that held themselves to a higher standard and lived ascetic lives in pursuit of this goal, but that simply allowed for imposters to flourish in their shadows.

These "fake" orpheotelestae claimed to know many things outside of the range of the average person, and boasted of the ability to cure the sick of any illness, no matter how serious, often through the use of dance. A group of said devotees would presumably join hands and dance in a ring around the afflicted, which they confidently assured would bring about the desired healing. They even said that the crimes of both the living and dead could be exonerated with their mystical and magical capering.

It goes without saying that this type of treatment rarely worked (though we don't really have any information on the efficacy of the forgiveness of the dead's sins by dancing), and that these Orphic folks gained a bad reputation among many as being the charlatans and frauds that they were. Some saw them as little more than beggars, carrying their books and magical supplies on the backs of donkeys and preying on the gullible, but enough simple-minded people of all social classes believed them and their crazy dancing that they persisted far longer than they probably should have.

CINESIAS (CA. 450–390 BCE)
⟵⟶ *Flapping in a slough of ever-flowing dung* ⟵⟶

Cinesias merits inclusion here for being an unusual entry from this far back: a choreographer who was known (rather infamously) for his work on a particular kind of performance, the dithyramb, which was hymn and sometimes a dance piece in honor of Dionysus that preceded some dramas. In fact, the theatrical genre of tragedy may well have developed from these pieces. It was a ritual piece that probably included movements that we might not today associate with dancing, such as acrobatics and intricate hand gestures, or *cheironomia*.

Cinesias came from a line of musicians, which may have affected how he viewed dancing, but he seems to have been more interested in choreographing things that delighted the crowds, rather than aspiring to any kind of "higher art." His contemporaries Aristophanes (ca. 446–ca. 386 BCE) and Plato (yes, that Plato), considered him to be really bad at it, wallowing in bad morality. They also noted that he was somewhat sickly (possibly tuberculosis), emaciated, and may have had short or bowed legs. But that didn't stop Cinesias from choreographing work that might be more at home in post-modern performance art than in the ancient Greek amphitheater. One account hints that his dancers are made to flap their arms like birds in a manner that was out of the ordinary, and may have looked unintentionally comic or obscene. He may also have used sharp motions and gestures, and perhaps positions that were considered inappropriate for a "true" dithyramb, but which apparently delighted audiences anyway. They are described as having many twists and turns, but no real harmony; maybe some dancers were allowed to improvise, or do things against the rhythm of the music, all of which would have been abnormal, to say the least.

Aristophanes was clearly not impressed. In his comic play *The Frogs*, Dionysus and Heracles (Hercules) are at the shores of the river Styx, waiting for the ferryman, Charon, to take them to the underworld. Heracles tries to describe the horrible things that even the god of wine will see. Dionysus gets in a good dig at Cinesias, claiming that even his students belong there:

Heracles: Theseus introduced them. And after this you'll see ten thousand snakes and terrible wild beasts.

Dionysus: Don't frighten me or make me scared. You won't turn me aside.

Heracles: Then a great slough of ever-flowing dung, and in it lie any whoever wronged his guest, or screwed a boy and took back the pay, or thrashed his mother, or smacked his father's jaw, or swore a perjured oath, or copied out a speech of Morsimus.

Dionysus: Now, by the Gods, besides these there should be whoever learned Kinesias' pyrrhic dance.

Centuries before Dante, Aristophanes was declaring Cinesias' devotees worthy of a place in the underworld! Cinesias is one of dozens of characters—real and fictional—who populate the play, and he receives a good humorous poking. Pisthetaerus, a citizen of Athens speaks to him, when receiving him:

> **Pisthetaerus:** Welcome, Cinesias, you lime-wood man! Why do you come here twisting your lame leg around in crooked, cyclic dances?

So, the establishment didn't like his appearance, behavior, or the way he was cheapening the sacred dithyramb, and they weren't shy about putting him in their own plays and mocking him. That he continued doing what he did and being popular for it shows exactly what he thought of their elevated opinions! You do you, Cinesias.

A MULTITUDE OF UNUSUAL GREEK GAMBOLS
↜ *Acrobatic, erotic, comic, and leave my cows alone* ↝

Dancing existed in countless forms throughout the Greek period, from the most exalted to the most salacious. Dances for worship and formal occasions were often miles away in style and content from popular dancing, then as now. Here, we will look at a few of the more unusual examples of dances depicting war, sex, and crime.

In his work, *Anabasis*, the historian Xenophon (ca. 430–354 BCE) describes some unusual dancing entertainment at one particular festival in Trapezus (now Trabzon, a city on the Black Sea in modern Turkey) to celebrate a military victory:

> Up got first some Thracians, who performed a dance under arms to the sound of a pipe, leaping high into the air with much nimbleness, and brandishing their swords, till at last one man struck his fellow, and everyone thought he was really wounded, so skilfully and artistically did he fall, and the Paphlagonians screamed out. Then he that gave the blow stripped the other of his arms, and marched off chanting . . . whilst others of the Thracians bore off the other, who lay as if dead, though he had not received even a scratch.

Well, things were off to a good start with some convincing simulated death! It got a bit weirder with the next performance:

> After this some Aenianians and Magnesians got up and fell to dancing the Carpaea, as it is called, under arms. This was the manner of the dance: one man lays aside his arms and proceeds to drive a yoke of oxen, and while he drives he sows, turning him about frequently, as though he were afraid of something; up comes a cattle-lifter, and no sooner does the ploughman catch sight of him afar, than he snatches up his arms and confronts him. They fight in front of his team, and all in rhythm to the sound of the pipe. At last the robber binds the countryman and drives off the team. Or sometimes the cattle-driver binds the robber, and then he puts him under the yoke beside the oxen, with his two hands tied behind his back, and off he drives.

Ah yes, the beloved "don't steal my cattle" dance, all the rage in Trapezus this year! Finally, after more war dancing, Xenophon mentions this fascinating finale:

> The Mysian . . . persuaded one of the Arcadians who had a dancing girl to let him introduce her, which he did after dressing her up magnificently and giving her a light shield. When, lithe of limb, she danced the Pyrrhic [a war dance], loud clapping followed; and the Paphlagonians asked if these women fought by their side in battle, to which they answered, "To be sure, it was the women who routed the great King, and drove him out of camp." So ended the night.

Facetious answer or an amazing insight into Greek military strategy?

War was not the only subject of dancing, of course. Erotic dances of all kinds were performed by both male and female dancers, who were most often slaves, courtesans, or otherwise of the lower classes, since such things were forbidden by people of "respectability," though it was perfectly all right for them to view such dancers, of course. Such dancers often performed at *symposia*, which were private parties, where the privileged could indulge in whatever they wished, away from the prying eyes of disapproving neighbors and the law. It was implied that such dancers be sexually available for the entertainment of guests, and their dances were intended to be suggestive and inviting.

This type of "lewd" dancing also found its way into comic plays, with the cordax dance being the most famous/notorious. This dance was performed while wearing a mask, and was highly sexual and suggestive, but in comical ways. Actors in these plays might also wear padded clothing to exaggerate their behinds, with large stuffed male members dangling from between their legs. The dance included pelvic thrusts and hip rotations, bending over to moon the audience, and other bodily gyrations, all of which presumably amused spectators to no end. It was very lowbrow and puerile humor that had its fans and its detractors.

Our old friend Aristophanes argues in his play, *The Clouds*, that the use of the cordax in plays is a sign of poor comedy writers, who have nothing better to offer. He says, with smugness, that his play is like the character of Electra:

But see how modest she [i.e., his play] is by nature, who, in the first place, has come, having stitched to her no leathern phallus hanging down, red at the top, and thick, to set the boys a laughing; nor yet jeered the bald-headed, nor danced the cordax.

And I, although so excellent a poet, do not give myself airs, nor do I seek to deceive you by twice and thrice bringing forward the same pieces; but I am always clever at introducing new fashions, not at all resembling each other, and all of them clever.

Bouncing butts and dangling dicks were for amateurs, he insists, and he is far more creative than that.

But this didn't stop the dance and similar such crude capering from surviving well into Roman times where they were equally appreciated . . . or not. The Roman poet Juvenal (late first–early second century CE), in his *Satire XI*, notes that a form of the cordax was performed by certain female dancers of Roman Spain during his time—without the bulging bums and wobbly willies—and was known for its suggestiveness and lack of respectability:

> You may look perhaps for a troop of Spanish maidens to win applause by immodest dance and song, sinking down with quivering bottoms to the floor—such sights as brides behold seated beside their husbands, though it were a shame to speak of such things in their presence . . . My humble home has no place for follies such as these.

Speaking of Rome . . .

THE ROMANS AND DANCING
ᔐ *A love/hate relationship* ᔐ

Roman society, especially by the imperial era beginning in the first century BCE, was very much about the proper order of things. Maintaining that order—and basically, civilization—depended on citizens' activities being monitored and controlled, at least to a certain extent. Dance, as you can imagine, was a suspicious activity, because it could get out of control very easily, defying established and acceptable behaviors. This male-dominated and military-focused society was ill at ease with letting go; dirty dancing was not an option, at least not in public. What people got up to in their own homes was a different matter. Out of sight, out of mind, as they say. The upper classes often didn't dance themselves, but brought in dancers for their entertainment who were slaves from, as we've seen, as far away as Spain. This only further promoted the idea that dancing was not a proper pastime for proper Romans.

Certain types of ritual movement were acceptable in the complex Roman religious rites and processions, and later, pantomime was greatly appreciated by the upper classes, including Roman emperors. Everyone's favorite crazy emperor Nero was especially enamored of pantomime (see the next entry for how that ended in a predictably bloody way). This dance was a style performed by a masked man to music and singing, who acted out scenes through movement in graceful and restrained sorts of ways.

But unrestrained, ecstatic dance was a very different story. The frenzied religious cults of Asia Minor and Greece were of particular concern to nervous Roman conservatives, because they encouraged free expression, free social interaction, and all sorts of alleged forbidden festive follies. While Rome tended to tolerate foreign gods, some of them were definitely problematic. Around 204 BCE, the cult of Cybele found its way to Roman lands from what is now Anatolia in Turkey. With its female priesthood and followers who would dance publicly in ecstatic ways, it was unsettling to Roman sensibilities, to say the least. Further, male priests of the goddess were expected to castrate themselves publicly as a sign of devotion, and cut themselves with knives in future rituals.

This kind of behavior was a direct challenge to the staid and proper Roman priests and signaled that they were not needed for people to have a connection to the divine. It was the kind of popular movement that should have been banned immediately . . . except that there was one little problem. Cybele was credited with aiding Rome in its defeat of Carthage during the Second Punic War, which was wrapping up just as her cult was appearing. In fact, it was quite possibly due to her presumed involvement in said victory that her worship was spreading. So, the authorities couldn't exactly ban her and her followers (though later on, they would); that would have been ungracious to the goddess and bloody rude, to say nothing of dangerous if she took offense. Perhaps she would reverse Rome's fortune? So they had little choice initially but to endure the spectacles of the tortuous ecstasies in Cybele's worship with clenched jaws and revolted sensibilities.

However, another cult didn't get away with the same begrudged freedoms. This group was the equally ecstatic worshippers of Dionysus—called Bacchus in Rome—who spread a particularly popular form of social interaction (i.e., drunken revels) and protest in southern Italy at about the same time. While Cybele's men were lopping off their bits, the Bacchics were accused of gathering without authorization, indulging in sexual deviancy, drunkenness, homosexual activity, and actively plotting against the Roman state, up to and including murder.

Livy (ca. 59 BCE–12 or 17 CE) wrote about some of their alleged practices, or rather spread the popular myths:

> Whoever would not submit to defilement, or shrank from violating others, was sacrificed as a victim. To regard nothing as impious or criminal was the very sum of their religion. The men, as though seized with madness and with frenzied distortions of their bodies, shrieked out prophecies; the matrons, dressed as Bacchae, their hair dishevelled, rushed down to the Tiber with burning torches, plunged them into the water, and drew them out again, the flame undiminished.

A crackdown on the cult came in 186 BCE, when a former member decided to rat them out and accused them of all manner of perversions, as well as forgery and perjury, the latter two of which seem rather odd accusations for an ecstatic cult of dancing and drinking. The authorities came to believe that Rome was crawling with Bacchic devotees who were secretly plotting to overthrow the republic. Thousands were said to have been arrested and executed. Obviously, worship of Bacchus continued, but it had to be considerably less blatant and way more subtle in the future. Those worshippers that remained were forced to reshape the religion into something state-approved; the Romans couldn't risk offending the god by banning his religion entirely, of course. And it goes without saying that ecstatic rites of dance, alcohol, and free love continued (especially in the south of Italy). Those who partook were just way quieter about it in the future.

PYLADES AND BATHYLLUS
(LATE FIRST CENTURY BCE)
A hate/hate relationship

Not much is known about the lives of these two, but they had a great effect on their fans. Well, "great" may not be the best word for it. Pylades and Bathyllus were pantomime dancers credited with introducing the art form to the Roman world and probably making a number of improvements to it. Pantomime was a dramatic dancing style that blended acting and dance in a silent format, a bit like modern mimes, but with less creepiness and invasiveness in public parks. The performers told a story through masks, costumes, and movement, accompanied by music.

Both Pylades and Bathyllus were former slaves of high-ranking Romans (Pylades to Emperor Augustus himself and Bathyllus to Maecenas, public relations minister to the emperor), but each approached the style differently. Bathyllus was the joker, who gave comic performances not unlike the raunchy cordax dances, while Pylades preferred a "higher art" and gave himself over to evoking tragedy. The two not only became rivals, their fans and admirers also began to hate each other, rather like fans of one band telling fans of another that their favorite group sucks, or the rivalries that plague some over-zealous sports fans. Everyone was a Bathyllian or a Pyladian; maybe they wore togas with their respective logos. The problem is, this rivalry went way beyond name-calling, and graduated into open violence. Such was their popularity that their devoted followers engaged in riots in defense of their respective favorite.

Emperor Augustus wasn't too pleased with this, being all about restoring order to Rome after a civil war and such, and at some point, he exiled his former slave Pylades. This may have been because of the increasingly violent rivalry, or possibly because his performances were a bit too critical of the emperor's authoritarian decrees. Regardless, this was a bad move, and allegedly almost provoked another civil war. The decree was recalled and the revolution was averted, but that only left more room for riots between the two factions. Cassius Dio (ca. 155 CE/163-64–235 CE) recorded long after their lives:

> He [Augustus] restored one Pylades, a dancer, who had been exiled on account of sedition . . . Hence Pylades is said to have rejoined very cleverly, when the emperor rebuked him for having quarreled with Bathyllus, a fellow-artist, and a favourite of Maecenas: "It is to your advantage, Caesar, that the people should devote their spare time to us."

And presumably, not pay attention to whatever governing actions Augustus was taking at any given moment. Pylades was suggesting an early example of the "bread and circuses" strategy, i.e., keep the populace preoccupied with trivialities so that they ignore the big picture. It has worked well for authoritarian regimes ever since.

Bathyllus seems to have been far less politically minded, and certainly less fearless of authority than Pylades, but he had his own passionate devotees. Juvenal described a dancer named Bathyllus and his erotic effect on women in the audience, but it's unclear if this is the same dancer as our obscene riot-inducer, or a later dancer of the same name:

> When the soft Bathyllus dances the part of the gesticulating Leda, Tuccia cannot contain herself; your Apulian maiden heaves a sudden and longing cry of ecstasy, as though she were in a man's arms; the rustic Thymele is all attention, it is then that she learns her lesson.

Wow. Apparently, Pylades was less charming. Once, when a crowd demanded that he dance for them, he simply sat down and, motionless, appeared to be in deep thought. When they asked what he was doing, he said that he was performing the role of a general planning a military campaign. If someone didn't appreciate his tragic art, he had no qualms about telling said offender where to get off. One time, when an audience member hissed at his work, he stopped mid-performance and made an obscene gesture to the rude man in response. On another occasion, when an audience member showed dislike for his movements in a piece called "Mad Hercules," he stopped, removed his mask, and reminded them: "Fools! I am dancing the role of a madman!" Apparently, he became so incensed with this criticism that he took up a bow and shot arrows at the audience! Well, that's one way to deal with hecklers.

The form of dance that these two perfected would endure for centuries, but it was Pylades' tragic interpretations that became the norm and elevated such dancers to the status of modern-day rock stars and athletes. Pylades himself became immensely wealthy, and pantomimes would soon dance for emperors. Actually, some emperors, such as Caligula and Nero, fancied themselves as fine dancers as well, which was not a good thing, especially given that both were completely off their respective rockers.

Nero, in particular, thought of himself as an expert singer and performer, even though such activities were supposed to be beneath the dignity of a Roman emperor—this is the man who, at his assassination, uttered the words "what an artist dies in me!" after all. But actually, he was average at best and inept at worst. No matter, he loved all things artistic and Greek, and gave agonizingly long performances that no one in attendance was allowed to leave until he was finished. But he was also extremely jealous of genuine performers who might outdo him, which was not a difficult task. Cassius Dio records that one time a certain pantomime dancer ran afoul of the disturbed emperor, and asks:

> Is it worth while adding that Nero ordered Paris the pantomimic dancer, to be slain because the emperor had wished to learn dancing from him but had not the capacity?

Why, yes. Yes, it is. Suetonius records that Nero murdered Paris because he saw him as "a dangerous rival" who would take away glory from the emperor. Either or both may be true, but regardless, poor Paris the dancer was still dead.

3

The Middle Ages

The "Middle Ages" is an odd term, and not a very accurate one. It was coined in the nineteenth century to describe the time, roughly from about 500 to 1500, that was between the greatness of the Greco-Roman world, and our own obvious modern greatness. If you're skeptical about that assertion, you're not alone. The problem, of course, is that as time marches ever on, who's to say when this middle period actually ended? In any case, it's the term we've been stuck with, so we'll have to live with it.

The early medieval period in Europe was characterized by the breakdown of the Roman Empire, its fragmentation into tiny states and nations, and the rise of the Christian Church. During this chaotic time (once known as the "Dark Ages"), dance, as you can probably imagine, wasn't exactly on most people's minds. Running away from the big, scary barbarian men with axes was a bigger priority. Still, that didn't stop early Christian writers (both in the Roman Empire and later) from chiming in about what was wrong with dancing, often in exhaustive detail.

It wasn't so much that dancing represented pagan practices (though that didn't help, let's be honest), but that the wild, uncontrolled dances of Bacchus and others were exactly that: free of control. Such a lack of control could lead to a further breakdown in a society that was in many places already coming unglued, and this worried the authorities that still remained.

It was a threat to the new order that the church was trying to establish, one that was based on a belief that everything had its place in God's cosmos. To be fair, certain types of controlled dancing were permissible, such as devotions to saints at certain times of year, or processions at religious festivals. These were often led by priests, but the free-dancing, Roman raves had to go. This attitude would remain throughout the Middle Ages, though dancing most definitely did not disappear. Often it was the timing of events set aside for dancing that irked churchmen, as much as anything else. They took place on holidays and times of religious observance, or at the same time that church services were happening. It was seen as an offense on those days and times that should have been devoted instead to God.

In this chapter, we'll look at a few of those early condemnations and their medieval counterparts. And then we'll see how dancing survived, sometimes in pretty subversive ways, even among representatives of the clergy themselves. No amount of authoritarian huffing and puffing can quell people's desire to kick up their heels and have a bit of fun, after all.

THE SINFULNESS OF DANCING: IN CHURCH, IN THE STREETS, AND PRETTY MUCH ANYWHERE
&ce&o; *Jumping like camels, and other offenses* &o&e;

As you can probably imagine, the medieval church was not always the biggest fan of dancing. Even so, there were a variety of opinions, from relative tolerance to outright condemnation. There was already a long history of such cranky anti-dance tirades, so medieval thinkers had a lot of material to draw from in crafting their own fire-and-brimstone sermons against the moving of bodies in sinful ways. Many churchmen believed that all dance had diabolical origins, being held over from pagan (i.e., diabolical) practices and rituals designed to worship other (i.e., diabolical) gods. So dance was, for many, a form of idolatry at best and devil-worship at worst. A common image used was that of the Hebrews dancing before the idol of the golden calf, a sight that made Moses so angry he smashed the first edition of the Ten Commandments (a second printing appeared shortly afterward). And if dancing could rile up Moses to commit such an act, that was good enough for the medieval church.

Here are a few thoughts from the early church movers and shakers (no pun intended) that set the tone for the next thousand years, give or take a century:

Ambrose of Milan (ca. 340–397), in *Concerning Virgins* (great title!), Book 3, chapter 6: 27, writes:

> Is anything so conducive to lust as with unseemly movements thus to expose in nakedness those parts of the body which either nature has hidden or custom has veiled, to sport with the looks, to turn the neck, to loosen the hair? Fitly was the next step an offence against God. For what modesty can there be where there is dancing and noise and clapping of hands?

John Chrysostom (ca. 349–407), writes in his Homily 48 on Matthew's Gospel, chapter 4:

> For where dancing is, there is the evil one. For neither did God give us feet for this end, but that we may walk orderly: not that we may behave ourselves unseemly, not that we may jump like camels (for even they too are disagreeable when dancing, much more women).

Ah, yes, nothing worse than a camel prancing about, except for a woman doing the same thing.

Cyprian (ca. 200–258), also known as Novatian, has his own ideas about how dancing in the Bible differed from what those obvious sinners around him were doing:

> The fact that David led the dances in the presence of God is no sanction for faithful Christians to occupy seats in the public theater. For

David did not twist his limbs about in obscene movements. He did not depict in his dancing the story of Grecian lust.

The Council of Laodicea (390) declared, in Canon 53:

Christians, when they attend weddings, must not join in wanton dances, but modestly dine or breakfast . . .

Wow, even breakfast has to be a sedate affair; no morning mambas for you, young man!

Later on, religious writers in the Middle Ages had many of the same fears and anxieties. For them, as for their Roman moralist predecessors, the biggest concern was wild, unrestrained dancing, like that of the Dionysian and Bacchanalian bashes of antiquity. This kind of uncontrolled revelry could lead to drunkenness, gluttony, casual sex, disrespect for authority . . . pretty much everything every teenager has enjoyed since the beginning of time.

And speaking of youthful enjoyment, various academics and clerks (students) at the University of Paris in the thirteenth century had various things to say about dancing. Like most students, their attentions were frequently directed away from their studies, which could lead to all sorts of problems. The university was always at the center of "town-gown" conflicts with the city. Each year, an influx of students—both domestic and foreign—brought the potential for law-breaking, drunken disturbances, public brawling . . . basically, all of the typical indulgences of a university frat house.

One such student, Henri Bate, insisted in the mid-thirteenth century that dancing and singing were "not especially injurious to studies among the young." Well, he may have been white lying, just a little. Among those with university educations, opinions of dancing were, as you might expect, considerably more favorable than those with strictly monastic and priestly backgrounds. Curiously, this was often the case for those churchmen with university degrees; the Franciscan and Dominican friars who studied at the University of Paris often had less hostile views toward the carol and other dances (more on the carol below). Some early biographies of St. Francis even declared that he danced as a part of his worship. That being said, other sources were keen to point out that the dance floor was the devil's playground. The Dominican John Bromyard (d. ca. 1352) told a story about a group of friars going to a town and seeing a demon sitting on the walls (as you do). They asked him why he was there, and he answered, "the city is obediently subject to us [demons]." When they went in, they saw the people "dancing caroles and occupied with diverse other entertainments." It was enough to drive the friars away in fear.

As far as we know, there weren't actually any demons sitting on the walls of Paris. Still, prohibitions persisted. Students at the university during the second half of the thirteenth century, for example, were warned on several occasions not to dance (carols and other things) on feast days, or at graduation celebrations that turned into street processions. This was as much as anything meant to quell the tendency that such song and dance parties had to become violent. Dancing in the streets was a no-no for not only the church, but also the city authorities, who invariably had to send out the guard to bust some heads when things inevitably got out of control. Better to nip it in the bud before it started, but as you can imagine, university students were not so easily suppressed, and the problems of student dancing persisted right down the centuries.

THE CAROL, FOR TO DAUNCE
ⅇ☙ *It's for life, not just for Christmas* ☙ⅇ

When we think of "carols," we immediately think of the holidays, and singers gathered in shopping malls, or going door-to-door to spread cheer and fa-la-las to a not-always-appreciative audience. Or even worse, we shudder at piped-in music in stores that usually begins sometime in the second half of September. But the carol, or *carole*, had a very different meaning in the Middle Ages and was most closely associated with dancing. That made it an instant target for its critics.

The word may derive from the Latin *chorea* ("dance") but some debate that. In any case, it most often described a dance piece that was sung (rather than needing instruments, though these certainly could have been included), with a simple refrain, easy lyrics, and a catchy tune. The dance was probably circular, with the dancers joining hands and proceeding to move in one direction or the other. As such, it was a "portable" dance that could be taken up anywhere, and of course, that was part of the problem, because "anywhere" could be homes, taverns, streets, or even churchyards. Unfortunately, even though it was a very common form of entertainment, there aren't many good surviving descriptions of exactly what it looked like, or what steps were done. It was apparently so common that writers both pro and con just assumed that the reader knew what they were talking about and would be either shocked or delighted accordingly.

The lyrics to the accompanying songs could be in Latin or vernacular languages and were usually very secular in content, arousing suspicions in many. The *Cambridge Songs*, a collection of lyrics in Latin from the eleventh century, (sadly, with no surviving music) originated in Germany, and was possibly meant for courtly enjoyment. Some of them seem to be dance songs, and the words to one give you an idea of how saucy they could be:

> Come to me, my dearest love—with ah! and oh!
> Visit me—what joys you will have! with ah! and oh!
> I am dying with desire—with ah! and oh!
> How I long for the fire of Venus! with ah! and oh!
> If you come and bring your key—with ah! and oh!
> Your entry will be easy! with ah! and oh!

Oh my. Although something like this could have been only for the private entertainment of the eleventh-century one-percent, similar bawdy lyrics undoubtedly permeated the songs in everyday languages, enjoyed by the common people. The church's solution to this ribaldry was often quite simple, even ingenious: take these popular tunes and substitute religious words for them, and then encourage folks to sing (and maybe even dance, if they must) these lyrics, instead. One bishop in Ireland wrote in the fourteenth century that this was done so that the dancers' "throats and ears, consecrated to God, might not be sullied by dramatic, lewd, and secular songs."

It also wasn't uncommon for said clerics to kick up their own heels a little, at least at certain times (such as on important feast days) and under controlled conditions, singing and dancing those very songs that had been altered away from lewdness and molded into dance tunes for spiritual betterment. The church seems to have gone back and forth, prohibiting dancing of any kind in certain areas (churches and cemeteries), while allowing it on those holidays and in approved places.

Musical theorist Johannes de Grocheio (ca. 1255–ca. 1320) gave perhaps the best defense of the secular version of the dance, saying that it, in fact, did the opposite of what so many church moralists claimed. Writing around 1300, he declared that it "guides the hearts of young women and men and keeps them from vanity, and it is said to be effective against that passion which is called erotic love." It's doubtful that many churchmen were convinced.

The music for carols was also a cause for concern for some, because it was simple, catchy, and could stay in the mind long after hearing it: these were the original musical ear worms. There was a popular story that one priest had heard such a tune and it had stuck in his head, so that when it came time to sing a certain line of music at mass, he accidentally sang the dance tune instead! Oops. Some theologians insisted, therefore, that anyone who had such a song stuck in their heads needed to tell their priest during confession; if they didn't do so, they incurred an additional eighteen days in Purgatory for their neglect. Remember this next time you've got the latest radio hit repeating in your head.

One of the most splendid condemnations of carol dancing came from the Dominican preacher, Guillaume Peyrault (ca. 1190–1271). In his

Summa de virtutibus et vitiis ("Sum of Virtues and Vices," ca. 1250), he goes on a lengthy tirade, invoking apocalyptic visions worthy of a modern horror movie:

> The smoke rising from the bottomless pit is the stench and heat of lust which has darkened the sun . . . Out of the smoke come locusts, that is female singers and dancers, not governing themselves in a sane way but advancing in chaos as if they were brute beasts.
>
> Caroles principally injure the Church from Easter until Autumn. Just as kings are accustomed to go to war during this season, so that they can bear away the things which their enemies have produced by labouring during the winter, so the Devil, as soon as it is Easter, musters an army of carollers and carries off what the Church has produced during Advent and Lent.

Who knew that simple circle dances could cause so much end-of-the-world devastation? Peyrault's colorful attack was popular and widely circulated, but dancing persisted, and no doubt, many quietly laughed at his hysterics.

His fellow Dominican, Albertus Magnus (ca. 1200–1280), had a somewhat more lenient view toward dancing the carol. "Dancing" and "leaping" he said, were potentially "worthy of a free man" (along with singing and instrument playing), if pursued correctly. While wary of dancing's potential to lure people into sin, he granted that there were certain circumstances when dancing a simple dance could be acceptable:

- Such dancing should only be for actual celebrations: a wedding, a military victory, the return of someone from a foreign land (such as a crusader), and so on.
- The dance must be done without the intent to be lecherous (well, that's no fun!).
- Clerics—those in holy orders—should not take part in it, regardless.

- The dance movements should not be overly showy, but should strive for beauty instead.
- The words sung to the music must be uplifting and not lewd or impious.

With these five elements satisfied, it is permissible, he asserts, to dance. This is still a pretty strict set of guidelines that would be difficult for many revelers to follow, but it shows that he, like Thomas Aquinas, acknowledged that some kinds of recreation could be healthy and valuable in certain situations. Hey, it's a start.

THE SALISBURY HARE
ᴄᴧᴐ *Lucky rabbit feet* 🕭

One day in 1318, an English shepherd named John Godwin claimed he was confronted with a rather extraordinary sight while tending to his flock somewhere on Salisbury Plain near Imber, a village to the west and slightly north of Stonehenge. Maybe it was because of the long history of mystical goings-on in that area. Maybe it was the midday sun. Maybe his ale was off, but John later reported a strange encounter with a rabbit. He asserted not only that said beastie was not afraid of him, but also that it actually began to dance around him. It started slowly, but gradually built up speed, stamping its hind feet on the ground while moving around him in a circle, which sounds very much like a medieval carol or ring dance; at least there was only one leaping leporid and not a group joining hands (paws?). In any case, it must have been an astonishing, and maybe even unnerving, sight!

Now, we don't know how true this is, of course, the story being exactly eight hundred years old, so any proof of it is long lost in the mists of time. But it was recorded in the Imber parish church records, so someone literate thought it was noteworthy (or amusing) enough to commit to parchment for posterity.

This apparently wasn't the only incident, though, because over time the dancing hare became a part of local folklore. The boogieing bunny was said to favor dancing under the full moon, and if any were fortunate enough to see it, good luck would be theirs for the rest of their lives. Apparently, only those of a certain level of purity were privileged with seeing the hare do its thing, and these were the ones most in need of its blessings. Obviously, this has more than a whiff of older pagan folk belief about it (though Christians came to believe that the jaunty little animal was sent by God), and stories about hares are fairly common in Celtic myth, where they are associated with the Otherworld and good fortune—think of the "lucky rabbit's foot." The Romans and Germans saw the beast as a symbol of fertility—think of "breeding like rabbits." In the later Middle Ages and into the witch crazes of the Renaissance and seventeenth century, some believed that witches could transform themselves into hares to work their mischief. But in this region of England, the benevolent little dancer reigned supreme.

Indeed, the bunny has never completely gone away. As recently as fifty years ago, a farmer in the same area claimed to have seen a dancing rabbit one night while he was helping with lambing. The local newspaper picked up the story and the dancing hare lived once more.

BERNARD LE FOL
(FOURTEENTH CENTURY)
Dirty dancing

Bernard "the fool" was a French entertainer at the royal court, whose job included making music, making jokes, and doing whatever was necessary to please grumpy royalty and courtiers. Fools often had quite a bit of leeway and freedom of speech. They could say what they wanted with impunity (up to a point, of course). We can look to the Fool in Shakespeare's *King Lear* for an example of this relative autonomy of thought. Kings turned to their fools for amusement, advice, and honesty when sycophantic courtiers only told them what they thought would please them. It must have been refreshing to hear an honest voice, even one telling off the monarch.

We know nothing of Bernard except that he was present at a grand celebration in June 1313 that King Philip the Fair (who really wasn't so fair; in fact, he was rather horrible) held for the knighting of his sons. It was a big deal and one to which the King of England, Edward II, was invited, and expected to attend. Edward, however, wasn't having a good time. While staying north of Paris, a fire had broken out in his wardrobe (um . . . how?), destroying many of his fine clothes and forcing him and his wife to flee into the streets in their nightgowns.

More upsetting for the king, June 19 was the one-year anniversary of the murder of his favorite courtier, Piers Gaveston, who was hated by Edward's nobility for the preferential treatment the king showed him. It has long been suspected, then and now, that the two were lovers. As you can imagine, the king was in no mood for fun.

But Bernard came up with an idea, a daring idea worthy of a fool. Sadly, we don't know the details, but Bernard rounded up fifty-four dancers (and the record is specific about that number) to provide a special entertainment for the sad and sullen monarch. A register from the time gives us only a brief, but tantalizing detail of the show: "To Bernard le Fol and 54 of his fellow actors, coming naked (*nudis*) into the presence of the king and dancing, of the king's gift, 40 s[hillings]."

So, the fool put on a nude dance review for Edward, presumably including Bernard himself. If fifty-four naked dancers don't cheer up a king, then who knows what will. The fact that this is mentioned so casually and no other explanation is given is both frustrating and intriguing. What exactly did they dance? Did they get cold? Did Bernard play a citole (a medieval guitar) and was it uncomfortable? So many questions! Apparently, the king was amused enough to reward them with a generous sum of money, so maybe it lifted his spirits a little.

Were these kinds of shows for royals fairly common? Well, more than a century later, the very religious King Henry VI of England was recorded as having fled from a Christmas feast when nude dancers made an appearance at one point. Now *they* must have been cold!

4

The Renaissance

the "rebirth" of civilization following the long period of medieval decay was an idea proudly promoted by nineteenth-century scholars. The emergence of scientific advances and a new humanism as Europe shrugged off centuries of mysticism and church oppression appealed very much to Protestant scholars working in Victorian England, as they were keen to promote the Reformation, the Elizabethan Age, Shakespeare, and other such national treasures.

The Renaissance actually began, of course, in Catholic Italy in the later fourteenth century, but let's not let those details trip us up. It was true that there was a great interest in Greco-Roman achievements and classical learning, philosophy, and mythology, all of which were reflected in art, music, theater, and dance. Dance in courtly circles started to come into its own in the fifteenth century, from which the earliest choreography and dance step manuals survive. While the church still remained opposed to certain types of dancing, there was a greater interest not only in how the upper crust were kicking up their heels, but also in what common people were doing. Painters like Bosch and Bruegel depicted various dances in their art, and Bruegel was noted for showing peasants engaged in country dances, which must have been a revelation for some. The little people enjoyed dancing, too! Who knew? Still, his peasants often had a misshapen and grotesque air about them, lest anyone think he was being too kind to the lower classes.

The Renaissance period was unusual in that thoughts about dance belonged mostly to either those that condemned it, or those that praised it; it seems like a middle ground was not even possible. On the negative side, religious reformers pointed out that dancing was often done on the days of various saints' feasts, and so, they insisted, it was actually a form of Catholic worship to be condemned! They associated dancing with gluttony and lust, and a lack of self-control that led to wanton behavior. Men and women dancing together could lead to "forbidden" behaviors. There was even a French proverb, "après la panse vient la danse," translated to "after the paunch, the dance comes" and meaning that dancing was bound up with gluttony. Interestingly, music was generally seen much more favorably by these preacher moralists. Some even held that dance "corrupted" music.

Still, outright prohibitions on dancing were rarely successful, and even if they were enacted, they didn't last long. Bans could risk public unrest, so most authorities were content to leave the common people to the things that amused them, while tut-tutting and paying lip service to moralizing to satisfy the church.

Treatises in praise of dance often came from lawyers; there has to be a pile of jokes in this somewhere . . . There was also recognition that dancing could be good for health, and doctors saw it as a form of physical exercise, within moderation of course. It was not good to dance after a meal, since this was bad for digestion, and overly wild dancing was viewed with suspicion. But in controlled amounts, many physicians saw dancing as a good and healthy thing.

Of course, with all this renewed prancing and capering, it was inevitable that some strange and gruesome stories would find their way into the mix, perhaps none more so than the poor supporters of György Dózsa, who we'll come to in a moment. Political intrigue, cross-country dancing marathons, dangerous wooden poles, and perhaps even assassination all found their way into the world of Renaissance dance, and while the church was forced to retreat a little, the religious reformers weren't always keen on these new crazes, to put it mildly. Witches, those ever-popular enemies of all things good (at least in the minds of said reformers), were known to enjoy dancing, after all, as we will see.

GYÖRGY DÓZSA (1470–1514)
ᶜᵉ⁻ᵒ *Hot under the collar, hot underfoot* ᶜ⁻ᵛ

Dózsa is a national hero in Hungary, famed for leading a peasant uprising against the oppressive and cruel nobility that were crushing the people under the proverbial iron fist at the time. Hungary was an area of many conflicts and little certainty. The Ottoman Turks were continually knocking on the door, militarily speaking, and it was the need to resist them that started what ended up becoming a bloody mess, literally.

In 1514, the Hungarian papal legate returned from a social call with the pope (okay, it was more complex than that) with a nifty little gift: a papal bull (that's an edict, not a large, holy bovine) authorizing the Hungarians to go on crusade against the impending Ottoman invasions. Dózsa—who may have been a nobleman himself—was tasked with assembling the army, and succeeded in gathering thousands of hajdúk, or mercenaries, for the job, mainly drawn from the peasantry and lowest of society. The problem was the nobles had little interest in training them properly or giving them trivial things like food and clothing. Also, their aristocratic landlords weren't happy about them leaving their fields to go fight and probably die. Who was going to harvest the cabbage if the peasants died in the crusade?

Soon, rebellion was in the air, and Dózsa, whether he liked it or not, found himself as the uprising's leader, at least in theory, but he didn't have much control. The peasant armies began ravaging the land, burning castles and crucifying or impaling the nobility, which was most definitely not how said nobles thought things would turn out. The peasants had decades of rage and frustration on their side, but the upper class still had guards with training, and in the end, the revolt failed.

Dózsa, as the figurehead of the rebellion, was made an example of, in the most grisly way imaginable. There are different accounts—no doubt each historian wanted to add his own particular ghoulish spin—but most agree that he was stripped naked and made to sit on a red-hot iron throne. An equally hot scepter was placed in his hand, along with a crown of the same unpleasant temperature, mocking his alleged desire to crown himself king. But that wasn't the end of it, oh no.

A group of his followers (the number varies) were brought to him; they had been deliberately starved for days. Dózsa's torturers removed some pliers from a fire and dug them into his flesh, tearing off pieces. The hungry onlookers were then told to set upon him and eat flesh from where they had torn the skin away or else be cut to pieces; apparently they did, eating away at him with their teeth, like wild animals. You're probably wondering what all this has to do with dance. Well . . .

These unfortunate folks were then made to dance a Hadju tánc, a traditional Hungarian military dance, commonly performed with swords. They did this around the heated throne while a bagpipe and/or other instruments played and their leader died in agony. Despite this grisly spectacle— torture, cannibalism, impalement, manic military dancing, and worst of all, a bagpipe—Dózsa was said never to have uttered a sound in pain, but actually encouraged the horrific proceedings. When the sentence was pronounced, he replied, "If a single groan escapes my lips, may my name be covered with eternal infamy!" As his flesh was being eaten, he defiantly yelled to them, "To it hounds! Ye are of my own rearing!" What he thought of their dancing, however, we don't know.

THE REFORMERS AND DANCE
⤜ꝰ *Off with their heads, and they'll drink in hell* ꝰ⤏

Well, here we go again; first the Greek and Roman moralists, then the Catholic Church, and now, the Protestant Reformers. Various members of all of them had a thing or two to say about dancing, and as we've seen, a lot of it was not good. Given the strictness of some Protestant reformers, you can imagine that their tirades against dance would be pretty intense. Actually, they could be even worse than their Catholic counterparts. Three names stand out for their wise (or not) pronouncements on all things dancing: Calvin, Knox, and Luther.

In the Geneva of John Calvin (1509–1564), dance was always a no-no, and only certain types of music were allowed. He wanted the city to follow his particular brand of theocracy, and so the Geneva Ordinances of 1547 laid down the law on what was and wasn't permissible. As you can imagine, all things fun came under scrutiny, and many were rejected. Taverns had to be closed during church services and were fined if they remained open. Drunkenness was a "three strikes and you're out" sort of deal, with fines for the first two offenses, and prison for the third. And of course, here is what the law had to say about music and dance:

> If anyone sings songs that are unworthy, dissolute or outrageous, or spin wildly round in the dance, or the like, he is to be imprisoned for three days, and then sent on to the consistory [church court].

Damn, that's pretty harsh! Of course, this is coming from a guy who thought it was fine to behead a child who struck his parents, and who had no problems when his son-in-law and stepdaughter were convicted of adultery and executed, so consider the source.

The Scotsman John Knox (1505–1572) was Calvin's chip off the old block. He held to many of the same rigid positions, but he had to be a bit more careful, living in Scotland under a Catholic queen, Mary Stuart (1542–1587). Still, he was not about to let that keep him quiet; in a famous sermon he criticized her love of dancing, especially since, on one occasion in 1562, he assumed it was in celebration of renewed persecution of Protestants in France. For this, he said, she would "drink in hell."

Getting wind of this, Mary summoned him to court to answer for it. Knox was able to backpedal a bit and use some weasel-wording to get out of trouble. He admitted to her that dancing was lawful and not always sinful, provided that those engaging in it didn't neglect their primary duties, and didn't do so out of pleasure at hearing of the misfortunes of God's people, i.e., Protestants. This was still a pretty bold thing to say, but Mary seemed content to let it go. Though realistically, Knox was probably lying, and seemed to have a spring in his step (though not a dancing one) as he left, fairly certain that he'd gotten away with something.

Martin Luther (1483–1546), on the other hand, had a much more tolerant view of dancing. In a sermon on the wedding feast at Cana, he wrote:

> Now is it a sin to play and dance at a wedding, inasmuch as some declare great sin is caused by dancing? I see no reason to condemn it, save its excess when it goes beyond decency and moderation. That sin should be committed is not the fault of dancing alone; since at a table or in church that may happen . . . Where things are decently conducted I will not interfere with the marriage rites and customs, and dance and never mind. Faith and love cannot be driven away either by dancing or by sitting still, as long as you keep to decency and moderation. Young children certainly dance without sin; do the same also, and be a child, then dancing will not harm you. Otherwise were dancing a sin in itself, children should not be allowed to dance.

Luther, of course, was accepting of many things that drove his more zealous colleagues into a tizzy, including—gasp—singing religious music in Latin and even Hebrew. Luther was also a big fan of music and a noted composer himself, so it's no shock that his views on dance were on the more lenient side. It's just that many of his colleagues weren't on the same page and were hell-bent (pun intended) on eradicating the curse of dancing once and for all. They failed.

THE DEADLY MAYPOLE
〜 *Timber!* 〜

The Maypole and the dance associated with it have a long and controversial history in Europe. Most often found in the Germanic regions, Scandinavia, and England, some believe that dancing with ribbons about the pole and weaving them into a pattern is a remnant of an ancient pagan fertility dance undertaken on May Day or thereabouts, or sometimes at summer solstice. We can say "some believe" because, as with so many folk customs, its origins are lost in the mists of time and people tend to freely invent what they want to fill in the gaps.

What is known is that moralists and theocrats from the later Middle Ages and into the Renaissance tended to hate the whole business, with all that skipping and dancing and lusty fertility stuff, though it was really the Protestants in England and Scotland that led the charge to stamp out its (to them) obvious idolatry. The pole itself may have originally represented the World Tree of Germanic paganism, the idea that the cosmos and various realms were accessed via a giant tree, called Yggdrasil in Norse belief. And of course, the long, tall wooden log was full of suggestive symbolism. You can figure that out for yourself.

Despite opposition, it was a (mostly) harmless folk custom that persisted in the face of periodic attempts to stamp it out. Yes, mostly harmless. There were a few incidents that proved that making merry could be a dangerous business, before one even got out on the green and started to dance about. Let's look at three English reports.

One unfortunate fellow discovered that what goes up can most definitely come down. In the city of Coventry on April 26, 1558, a large maypole collapsed, hitting the city stone wall. A certain Thomas Alsopp had the misfortune of being in the exact vicinity of this plunging plank. The pole dislodged a large stone from the wall, which fell and struck the left side of his head, causing a terrible indent into his skull, squishing his brain, and killing him instantly.

William Cerbe also suffered a similar fate, though his came about before the pole had even been set up. He was transporting it on his cart to Little Wakering (no, not Wankering) in Essex on April 30, 1592. The roads in those days weren't paved, and were pretty miserable, bumpy affairs that made a trip anywhere decidedly uncomfortable. This day was, unfortunately for William, the most uncomfortable of all. For whatever reason, his cart overturned and the pole that was intended to bring fun to everyone instead brought him death, when it struck his head, also killing him instantly.

Finally, a few years later on May 5, 1594, on the Abbey Green in Bath, one John Richardson suffered a similar fate, when a "maye poll or somer lug" slipped from the grip of those trying to raise it, and landed on poor John's head and shoulders, killing him in an instant. One can only imagine that the celebrations must have been pretty muted in the wake of all of these disasters, and perhaps made some fear that the pole was the work of evil forces after all. The Puritan government established after the English Civil War called them "a Heathenish vanity, generally abused to superstition and wickedness." Despite condemnation and the occasional horrific accident, they survived and continue to be erected and enjoyed, presumably just like what they allegedly symbolize.

DANCE AND THE SAINT BARTHOLOMEW'S DAY MASSACRE (1572)
ᴄᴏ *Trouble in paradise* ᴏᴏ

France, like so many regions of Europe, was in a state of pretty awful religious turmoil in the 1560s and '70s, the aftershock of the Reformation unleashed by Luther, Calvin, and company. But Catherine de Medici (1519–1589)—Italian noblewoman, Queen Mother of France, and noted patron of the arts— had an idea to try to quell at least some of the rage and violence, with a wedding, and a pageant with lots of dancing. It backfired spectacularly. Catherine's idea was to marry her Catholic daughter,

Marguerite of Valois (1553–1615) to the very Protestant Henri of Navarre (1553–1610), future king of both Navarre and France. But basically, no one liked it: not Catholics, not Protestants, and certainly not the pope, who refused to recognize and authorize it.

Catherine would not be deterred. The wedding went ahead on August 18, 1572, and was followed by spectacular celebrations, one of which was the pantomime-ballet, *Le Paradis d'Amour* ("the Paradise of Love"), rather ironically named for what was about to follow. One can imagine two sets of noble families, basically mortal enemies, sitting through the banquet and the entertainments that followed, keeping a constant watchful eye on each other; you could have cut the tension with a knife. And pretty soon, people were being cut, too.

The *Paradis* featured many scenes from myth and legend, blended into much dancing and pageantry. In one such scene, King Charles IX of France (1550–1574) took part and led his brothers in a symbolic defeat of the Huguenots (French Protestants), saving a group of nymphs and dispatching the dastardly Protestants to a hell populated by noisy demons. Yeah, that probably didn't send the best message to the Huguenots in the audience. The nymphs then danced to show their gratitude at being saved by the Catholic heroes because of course they did. But, in the spirit of "fun," Henri himself was among those so consigned to damnation and the king and his siblings obliged by "rescuing" the Protestants from hell, so that all was made right again. Well, that was the intent, anyway. If the piece wanted to show a way of reconciliation between the two warring factions, it didn't work.

Two days later, one of the leading Huguenots, Gaspard de Coligny (ca. 1519–1572), was nearly assassinated when he was shot in his shoulder and hand. What happened next still puzzles historians, but the Catholic forces began a wholesale slaughter of all Protestants in Paris and beyond, later dubbed the Saint Bartholomew's Day Massacre. This may have been done as a pre-emptive strike against what the Catholic leaders feared would be Protestant retaliation for the attack and many believe that Catherine herself was in on it, realizing that her attempts at brokering peace were going to fail. In any case, the king ordered the murders of the Protestant nobility, and they were carried out ruthlessly. But soon the bloodbath spread to the common people as well and King Charles was powerless to stop it. Coligny himself, after surviving his gunshot wound, was beheaded and his body thrown into the streets.

The massacre was just that: it's thought that between ten and thirty thousand Huguenots were killed in Paris and across France over the next few months. Untold numbers of Parisian Protestants were murdered and their bodies dumped in the Seine, even though it is recorded that many Catholic courtiers, appalled by what they were seeing, tried to intervene and save the victims.

At some point after this horrific bloodbath, rumors circulated that the dance spectacle itself, with its scenes of thinly veiled religious conflict, had given clues to the slaughter. In other words, some believed that the attack was already planned and the wedding was just a pretext for gathering the many French Protestant nobles and their retinues into the city so that they could be eliminated. It brings to mind the "Red Wedding" from *Game of Thrones*. But was this true? Was Catherine a monster after all, who elaborately plotted mass murder to remove the perceived Huguenot threat? Historians have tossed it back and forth, and the actual answer may never be known. But hey, at least the dancing was apparently spectacular.

HENRI III (1551–1589)
ເ☉ *Live by the dance, die by the dagger* ☉ⱻ

On the evening of August 1, 1589, a visitor came to see King Henri III of France. Henri had struggled to be a strong ruler, seeing as the Catholic League, a group opposed to many of his policies, had driven him out of Paris. So just outside the city, the king prepared a military campaign to retake the capital. The visitor in question was Jacques Clément (1567–1589), a radical friar who was deeply opposed to the king and all he stood for. And a card-carrying member of the Catholic League. Clément claimed to have an important message for the king, and was granted an audience. Not one of Henri's better decisions, but like we said, kingship wasn't one of his strongest attributes. As Henri leaned in to hear the religious fanatic's "secret" message, Clément drew his dagger and stabbed the king in the abdomen. Sadly for poor Henri, the metal detector wouldn't be invented until the end of the nineteenth century.

In any case, the king seized the weapon and struck his would-be assassin with it, crying out for his guards, who rushed in and killed the friar on the spot; his body was later mutilated and burned. Henri didn't die right away, but the wound was fatal, and he passed away the following morning. He has the dubious distinction of being the first French king to be murdered by one of his own subjects. So what prompted the murder of a monarch by someone willing to face his own death? Well, at least in part, it included dancing.

Henri was passionate about dance, even obsessed with it. It was one of several indulgences and personality quirks that irritated his court and alienated his people. Being a king: You're doing it wrong. He came to the throne at a very turbulent time in France's history, when Catholics and Protestants were at each other's throats and struggling for theological dominance. Both sides had no qualms about plotting slaughter (see the St. Bartholomew's massacre above). Henri inherited this mess, and he probably wasn't a bad king, really, but his priorities were different from his predecessors, and that kind of change didn't sit well with many.

He made himself far more remote than those before him, harder to reach, and seemingly more aloof. He played favorites and rewarded his group of close associates—known as *mignons*—with lavish gifts and favors. This stirred up jealousy and sparked rumors that these young men were having sexual liaisons with the king, a suspicion both then and now, though there is little evidence for it outside of gossip. He also refused to travel, another break with tradition. He preferred to stay at the Louvre—yes, that Louvre, only it wasn't a museum back then—rather than have a mobile court that traveled about the country, which left many regular French folk feeling alienated.

But it was his devotion to all things dance that irked quite a few of his courtiers. Henri commanded that dancing take place at least twice a week in the evenings, and his nobles were expected not only to be up on all their moves, but also to provide costumes and even pay for entertainments out of their own pockets. The king himself loved to lavish money and time on full-on spectacles of dance and masquerade, prompting many to resent his use of these funds when the money could have been better spent elsewhere. Also, some felt that by devoting himself so much to dancing, he was neglecting affairs of state. He *did* lose the city of Paris to a group of Catholic fanatics. And perhaps he was just carrying on a family tradition. An English ambassador to the French court once complained that the king (possibly Henri's predecessor) had no time for him because the king was too busy dancing.

Some in his own court feared that Henri was harming his health with so much devotion to prancing about. Others suspected that he used these spectacles to subtly manipulate attendees and promote his political agendas. There was often an element of propaganda where the king—who performed in his dance spectacles—used classical motifs in the stories to assert his own ability to restore order by having his character receive power from a mythological figure at the end of the piece and then use it for good.

Was Henri assassinated for loving dance too much? Well, it wasn't the only reason, of course. There was the usual tangle of politics, court intrigue, religious conflicts, and all of the other things that simmer and threaten to boil over. But his dance obsession played a part in alienating him from his courtiers, their traditions, and even the French people. His dismissal of some of their concerns—like the much later Louis XVI—resulted in a violent end from which no amount of skillful strutting could save him.

WILLIAM KEMPE (D. 1603)
❦ The nine days' wonder ❦

Kempe was an actor and dancer with a keen eye for comedy, who entertained the rich and famous throughout much of the 1580s and '90s, both in England and Denmark. In the second half of the 1590s, he was closely associated with Shakespeare and was a member of the Lord Chamberlain's Men, the acting company that also included famed actor Richard Burbage and Shakespeare himself. It's likely that Shakespeare wrote various comic roles for Kempe into his plays, including Dogberry from *Much Ado about Nothing*, Peter from *Romeo and Juliet*, and maybe even Falstaff himself (though many dispute this one).

He parted ways with the company in 1599, and it may have had something to do with his style of improvisational acting being unsuited for what the rest of the crew wanted to do, performance-wise. Hamlet famously says words which may have been the bard's own sentiments (Act II, Scene 2):

And let those that play your clowns speak no more than is set down for them; for there be of them that will themselves laugh, to set on some quantity of barren spectators to laugh too.

In other words, clowns were getting a bit too uppity and improvising too far away from the scripted page, to the annoyance of other actors.

Kempe was also famous for his jigs, which were slapstick comic pieces that included dance, often performed after a tragedy to lighten the mood. Not a bad idea considering how awful so many Elizabethan tragedies were. But many playwrights felt that these skits ruined the effect of their "elevated" tragedies and didn't like including them. The clash between comic and tragic in the theater that began with the Greeks was still going strong in the later sixteenth century.

For whatever reason, Kempe found himself out of a job (voluntarily or otherwise) and schemed up a clever publicity stunt to bring him some public attention and raise money. He resolved to perform Morris dances from London all the way up to Norwich—a distance of over one hundred miles—and later wrote about it in his pamphlet, *Kemps nine daies wonder*. He described his journey so that no one could say he had lied about doing it, "to reproue lying fooles I neuer knew," as he put it. Despite the title, he danced his amazing journey over a period of a little more than three weeks, stopping to rest along the way, of course; it wasn't meant to be a dance marathon! The actual year that it took place varies in different accounts, believe it or not, due to whether the Julian or the Gregorian calendar was referenced, but it's listed as happening either in 1599 or 1600.

He and his piper were met with curiosity and encouragement everywhere that he danced, but this being the time when highwaymen were rampant, he was not immune to the dangers of the open roads, as he notes on his second day:

> In this towne two Cut-purses were taken, that with other two of their companions followed mee from Lōdon (as many better disposed persons did): but these two dy-doppers gaue out when they were apprehended, that they had laid wagers and betted about my iourney; wherupon the Officers bringing them to my Inne, I iustly denyed their acquaintance, sauing that I remembred one of them to be a noted Cut-purse, such a one as we tye to a poast on our stage, for all people to wonder at, when at a play they are taken pilfring.

This is an interesting record of what was done to thieves caught at a theater, i.e., tying them up for public shaming. He continues:

> This fellow, and his half-brother, being found with the deed, were sent to Iayle: their other two consorts had the charity of the towne, and after a dance of Trenchmore at the whipping crosse, they were sent backe to London, where I am afraide there are too many of their occupation. To bee short, I thought myselfe well rid of foure such

followers, and I wish hartily that the whole world were cleer of such companions.

It wasn't all menace, however. He describes many friendly interactions, including this amusing incident where a certain strapping butcher wanted to dance part of the journey with him. It didn't quite go as planned:

> In this towne of Sudbury, there came a lusty tall fellow, a butcher by his profession, that would in a Morrice keepe mee company to Bury: I being glad of his friendly offer, gave him thankes, and forward wee did set: but ere ever wee had measur'd halfe a mile of our way, he gave me over in the plain field, protesting, that if he might get a 100 pound, he would not hold out with me, for indeed my pace in dauncing is not ordinary.

One can just see the picture of this strong fellow, doubled over and out of breath. After the poor man's defeat, however, another challenger emerged:

> As he and I were parting, a lusty Country lasse being among the people, cal'd him faint hearted lout: saying, if I had begun to daunce, I would have held out one myle though it had cost my life. At which wordes many laughed. Nay saith she, if the Dauncer will lend me a leash of his belles, Ile venter to treade one mile with him my selfe. I lookt upon her, saw mirth in her eies, heard boldnes in her words, and beheld her ready to tucke up her russet petticoat.

And off they went. This "merry Mayde-marian" not only kept up with him, but he rewarded her with some substantial drink money at the end of their journey.

Eventually, he made it safe and sound to Norwich, where the gathered crowds greeted him with welcome and wonder. After three weeks and no doubt some very sore feet and legs, he'd done it. He'd made money along the way, brought himself back into the public eye, and just maybe got one over on his former theater partners. He was always happy about undertaking the trip, from beginning to end; even England's notoriously unpredictable weather didn't faze him. In his dedication to his patron, he describes his feelings on that first day:

> I lowly begge pardon and leaue, for my Tabrer strikes his huntsup, I must to Norwich: Imagine, noble Mistris, I am now setting from my Lord Mayors, the houre about seauen, the morning gloomy, the company many, my hart merry.

But, as all these stories must take a grim turn, it seems that he didn't have long to live, and was probably carried off when a bout of the plague struck London in 1603. The dance of death ultimately claimed the dancer of jigs. You could say that for Kempe, the jig was up.

WITCHES' DANCES
⁃⁊ *Branle double, toil and trouble* ⁊⁃

The belief in—and fear of—malevolent witches is something that is seen as a remnant of medieval superstition, back when people were plagued by plague, feared the imminent end of the world, and thought that said world was flat. But interestingly, the wholesale persecution of witches in Europe really only got underway at about the same time as the Renaissance. It's not difficult to see why; periods of rapid social and cultural change frequently induce anxiety in those fearing that they are being left behind, and in those who want to cling to something, anything, as a measure of certainty. With the "rebirth" of interest in classical art, philosophy, humanism, and other such treasures beginning in the fourteenth century, many feared that the traditional ways of doing things would be eroded, and they were right. Throw in wars, famines, and successive waves of the bubonic plague beginning in the mid-fourteenth century, and things began to look downright scary. It seemed like the whole of society was being turned upside down.

Scapegoats for such turmoil are all too common, and for various reasons, witches (both men and women) fit the bill nicely. Witchcraft, previously seen by many medieval churchmen as superstitious nonsense, became a deadly serious concern in the fifteenth century. Witches, this new generation of clergymen believed, served the devil, subverted the natural order, caused evil, and engaged in all sorts of perversions in mockery of good Christian society. It almost went without saying that wild, uninhibited dancing was a central part of their activities.

The inquisitor Heinrich Kramer (ca. 1430–1505) believed that something had to be done, so he wrote the *Malleus Maleficarum* in 1487. This book is an exhaustive tome on the supposed activities of witches and the dangers they represent, and is an encyclopedia of paranoid delusion never before seen and rarely since surpassed. It says far more about the disturbed mental conditions of this extremely repressed man than it does about anything in the real world and is practically a textbook for psychologists.

The name of a second author, Jacob Sprenger (ca. 1436/38–1495) was added as a co-contributor in a sixteenth-century edition, but Sprenger (a well-respected inquisitor) apparently had no interest in witches, hated Kramer, and even tried to hinder him, so their supposed collaboration was probably a blatant lie to give Kramer's work more credibility. Hey, whatever works.

In addition to everything else that witches do, they dance, of course, or even better, use seemingly innocent celebrations as a way of working their evil. One German witch who was not invited to a wedding decided to take revenge on those dancing in celebration:

Being indignant because of this, and wishing to be revenged, she summoned a devil and, telling him the cause of her vexation, asked him to raise a hailstorm and drive all the wedding guests from their dancing; and the devil agreed, and raising her up, carried her through the air to a hill near the town, in the sight of some shepherds. And . . . she made a small trench and filled it with her urine instead of water, and stirred it with her finger . . . with the devil standing by. Then the devil suddenly raised that liquid up and sent a violent storm of hailstones which fell only on the dancers and townsfolk.

Talk about pissing on other people's fun! The devil didn't just help out in this one case, and had been causing such mischief for a long time. Dance originated with devils in the ancient world, of course:

Owls shall dwell there, and Satyrs shall dance there. By Satyrs here devils are meant . . . Satyrs are wild shaggy creatures of the woods, which are a certain kind of devils called Incubi.

From these devils, the pagans learned to party and dance in celebration of their gods, who were actually demons in disguise:

And in honour of him [the god Janus], or rather of the devil in the form of that idol, the Pagans made much boisterous revelry, and were very merry among themselves, holding various dances and feasts.

And so it continued through the late fifteenth century. People who still engage in dancing may not realize that they are doing wrong, but secretly underneath it all, evil works its ways:

So much that was heathen, so much that was bad, was mixed up with what might seem to be simple credulity, and the harmless folk-customs . . . a song or a country dance mayhap, innocent enough on the surface, and even pleasing, so often were but the cloak and the mask for something devilish and obscene, that the Church deemed it necessary to forbid and proscribe the whole superstition even when it manifested itself in modest fashion and seemed guileless, innoxious, and of no account.

The trend toward paranoid thinking continued as the Renaissance flowered. A French jurist, Florimond de Raemond (1540–1601), wrote a detailed description of a black mass in his *L'Anti-Christ* of 1597, in part to refute the Protestant idea that the pope was actually the Antichrist. He claims that in this case, some sixty people attended:

> . . . all of whom carried a black candle, lighted from the candle that the goat had between his horns. After that they all began to dance in circles, their backs turned to one another. The person who was performing the service was clothed in a black robe without a cross. He raised a round slice of turnip, dyed black, instead of the Host, and cried at the Elevation: Master, help us.

A turnip? Not very diabolical; now if it had been Brussels sprouts . . .

Similarly, Francesco Maria Guazzo (1570–ca. 1640) in his *Compendium Maleficarum* (1608), describes a witches' Sabbath made up of participants who are "riding flying goats, trampling the cross, and being re-baptised in the name of the Devil while giving their clothes to him, kissing his behind, and dancing back-to-back forming a round."

Clearly, dancing was seen as an important element of these satanic celebrations, precisely because it was forbidden in the actual mass, and these celebrations were blasphemous parodies of Christian practice. It's not hard to see how easy it was to associate evil with *any* kind of dancing.

The idea of celebratory witches' dances was alive in folk tradition for centuries. Robert Burns' famed poem "Tam o' Shanter" told the story of a farmer who spied a group of witches dancing in a ruined church and had to flee on horseback for his life and soul. Burns claimed that the account given to him was true and described the scene in a prose summary:

When he had reached the gate of the kirk-yard, he was surprised and entertained, thorough the ribs and arches of an old gothic window which still faces the highway, to see a dance of witches merrily footing it round their old sooty black-guard master [i.e., the devil], who was keeping them all alive with the power of his bagpipe. The farmer stopping his horse to observe them a little, could plainly desern the faces of many old women of his acquaintance and neighbourhood.

Well, it figures that the bagpipe would be a satanic instrument (no angry letters from bagpipe players, please!). Obviously, there was still a great appetite among rural populations for such stories, even at the birth of the "modern" world. Old legends die hard, and for many, a cabal of witches and their demonic (if musical) master cavorting in a local ruined church on certain nights was entirely believable, if more than a little unsettling.

5

The Seventeenth Century

the seventeenth century in Europe was another of those times of great change, and with that change came great violence. Religious wars seemed to erupt constantly on the continent, while England fought a civil war that cost the king his head and saw a puritanical government claim power for over a decade. At the same time, scientific advancements began to take off, "classical" music took on the structural forms that it still uses, theater flourished and reached new heights, and ballet as an elevated and virtuosic art form began to come into its own. These ballets were unlike modern productions, being over-the-top spectacles, starring a host of nobility and other well-off folks, and could last for hours or days at a time. Remember that during your child's next ballet recital. They featured large numbers of dancers, sometimes marching in military fashion and outfits, and including horses (horse ballets were a thing of their own, in fact). Men played many of the main roles and it was only in the latter part of the century that ballet began to feature virtuoso women dancers and be performed on stages in concert halls, rather than being the grand festive shindigs that they had been.

Even with this newfound public approval, dance was controversial and even contradictory: the English Puritan Oliver Cromwell, while banning public theater and Christmas holiday celebrations, privately enjoyed music (as well as smoking) and tolerated dancing, probably to the chagrin of some of his more religiously extreme colleagues. Meanwhile, the French king Louis XIV effectively used ballet as a way of manipulating and controlling his courtiers. In Spain, someone devised a clever, if not always bloodless, way of settling disputes by using dancing in lieu of dueling. And speaking of duels, the famed English diarist Samuel Pepys had a bone or two to pick with his wife's dancing instructor, but found out that his wife had her own pointed opinions about things.

LOUIS XIV (1638–1715)
ᶜᵉᵒ *The Sun King in Machiavellian splendor* ᶜᵛ

Louis XIV, of course, was famous for so many things, among them the palace of Versailles, the Three Musketeers, and men wearing very long and large wigs. All right, he was famed for a few other things as well, most notably (at least for this book) being an excellent and passionate ballet dancer in his early years. Over the course of his "career," he is said to have performed in some eighty ballet roles in more than forty ballets, a remarkable achievement for one who was supposed to be attending to his kingdom. At the height of his interest, he was known to have practiced dancing for up to six hours a day.

It was Louis' appearance in the *Ballet de la Nuit* ("Ballet of the Night") in February 1653 that not only showed off his talent, but established what kind of monarch he would become. This spectacle of forty-three smaller ballets lasted for over twelve hours (presumably with breaks!) and included, as its title suggests, a representation of some of the terrors of the night: werewolves, demons, and witches (who performed black masses), as well as Greek gods and goddesses, including, of course, young Louis as Apollo the sun god, who vanquishes the dark and is the light in the world. The political message was clear, and the performance gave him the nickname he would have ever after: the Sun King.

He was able to channel his interest in the art into a skillful manipulation of his royal image and he used some concepts derived from dance to do so. An attempted rebellion by a group of nobles against the monarchy when he was young impressed on him that he would have to rein in his courtiers and control them. As some historians have noted, he became a kind of political "choreographer," with his court dancing to his directions and always remembering who was at the center of the performance, namely him. He called many of the courtiers to attend to him at Versailles, forcing them to stay there in a kind of extravagant prison, where he could keep an eye on them.

He imposed strict protocols on who stood beside whom, who was permitted to sit where, how close someone was allowed to be to the king, and dozens of other rules that were designed to keep his nobles constantly guessing about their status, rather than conspiring to plot against him. Further, the men were expected to have dancing skills equal to his own, and their failure to take it seriously or improve to his liking could lead to them becoming social outcasts. Yet another bit of anxiety designed to prevent any talk of insurrection. He was a dictator-by-dance, and his scheming worked. Louis made it clear that he was the absolute monarch by divine right, and his firm hold on power would be passed down to his descendants, never to know that his grandson would wind up on the chopping block during the French Revolution, a victim of an angry people who had had enough of royal excess.

But unlike his predecessor, Henri III, ballet was not his undoing. He hung up his dancing shoes in 1670, retiring but encouraging others in the art he loved. Why did he stop so young? There are a few theories. One is that his religiously-conservative wife disapproved of his constant attention to the art. The other is that, despite his efforts at staying fit, his appetite for rich foods was making his physique unsuitable for the rigors of six hours of daily dancing. His sister-in-law claimed that she saw him at one meal eat: "four bowls of different soups, a pheasant, a partridge, a large bowl of salad, two slices of ham, a slice of mutton and a dish of pastries, finished with fruit and boiled eggs." Wow, that could definitely slow down anyone except an Olympic weightlifter.

Despite his change in looks and the subsequent downplaying of ballet as an exclusively courtly occupation, the king still expected his nobles to display their skills. A story from the 1690s tells of a young courtier named Montbron who, newly at court, insisted that he could dance, only nearly to fall on his ass in front of Louis, and try to hide that fact by flailing his arms around and making faces. The result was that the king laughed his generous butt off at the poor fool, effectively ending his prospects. Tyranny by dance proved to be an effective method, after all.

CROMWELL AND PLAYFORD: THE PURITAN AND THE DANCING MASTER (1650s)
ᥱ⤳ *Light on the feet to saves one's neck* ᥆⤳

The modern popular imagination paints the English Puritans as a pretty dour lot, a group of (mostly) men who wanted to ban as much fun as they could, following their victory in the English Civil War and the execution of King Charles I in 1649. And to be sure, life in the Commonwealth of the Puritan leader, Oliver Cromwell (1599–1658), wasn't exactly a barrel of monkeys and uproarious laughs. Cromwell was determined to enforce his version of godliness on the population, and that included things like prohibiting celebrations at Christmas—no goose, puddings, or carols for you lot. In fact, it was said that Puritan soldiers would go from home to home, smelling for feasts, barging in and shutting them down . . . jerks! They also did this on the last Wednesday of each month, which was proclaimed a day of fasting. If you were caught sneaking a pasty or some bread and ale on the quiet, you could face fines and the stocks. Further, the Puritans closed all the public theaters (Shakespeare who?), something they had wanted to do since such places of iniquity had first become popular, way back in the 1570s. You couldn't even go for a leisurely walk on a Sunday; you had to rest whether you liked it or not!

Dancing, as you can imagine, wasn't exactly high on the list of approved activities, either, and the Puritan morality police made a point of pulling down and destroying the maypoles that country folk danced around on May Day, because of their presumed pagan origins. Public dancing was another thorn in their side, and they certainly did all they could to minimize it. Yet, perhaps surprisingly, they stopped short of a full-out ban. Indeed, Cromwell was known to have his private indulgences, which included a love for secular music, smoking tobacco, and if not enthusiastically supporting it, at least tolerating dancing. He even allowed full-on dances at his daughter's wedding.

The lawyer Sir Bulstrode Whitelocke (August 1605–1675, and what a magnificent name!), once shared England's stance on dance with the queen of Sweden: despite being pretty unpopular in some quarters, it was not specifically prohibited by law, provided it was done modestly and with respect. Dancing on Sunday was still a no-no, of course, but private dancing was generally allowed to continue as it always had, as long as things didn't get too out of hand. It tended to be public displays of potential lewdness that the new religious government wanted stamped out; for example, despite the public theaters being closed, private performances of plays for the wealthy tended to be ignored.

So, perhaps it's not surprising, or maybe it's even more surprising, that one of the greatest collections of English dance music ever published first appeared in 1651, in a collection titled *The English Dancing Master,* collected by John Playford (1623–1686/7). This splendid book included more than a hundred popular dance tunes from both his time and dating back several decades, and it presented them to a public eager to learn the music and the dances. The book was so popular that it was reprinted the following year, and again in 1657, and on and on until it had seen at least eighteen editions (in three volumes) by 1728. Why on earth would this collection of potentially lewd and pagan ditties have been permitted at the height of Puritan power?

Well, Playford was smart, and knew how to play the political game. During the Civil War, he had actually favored the king, and worked as a kind of war correspondent, but he was arrested by Cromwell's forces in 1649. They apparently told him that if he valued his continued ability to keep breathing, he would forget about publicly supporting the king and focus on other things. He was only too happy to oblige, and by late the following year, he had registered his dancing book.

Additionally, though the book contained so-called "country dances" and some of the tunes had been around in popular music-making for decades, the steps were not really the dances of the common folk, those potentially dangerous gyrations that gave Puritans fits and fevered dreams. Rather, these were dances of the educated, some perhaps in imitation of lower-class dances, but definitely belonging to polite society, and as we've seen, such things were tolerated by the Puritans, if done in moderation and not flamboyantly strutted about. Given that royalists had to keep a low profile in those years, anything that could provide some relief was welcome, especially a reminder of a common social pastime from the days of the now-headless king.

In fact, Playford thrived in the 1650s and eventually had almost a monopoly on printing music for quite a few years, well into the time of the Restoration (1660 onward), when King Charles II sat his decadent butt down on the throne and everything pretty much went back to the way it had been before. The new regime, incidentally, was delighted to sponsor and encourage dancing of all kinds, so if Playford was successful before, he was way more so then. He successfully navigated a dangerous time with a head for business (that stayed on his neck) and a spring in his step.

SAMUEL PEPYS (1633–1703)
ᥫᩬ *A dashing dancing master and red-hot tongs* ᥫᩬ

The Englishman Pepys (pronounced "peeps," like the yellow marshmallow birds) was a member of Parliament and a Navy administrator, best known for his detailed diary, which he kept between 1660 and 1669, and offers an invaluable look into daily life during the Restoration of King Charles II. It's quirky, amusing, tragic, and fascinating. In it, Pepys admits to having quite a fondness for young ladies. Though he married one such young woman, Elisabeth (1640–1669, the daughter of French Protestant immigrants), he was, of course, eager to explore other possibilities. And explore he did, apparently: though he came from Puritan roots, he had a string of mistresses, flings, and flirtations all across London.

Alas, as you might expect, what was good for the gander was not good for the goose, and Pepys became convinced in May 1663 that Elisabeth was having an affair with her dancing instructor, a dashing fellow named Pembleton. He recorded his irrational feelings in some detail in his diary:

> [Pepys was] a little angry with my wife for minding nothing now but the dancing-master, having him come twice a day, which is a folly."
> (May 12)

And they weren't just dancing; they would take time out to talk. But what were they talking about?

> I found it almost night, and my wife and the dancing-master alone above, not dancing but talking. Now so deadly full of jealousy I am that my heart and head did so cast about and fret that I could not do any business possibly . . .

The dancing man was married, after all! He resolved to put a stop to it:

> [Elisabeth] by my folly has too much opportunity given her with the man . . . [who is] married. But it is a deadly folly and plague that I bring upon myself to be so jealous . . . Which however shall be ended as soon as I can possibly.

Pepys even wanted to see if she was wearing underwear while she spent time with him, or whether she neglected that garment to make things easier:

> But I am ashamed to think what a course I did take by lying to see whether my wife did wear drawers to-day as she used to do, and other things to raise my suspicion of her, but I found no true cause of doing it. (May 15)

He tried to listen in on their conversations:

> Lord! with what jealousy did I walk up and down my chamber listening to hear whether they danced or no. (May 16)

Of course, this was all centered on his wounded male vanity:

> So that I fear without great discretion I shall go near to lose too my command over her, and nothing do it more than giving her this occasion of dancing and other pleasures, whereby her mind is taken up from her business and finds other sweets besides pleasing of me . . . (May 21)

Once, while they were in church, he was quite sure that the dancing master was ogling his wife and she was subtly acknowledging his leers:

> But over against our gallery I espied Pembleton, and saw him leer upon my wife all the sermon . . . and I observed she made a curtsey to him at coming out without taking notice to me at all of it, which with the consideration of her being desirous these two last Lord's days to go to church both forenoon and afternoon do really make me suspect something more than ordinary, though I am loth to think the worst, but yet it . . . makes me curse the time that I consented to her dancing . . . (May 24)

He checked out the beds, to make sure they were still made:

> And, Lord! to see how my jealousy wrought so far that I went softly up
> to see whether any of the beds were out of order or no, which I found
> not, but that did not content me . . . (May 26)

Finally, one morning, after peeing at 3:00 a.m., he talked with her and she
convinced him of her innocence:

> After an hour's discourse, sometimes high and sometimes kind, I
> found very good reason to think that her freedom with him is very
> great and more than was convenient, but with no evil intent . . .
> (May 27)

All was well. She may well have been leading him on to make him jealous,
though it's unlikely that she and Pembleton were doing any dirty dancing.
But again, with the usual array of male double standards, Pepys saw nothing
wrong in making his own many attempts at philandering. Elisabeth was
strong-willed and had a temper, and she was quite willing to retaliate against
him for his own awful behavior. She was also increasingly sick of his indis-
cretions. In one instance, Pepys was fondling their servant Deb Willet (with
whom he was hopelessly smitten), and got caught red-handed, so to speak:

> My wife, coming up suddenly, did find me imbracing the girl . . . and
> endeed, I was with my main in her cunny (October 25, 1668)

Elisabeth was not going to let it go, and quite rightly so, which he acknowledged. Three weeks later, she railed against him again:

> She instantly flew out into a rage, calling me dog and rogue, and that
> I had a rotten heart; all which, knowing that I deserved it, I bore with
> (November 14, 1668)

Deb left their service, but Pepys found her and they finally consummated their relationship. Almost immediately, Elisabeth found out about this and her anger was boiling hot and ready to attack Deb:

> But when I come home, hoping for a further degree of peace and quiet, I find my wife upon her bed in a horrible rage afresh, calling me all the bitter names, and, rising, did fall to revile me in the bitterest manner in the world, and could not refrain to strike me and pull my hair, which I resolved to bear with, and had good reason to bear it . . . but yet by and by into a raging fit she fell again, worse than before, that she would slit the girl's nose (November 20, 1668)

She pressed him to write to Deb, swearing never to see her again, and he grudgingly obliged, though her anger and resentment lingered long after and the threats of violence continued:

> At last, about one o'clock [in the morning], she come to my side of the bed, and drew my curtaine open, and with the tongs red hot at the ends, made as if she did design to pinch me with them, at which, in dismay, I rose up, and with a few words she laid them down . . . (January 12, 1669)

This put an end to things. Alas, poor Elisabeth died of typhoid in November 1669, and Pepys was genuinely distraught. While the charming dancing master may never have taken her in her bed, death most certainly did.

SPANISH DANCING DUELS
✑ *Throwing down the shoes* ✑

We've probably all heard of the "dance off," a competition between two or more dancers to see who's the best. These are usually in good fun, but that wasn't always the case. Rivalries between dancers and their fans could get fierce and lead to violence (see our Roman friends, Bathyllus and Pylades, for example), but in Spain, there was a unique solution to the problem of feuding foot-smiths: the dancing duel.

Dancing was long held to be a valuable skill for the male nobility (though it was also encouraged for women), on par with fencing; actually, there was at least one instructor in Madrid who taught both disciplines. So, it may not come as a surprise that some genius invented a way to combine them both to settle disputes. The procedure was similar to a typical duel: the wronged party issued a challenge, the offender accepted, they agreed on the time and place, and named their seconds. It was meant to be a contest of goodwill, to show off skills rather than threaten lives; however, it didn't always work out that way. Juan de Esquivel Navarro wrote in 1642 that sometimes things got out of hand and the duelers needed to be ready:

> Many friendships are lost, and in the studios many challenges have been issued which often end up in sword fights . . . because challenges often lead to quarrels, and because other quarrels may break out, the *maestro* should have his weapons close at hand, and they should never be absent from his side.

So, dance instructors were told to be armed at all times, in case of serious arguments between their student dancers; splendid. Navarro goes into some detail about how the challenge is to be made:

> The one who is offended goes to the studio from which the annoyance emanated. When he sees that it is most full, he request that the *alta* [a type of dance] be played.

While dancing the *alta* (wearing his cape, sword, and hat, of course), he then must issue the challenge, daring the opponent to dance several sets of eight dances "to see who does more and looks better." The challenger also offers money for the musicians (very nice of him!) and names the date. The dancer who accepts the challenge must also dance the *alta*, acknowledging that he has been challenged:

> He should do all this with his hat in his hand. And after saying this, he is to put on his hat with all the arrogance that he can, and continue by saying: "I accept the challenge exactly as he articulated it."

If this is all starting to sound rather silly and like some Monty Python sketch, just remember that it did sometimes lead to further violence, requiring the master to step in and settle things appropriately. During the actual challenge, the two dancers were to dance in alternation, and then the master took a vote from all of the spectators as to who they thought the winner should be. Often, it ended in a near draw, honor was restored, and both went away satisfied, at least in theory. It may all have been mostly for show, but the master always kept his weapons close by, just in case things got a little out of hand—or out of foot, as it were.

6

The Eighteenth Century

the eighteenth century and the beginning of the Enlightenment saw a major shift in the world of artistic dance. Louis XIV was just as eager to encourage virtuoso women dancers as he was men, setting the stage in France for the rise of professional ballerinas. Even though the previous century had more often focused on male dancers, the French ballerina came into her own in the 1700s. These young women now had the opportunity to learn and display a level of technical virtuosity previously unknown, and as you might expect, this was quite shocking and even offensive to some with a more conservative nature. But the genie was not going back in the proverbial bottle, and with these new and daring choreographies, jumps, leaps, and feats (feets?), women were well on their way to becoming the dance sensations that they would be known for in subsequent centuries.

This gave them a confidence and power that they wouldn't have had before, and led to such incidents as one dancer creatively taking her anger out on a musician as part of a legal dispute, while another ballet star created a very adult-oriented form of entertainment for her guests. A far cry from your holiday performance of *The Nutcracker*. Despite their newfound fame, dancers' lives were difficult, and having to deal with grumpy choreographers didn't help, as we will see.

At this time, France continued to cultivate ballet, though not with the fervor that Louis XIV once had. Across the channel, England was also beginning to enjoy ballet, imported from its French neighbors, but one of its most well-known native folk-dance traditions, as we will see, could produce some grisly results from time to time, which only furthered the negative stereotypes already dogging it.

Speaking of folk dances, the French brought a whole new level of gruesomeness to one little-known folk dance, which angry revolutionaries gleefully undertook around the guillotines of the condemned, to taunt them and mock them before they had a little taken off the top. That the doomed were sometimes forced to take part in this jaunty celebration before their bloody executions made it that much more delightfully awful.

MARIE-THÉRÈSE PERDOU DE SUBLIGNY (1666–1735)
⤙ঐ *The chamber pot of horrors?* ঐ⤙

How does one refer to her for short? Marie? Marie-Thérèse? Perdou? De Subligny? The possibilities are endless! In any case, she was a highly gifted dancer, and the first professional ballerina to appear in England. She was the daughter of an actor and playwright who may have had a hand in the creation of the publishing sensation known as *Letters of a Portuguese Nun*, which, unfortunately, isn't quite as salacious as it sounds; it was merely a series of love letters, but it was still quite popular. Despite this literary upbringing, she strangely never learned to read or write, which would play a role in another colorful (malodorous?) event late in her life.

In any case, she developed into a magnificent dancer, taking the lead at the Paris Opéra for more than seventeen years and spending enough time in London to influence the dancers there. She retired before the age of forty, but a curious anecdote survives from the year before her death. For reasons unknown, she had a quarrel with a certain violinist named Francoeur. Did he live nearby? Was he playing too loud? Practicing too late? We'll never know, unfortunately, but in the ensuing argument, she proceeded to dump a full chamber pot on his head. Musicians just never get any respect. Along with a certain Madeline de Bailleul (they were listed as being "of age"), she also sued him; he must have really been playing too late! Apparently, said lawsuit was tossed out of court, because she couldn't sign the plea; that whole illiterate business came back to haunt her. Some have argued that this couldn't have been the demure and talented ballerina, and have insisted that it was another lady of the same name, but it's fun to think that this matronly dancer, long retired and weary of everyone's nonsense, had finally had enough of an obnoxious neighbor playing too early or too late, and took matters into her own hands.

WILLIAM KEELEY,
THE MORRIS-DANCING MURDERER (D. 1772)
᧒ *Dancing the Tyburn jig* ᧒

On May 24, 1772, a gardener named Joseph Dyer took a long walk from his home near the town of Chipping Campden in England's idyllic Cotswolds. He went to collect some money he was owed, and while walking home, decided to stop at an inn to refresh himself. Thus satisfied, he left and began to wander home. He never made it. Sometime later that afternoon, his body was found, the victim of terrible violence. His throat was cut, one of his ears was mostly torn off, his head showed signs of being beaten, and some of his teeth were no longer in his mouth. They had been placed in his hat, lying on the ground next to him.

This appalling murder immediately became the talk of the area. Soon, a girl claimed she had seen a laborer named William Keeley on the same road and that he had blood on his pants. Keeley was arrested, and though denying everything at first, he soon confessed, but claimed that he wasn't alone. First, he tried to frame a man named Taylor, but it came out that his accomplice was actually one James Warner. These two weren't your average field laborers trying to make some extra cash in a robbery gone wrong. Oh no, they were far worse, as the *Oxford Journal* reported at the time:

> It seems that Keeley is a famous Morrice dancer, and on Sunday morning before the fact was committed, he was teaching a set of fellows to dance. Warner used to play on the tabor and pipe to the dancers. It is to be hoped the Justices will suppress such nurseries of idleness and drunkenness as morrice-dancings have generally proved.

Morris dancing already had a pretty bad rap among many in conservative and religious circles, who believed that this lively, jumping folk dance art with tricky footwork while wearing bells was inspired by lewd and pagan dances, or even worse, by the devil himself. So, it was no surprise to many that a Morris dancer and his musician would be involved in such a heinous crime. However, since there is no record of a trial for Warner, we can assume that he was acquitted, or the charges were dropped, or he somehow talked his way out of it. Actually, he may have had nothing to do with it at all.

Keeley was taken to Chipping Campden to be executed. There, he finally confessed that he alone had attacked Dyer for his money, picking up a hedge stake and hitting the poor man on the head, when he was climbing over a stile (a fence crossing) in front of him. Keeley admitted to hitting him again as he was lying on the ground, but then, strangely said that he couldn't bring himself to search Dyer's body for money and instead ran away. This brings up interesting questions: if this is true and he ran off, who cut Dyer's throat and knocked out his teeth? Presumably that person also stole the money. Was it Warner after all? Or some other unknown assailant? We'll probably never know.

In any case, Keeley was hanged. Hanging was sometimes known as "dancing the Tyburn jig," "jig" for the kicking and jerking that the condemned criminal did while being elevated and strangled by the rope (this was the preferred English method, rather than dropping victims from on high and breaking their necks). "Tyburn" after a village just outside of London where hangings took place. Whatever final performance he may have given, Keeley's lifeless, chained body was displayed swinging up on the gallows for some time afterward as a warning of the penalty for murder, and perhaps even worse, of the dangers of being a Morris dancer!

MARIE-MADELEINE GUIMARD (1743–1816)
ᏸ *Preaching to the perverted* ᏸ

Guimard was a ballet dancer at the center of attention during the reign of the ill-fated Louis XVI, who despite his grandfather, showed little interest in the art form (which didn't save him from a grisly fate). She was, simultaneously, a professional ballet dancer, a courtesan, a purveyor of eighteenth-century live sex shows, and a generous benefactor to the needy. By any reckoning, she had an inauspicious beginning, being the illegitimate daughter of one Anne Bernard, who seems to have forced her into a life of prostitution at a young age. Guimard had dance talent, however, and was able to make a name for herself. She was dancing at the court and the Paris Opéra by the age of twenty.

Ballerinas at the time frequently doubled as courtesans (by choice or by necessity; we'll look at them in more detail in act II), and Guimard played the game masterfully, lining up a string of wealthy lovers, including Charles de Rohan, Prince de Soubise, and no less than the Bishop of Orléans, one of the most powerful Catholic churchmen in France. At a time when the church tended to vehemently condemn dancers, to say nothing of courtesans, this was quite an achievement. Indeed, once when she fell ill, a sermon was given asking the congregation to pray for her recovery! Needless to say, she did very well for herself.

Despite these holy associations, her most notorious business venture was yet to come. In 1768, she adopted the idea of presenting decidedly pornographic ballets and stage shows to discriminating audiences in the upper classes. Dubbed the "Temple of Terpsichore," her shows featured scandalous live sex acts on stage—whether dances, burlesques, plays, or even operas—and private viewing boxes for audience members who wanted to partake in their own activities while watching. Yes, it was basically eighteenth-century porn to get people in the mood. The subjects varied, but they could be comedies, tragedies, or something in between, and were often based on Greek myths and the like, which were perfect for taking things to extremes.

These types of clandestine theaters were popular in pre-revolutionary France, and many saw them as on the same level as lavish dinners or dances. Sometimes, such shows were offered as an addition to one of these more respectable events, and it was common for them to be owned or run by women. The Duchess de Villerois, for example, produced explicit theater with exclusively female casts and lesbian themes. Because these entertainments were not anti-government (they *were* for the upper classes, after all!), they were often overlooked by the police, the church, and self-appointed enforcers of morals.

All during this time, Guimard continued to dance in an "official" capacity at public performances, and received much acclaim and praise for her grace on stage. Despite the popularity of her semi-secretive ribald repasts, Guimard's initial backer wanted out after a few years, so she turned, naturally, to her old friend the Bishop of Orléans, who seemed delighted to pitch in to keep the naughtiness flowing. With his financial help, she was able to build an even larger theater, which sat five hundred and nested inside an existing mansion (for privacy's sake, of course). There, she hosted three dinners a week, one of which was, according to a source at the time, "a veritable orgy . . . where luxury and debauchery attain their zenith." That's a lot to live up to once a week!

But even this ode to onanism flourished for only a relatively short time, and it folded in 1785, due to changing tastes and the increasing turmoil of the nation, as well as her own financial troubles from living lavishly. Guimard was smart and auctioned off the theater, but a storm was brewing in the form of that little event known as the French Revolution. One of her backers and the father of one of her children both lost their heads, and she was compelled to hide out in an attic in Montmartre where, apparently, she survived because revolutionary soldiers couldn't be bothered to climb the steep hill to find her. Who knew it could be that easy? If only Louis XVI had thought of it.

Though she couldn't dance publicly during those treacherous years, she came up with the ingenious idea of reviving her lewd theater by producing small shows using marionettes . . . yes, puppet porn. These shows earned her some money, because people still wanted their naughty entertainments any way they could get them. Somehow, she weathered the storm of flying heads and kept her own, dying at a decently old age in 1816.

THE CARMAGNOLE DANCE
AND THE FRENCH REVOLUTION
ᥱᥲᥩ *Dance-off with their heads?* ᧖

The Carmagnole was a song and dance popular during the French Revolution. Originally named for a type of peasant costume in Carmagnola, a town in northwestern Italy, "Carmagnole" was a fashion adopted by the Jacobins, those revolutionary hardliners that introduced lovely little things like the Reign of Terror. The all-singing, all-dancing bit came about when the name was given to a tune (allegedly also from Italy) to which appropriate words were added. It was both a satire and a condemnation of Louis XVI and Marie Antoinette. Here is one slightly abridged version (several others exist):

Madame Veto [Marie Antoinette] has promised
To cut everyone's throat in Paris
But she failed to do this,
Thanks to our cannons.

Refrain:
Let us dance the Carmagnole
Long live the sound
Let us dance the Carmagnole
Long live the sound of the cannons.

Mr. Veto [Louis XVI] had promised
To be loyal to his country
But he failed to be,
Let's not do quarters.

Refrain

Antoinette had decided
To drop us on our asses
But the plan was foiled
And she fell on her face.

Refrain

Her husband, believing himself a conqueror
Knowing little our value
Go, Louis, big crybaby
From the Temple into the tower.

Refrain

The Swiss had promised
That they would fire our friends
But how they have jumped!
How they have all danced!

Refrain

When Antoinette sees the tower,
She wishes to make a half turn,
She is sick at heart
To see herself without honor.

Not exactly the most pro-monarchist of sentiments! The song was very popular and a fairly energetic dance often accompanied it. Enthusiastic revolutionaries would sing and dance this around guillotines during executions. So, the last thing some of the condemned might have seen and heard in their lives was a taunting song and commoners kicking up their heels in celebration of the grisly acts about to follow. Sometimes the condemned were even forced to sing along with it before climbing the stairs to meet their ghastly fates, just to add insult to injury.

In August 1792, revolutionaries stormed Tuileries Palace where the royal family was staying, or rather, being held. They fled, and the Swiss Guard charged with protecting them were massacred. According to tradition, the attackers were "drunk with blood" and celebrated by singing and dancing the Carmagnole to mark their grisly victory. The song may actually have been composed afterward as a reminder of this event, but that does not, of course, preclude spontaneous singing and dancing in a fit of blood lust!

Even when not engaging in wholesale slaughter, the dancers could get pretty wild, and it seemed to some that the whole thing was little more than an organized riot. Charles Dickens' description in *A Tale of Two Cities* is vivid and while written long after the fact, captures the essence of the dance's vigor and its ability to stir up bloodlust and anger:

They danced to the popular Revolution song, keeping a ferocious time that was like a gnashing of teeth in unison. Men and women danced together, women danced together, men danced together, as hazard had brought them together. At first, they were a mere storm of coarse red caps and coarse woollen rags; but, as they filled the place, and stopped to dance about Lucie, some ghastly apparition of a dance-figure gone raving mad arose among them.

He continues with a description of the movements, which get pretty intense!

They advanced, retreated, struck at one another's hands, clutched at one another's heads, spun round alone, caught one another and spun round in pairs, until many of them dropped. While those were down, the rest linked hand-in-hand, and all spun round together: then the ring broke, and in separate rings of two and four they turned and turned until they all stopped at once, began again, struck, clutched, and tore, and then reversed the spin, and all spun round another way. Suddenly they stopped again, paused, struck out the time afresh, formed into lines the width of the public way, and, with their heads low down and their hands high up, swooped scream-ing off.

The whole thing was reminiscent of a mob or a brawl:

No fight could have been half so terrible as this dance. It was so emphatically a fallen sport—a something, once innocent, delivered over to all devilry—a healthy pastime changed into a means of anger-ing the blood, bewildering the senses, and steeling the heart. Such grace as was visible in it, made it the uglier, showing how warped and perverted all things good by nature were become. The maidenly bosom bared to this, the pretty almost-child's head thus distracted, the delicate foot mincing in this slough of blood and dirt, were types of the disjointed time. This was the Carmagnole.

This description is probably not far from the truth, since Dickens used a number of historical accounts in crafting his classic story. Other sources describe the song's verses as having slow dance movements, while the refrains become very rapid and lively for contrast. The song was even adopted into regimental music as a patriotic tune, but without the lively dancing. New verses were added over the decades, and it was still being sung by revolutionaries and anarchists at the end of the nineteenth century, a reminder of the grim days when the fed-up lower classes gleefully danced in mockery around those condemned to die a horrid death by decapitation.

CHARLES LOUIS-FRÉDÉRIC DIDELOT (1767–1837)
ᘓᗇᗇ *Spare the rod . . . well, not so much* ᘓᗅᗅ

Didelot was a French dancer and choreographer, but he is most importantly known for his work in Russia and for bringing Russian ballet up to equal status with its French counterpart. He is credited with inventing the precursor to the dancer's flesh-colored leotard, allowing for the appearance of being naked while still clothed, as well as introducing wires for his dancers to be lifted up off the stage floor to create the illusion of flying.

He came to Russia in 1801, having been invited by the director of the Imperial Theatres, but his dancing career came to an end in 1806, following an injury to his leg and the death of his wife. Undaunted, he continued as an instructor and choreographer, but he was more than a little cantankerous, quite possibly because of his personal misfortunes.

He was a harsh master and was not afraid of showing his displeasure when his students failed to live up to his expectations. He was known to give them beatings, and it was said that they would leave his classes with their arms and legs bruised where he had struck them. Now to us, this seems horrible and abusive, and it is, but given the harsh reputation of ballet at the time, and the strictness that most instructors required of their pupils, his punishments were probably not unusual or uncommon.

His stern watch continued during performances. He was very approving if his dancers did everything right, but if they messed up, he could be fierce:

> . . . he shook his fist at them, and, if they missed the figures, he made their lives a misery. He pounced on them like a hawk, pulled their hair or ears, and if any ran away he gave them a kick which sent them flying.

With one dancer, even though she received applause, he took hold of her backstage, shook her and punched her in the back to force her out onstage again, presumably to take more bows. The odd thing is, outside of classes and the theater, he was known to be very kind to all of his students, and it was said that he would even kiss those whom he had just hit an hour earlier. Whatever his failings, the company was said to be excellent, probably because they were too afraid not to be.

His grouchy nature eventually got him dismissed from the Imperial Troupe in 1810 after a fight with the director, who was probably sick of him and not as easily cowed as his young dancers. Didelot left Russia for a time and worked in England, but eventually returned six years later and remained for the rest of his life, no doubt temperamental until the end.

7

The Nineteenth Century

The nineteenth century ushered in enormous changes that altered the course of the world's history forever (and not always for the better), and the effects of which are still with us: the Industrial Revolution, Romanticism, the invention of amazing new technologies, colonialism, the expansion of the arts into the patronage of a wider populace, wars for independence, civil wars, revolutions, and just about everything else good and appalling that one can imagine.

With these transformations came the explosion of populations in cities, especially in Europe and North America, as families who had lived in the country for generations left behind old ways of life and sought to make their fortunes in the factories and other engines of industrialism. Most often, they failed, lived in squalid conditions, died young, and were miserable. The end? Well, no, not quite. Out of this squalor came new entertainments and a democratization of the arts; royalty and nobility were no longer the exclusive employers of artists, composers, dancers, and other entertainers. That role could be taken on by wealthy businessmen and the like, but this wasn't always an improvement.

The upper classes, of course, still had their upper-class entertainments, and ballroom dancing was a perennial favorite. From the shocking waltz to decidedly unsafe ball gowns, from the invented "exoticism" of a Middle

Eastern dance introduced to an intrigued Victorian populace to the crazy and outlandish habits of the quintessential English fop, the nineteenth century had no shortage of dancing weirdness, violence, ignominious tales, and even murder. Here is a sampling of some of the better tales.

THE SCANDAL OF THE WALTZ
The maelstrom of burning desire

The waltz is beloved today, a classic dance form associated with everything from the music of Johann Strauss to the TV shows of Lawrence Welk, and it's about as tame as can be imagined. Naturally, this means that at one time it was the epitome of evil, and the subject of much condemnation.

In its modern form, it seems to have appeared in Austria in the second half of the eighteenth century, its name meaning "to turn" or "revolve." Some have theorized that it came from rural peasant dances that were popular in Austria and Bavaria, which would have lent an even more unpleasant air to the whole thing in the eyes of its detractors, who wouldn't have wanted such rustic gyrations anywhere near polite society. Indeed, early forms of the dance were likely a lot less formal, and involved not so much gentle steps and polite holding of one's partner, but rather vigorous moves and the full-on swinging of whoever was nearby, touching them in forbidden places and potentially leading to who-knows-what.

Perhaps in an effort to quell this alarm, the dance became more formal and more reserved, but even then, its detractors continued their attacks. After all, it required a significant amount of touching of one's partner for long periods of time, completely oblivious to the other couples on the floor. Who knew what lascivious thoughts might enter their heads? One might have even seen their partner's ankles.

In 1797, German critic Salomon Jakob Wolf published a pamphlet titled "Proof that waltzing is a main source of the weakness of the body and mind of our generation," proof also that he wasn't messing around. It sold out two printings, which showed that a lot of people agreed with him; that's a lot of proof! One criticism levelled against this dance was that "the dancers grasped the long dresses so that it would not drag or be trodden upon, and lifted it high holding them like a cloak which brought both bodies under one cover, as closely as possible against them," and who knows what kind of sinful behavior they would get up to in that case!

In England, controversy over the dance led to a duel, as reported in the *Times* on July 22, 1812:

> Monday morning a duel took place between General Thornton and Mr Theodore Hook. After exchanging one shot each, the affair was amicably settled. It originated in a silly dispute on the subject of the dance called the waltz, the General having praised it in high terms, and the Author having bitterly reprobated it as leading to the most licentious consequences.

Later, in 1816, the *Times* again reported on the scandal of the dance, and the Prince Regent's shock upon witnessing it. It noted:

> National morals depend on national habits: and it is quite sufficient to cast one's eyes on the voluptuous intertwining of the limbs, and close compressure of the bodies, in their dance, to see that it is indeed far removed from the modest reserve which has hitherto been considered distinctive of English females. So long as this obscene display was confined to prostitutes and adultresses we did not think it deserving of notice; but now that it is attempted to be forced upon the respectable classes of society by the evil example of their superiors, we feel it a duty to warn every parent against exposing his daughter to so fatal a contagion.

The English waltz was apparently a slower affair than its Viennese cousin (though it got more energetic as time passed) and involved a lot of prolonged eye contact, which of course could lead to all sorts of naughty implications. Lord Byron, not exactly the most conservative fellow of his age, was critical of it and wrote a poem about the whole thing (first published anonymously), wherein he clearly noted that the movements were better suited to privacy and darkness:

> Endearing Waltz! – to thy more melting tune
> Bow Irish jig and ancient rigadoon.
> Scotch reels, avaunt! and country-dance, forego
> Your future claims to each fantastic toe!
> Waltz – Waltz alone – both legs and arms demands,
> Liberal of feet, and lavish of her hands;
> Hands which may freely range in public sight
> Where ne'er before – but – pray "put out the light."
> Methinks the glare of yonder chandelier
> Shines much too far – or I am much too near;
> And true, though strange – Waltz whispers this remark,
> "My slippery steps are safest in the dark!"

In his satirical poem, "English Bards and Scotch Reviewers," he also writes:

> Now round the room the circling dow'gers sweep,
> Now in loose waltz the thin-clad daughters leap;
> The first in lengthen'd line majestic swim,
> The last display the free unfetter'd limb!
> Those for Hibernia's lusty sons repair
> With art the charms which nature could not spare;
> These after husbands wing their eager flight,
> Nor leave much mystery for the nuptial night.

Given this controversy, there was a widespread interest in religious books condemning dance in general, apparently because of the fact that clergymen sometimes got a little bit carried away in their descriptions of what might happen to young ladies "corrupted" by dancing. Seeing this, American author Ambrose Bierce jumped on the critical bandwagon and wrote a critique of the waltz in 1877, splendidly titled *The Dance of Death*, under the pseudonym of William Herman. But he was lampooning the religious anti-dance screeds at the time (see the "Anti-Dance Books" chapter in act II for a whole lot more on these strange and wonderful tomes!). Knowing that his audience would initially be mostly devout readers looking for more ammunition in their war on the waltz, he decided to give them lurid descriptions (for the time) of the dance that might instead have gotten them a bit hot under the collar, offering up lengthy visions of waltzing that evoked seduction and sex:

> Her head rests upon his shoulder, her face is upturned to his; her naked arm is almost around his neck; her swelling breast heaves tumultuously against his; face to face they whirl, his limbs interwoven with her limbs; with strong right arm about her yielding waist, he presses her to him till every curve in the contour of her lovely body thrills with the amorous contact . . . his hot breath is upon her hair, his lips almost touch her forehead, yet she does not shrink; his eyes, gleaming with a fierce intolerable lust, gloat satyr-like over her, yet she does not quail; she is filled with a rapture divine in its intensity—she is in the maelstrom of burning desire.

Knowing that he was punking his upstanding readers makes this even funnier, because the language is much closer to erotic underground novels of the time than anything a religious campaigner would pen, and yet sincere audiences ate it up, probably never realizing that they'd been had! Bierce even gave it a bad review in his newspaper column as a further joke, but that only stiffened the resolve of his audience (so to speak) and the little volume sold at least eighteen thousand copies, so many a good moralist apparently bought it for its hot and steamy, er, good and decent content.

Later in the year, another book, *The Dance of Life: An Answer to the Dance of Death*, was published, allegedly by a Mrs. Dr. J. Milton Bowers as a response to "Herman's" licentious attack. Bierce probably wrote this one, as well, though he denied it. Nevertheless, a copy inscribed with the words "from the authoress" was written in handwriting very similar to Bierce's. It seems he wanted to extend the gag for a little longer.

Joking aside, given the prudery of the time, when the virtue of young ladies was paramount, it's no wonder that such an exciting and shocking dance would capture the imagination of the young and horrify their parents. But despite Bierce's prank, no amount of religious ranting and parental oversight could hold back the tide of a new dance craze. Just as the *Leave it to Beaver* generation was shocked by the gyrations of "Elvis the Pelvis," the Regency elites were equally appalled by "Lord Buster the Thruster." Okay, he wasn't a real person, but you get the idea.

Despite the hand-wringing and warnings of eternal damnation, the waltz persisted and prospered, becoming one of the most beloved dance forms of the nineteenth and twentieth centuries.

EMILY AND MARY WILDE (1847–1871 AND 1849–1871)
ೲೲ *The people who don't know how to play with fire get burned up* ೲೲ

Even as the fashion of the wealthy evolved from the elaborate excesses of the eighteenth century to styles that at least seemed a bit more practical, nineteenth-century clothing was not always safe. One fabric in particular, crinoline, was especially popular in the use of making those ridiculously wide Victorian dresses loved by upper-class ladies in the 1850s and '60s. It was also especially flammable, and thousands of women are said to have burned to death wearing the stuff. In this case, the two tragic victims, Emily and Mary, were half-sisters to none other than Oscar Wilde. They were the illegitimate daughters of the prominent surgeon, Sir William Wilde (1815–1876), but they managed to live respectable lives, being raised separately from the family by a relative of William's. They were welcome in the halls of high society and enjoyed attending balls and parties.

One such event was a Halloween ball held on October 31, 1871, at Drumacon House in Ireland. It was to prove far more ghoulish than they ever expected. The party was a great success and as the evening wore on, guests gradually made their ways home. The host, Andrew Reid, asked one of the sisters (both have been named in differing versions of the story) for a final whirl around the ballroom, and she was happy to oblige; it turned out to be a terrible idea. While she danced, her very flammable crinoline dress made contact with open flames; some reports say candles, others a fireplace. Either way, you can probably imagine what happened next.

As the dress went up like a bonfire, the other sister rushed to her aid . . . and promptly set her own dress ablaze. Reid tried to help contain the fire by wrapping his coat around the poor young lady he had danced with—the sister was apparently left to fend for herself; how thoughtful of him. To be fair, another report says he did try to help both of them. He may have rushed one or both outside and rolled them on the ground. One version said that there had been an early snowfall, so this would seem a good option, though even good old dirt and mud would help.

Ultimately, his efforts were for naught. Both sisters sustained terrible third degree burns that would prove fatal. Mary died on November 8 and her sister a few weeks later on November 21; they undoubtedly suffered terribly. The official coroner's report listed their name as "Wylie" and omitted their first names, probably to avoid any hint of scandal. Appearances in society were still everything in those days, after all. The story was actually hushed-up to avoid word getting out about their illegitimate status, and the family managed to keep it a secret for many years.

One creepy coda: after the sisters' deaths, it was said that a veiled woman dressed all in black would visit their graves and keep a silent vigil; she allegedly did this for some two decades. When asked about her relationship to the young women, she would only reply that they were close to her. Oscar Wilde would later write that a woman in black visited his father on his deathbed. Was the story of the veiled woman visiting the sisters merely an urban legend spun out from Wilde's own writings? Or did she really exist and was she the same person in both instances? Was she the girls' biological mother? Did Wilde even know of the existence of his half-sisters (there's some doubt). The family's success in keeping the incident out of the public eye has left all of these tantalizing questions unanswered.

FANNY ELSSLER (1810–1884)
⊷ꙮ *Family jewels and feline ammunition* ꙮ⊷

Fanny was an Austrian ballet dancer of considerable skill whose father was a copyist for the composer Franz Joseph Haydn, so she already had a good connection to the world of music and the stage. She was to become known for her excellent work *en pointe* and for introducing stylized folk dances into ballet performances. She traveled widely and received considerable acclaim throughout her career, living to an old age and dying very wealthy.

Two highly silly things merit her inclusion here. In 1840 she was invited to tour the young United States, and ended up being the toast of the town in Washington, D.C., literally. It was said that congressmen drank from a dance slipper in her honor, which can't have tasted very good. Politicians have been kinky for a long time, it seems.

On her journey to the New World, she had a very distressing experience, though one from which she extricated herself with great courage, if some savagery. The captain of the ship had given a dinner in her honor, and she wore her best jewelry to the affair. Well, said bling caught the eye of one sailor, who was determined to have it for himself, a shipman's pay being what it was in those days. Later in the evening, he snuck into her cabin with a knife, intent on stealing the stones. He had apparently forgotten that she was a dancer with great kicking ability. Instinctively, she kicked out in self-defense, her feet hitting . . . somewhere. It may have been in the head, it may have been in a place that was a bit more sensitive, but wherever she struck, it was enough to prove fatal. The hapless would-be thief died a few days later from the injury. She presumably pleaded self-defense and nothing more was said about it, though people probably gave her a bit of a wide berth for the rest of the sea voyage.

Fanny was used to rapturous applause and receptions, and flowers being thrown on stage, but once in Russia, she was inadvertently the cause of something a little less pleasant for a fellow dancer. She had secured a role at the Imperial Theater in St. Petersburg, where she had supplanted Elena Andreianova (1819–1857), one of the city's top ballerinas and mistress of the theater's director. The director tried to placate Elena by sending her to Moscow to dance for the Bolshoi Ballet, where she displaced the favorite ballerina and upset audiences there. Every dancer was shifting one space to the side, it seems, and no one liked it. During one of Elena's performances, instead of flowers, someone in the audience threw a dead cat at her. Way worse than rotten tomatoes! It was enough to make her faint, but when she revived, the crowd apparently felt remorse and gave her a standing ovation. Well, that's all right, then. Actually, this flattery must have worked, because she ended up staying at the Bolshoi for fifteen years; presumably no more dead creatures were lobbed her way.

Given the competitive nature of ballerinas, if Fanny ever heard about the incident, she probably would have been very amused. If it had happened to her, she no doubt would have just kicked the beast back into the audience.

THE ART OF BELLY DANCE IN THE WEST
ᴄᴇ᩠᪲ᴐ *Unseemly undulations* ᏸ᩠᪲

It can be argued that no dance has been so misinterpreted, abused, or misunderstood as the "belly dance." Men in Western Europe had long been obsessed with the "Oriental" belly dancer, particularly the Egyptian *ghaziyah*—Arabic for "invader of the heart"—or, dancing girl. The *ghawazi* (plural of *ghaziyah*)—likely related to the traveling Romany peoples from northern India—often made their living by dancing and performing. When economic times were lean (like when Muhammad Ali Pasha kicked them out of Cairo to appease conservative religious leaders, who didn't want the government to make money off of the taxes the dancers paid, because it was money made from vice), they would turn to sex work. Belly dancers around the world are still fighting this stigma, including those who perform in the Middle East today.

At the turn of the eighteenth century, when Napoleon occupied Egypt, the French considered the *ghawazi* as more of a nuisance than entertainment as they followed soldiers from camp to camp along the Nile performing dances and other "services." One French officer supposedly had enough, and ordered that four hundred *ghawazi* be beheaded and their bodies thrown into the river. More reliable sources suggest that an unspecified number of *ghawazi* were put in sacks and drowned after being blamed for bringing sexually transmitted diseases to the French camps; because that response is obviously so much nicer.

Writer Gustave Flaubert famously wrote about his encounter in Egypt with Kutchek Hanem, a professional public dancing girl. After "servicing" Flaubert and his traveling companion Maxime du Camp privately, she enthralled them with her "Bee" dance, in which an imaginary bee is trapped in the dancer's skirts and chemise, forcing her to, of course, ultimately remove all of her clothes to rid herself of the stinging insect. The Bee or "Wasp" dance as it was also known, was a popular shtick in pantomime at the time, but probably bears little resemblance to contemporary belly dance. It certainly created quite a buzz.

Belly dance famously (infamously?) came to the shores of Lake Michigan on the Midway of the World's Fair: Columbian Exposition in Chicago in 1893, where the mere mention of undulating ladies was enough to elicit moralizing protest and lurid obsession. The enterprising impresario Sol Bloom (1870–1949) capitalized on Victorian sexual repression when he booked acts for the Midway Plaisance, which placed exhibits featuring "human showcases" next to carnival amusements and conflating the two.

Western fascination with the "exotic Orient" was in full force and the Middle Eastern exhibits—which, of course, featured dancers—were, by far, the most popular, particularly after Bloom decided to translate the French *danse du ventre* (literally "dance of the stomach") into English as "belly dance," a term which has stuck ever since. For a culture who thought piano limbs had to be covered because they were considered to be too sexually suggestive (no, seriously!), even to mention the word "belly" was enough to send audiences into a tizzy. Indeed, the belly dancing at the Egyptian Street in the Cairo pavilion brought in more than two and a half million visitors in the fair's short six-month run.

Bloom was responsible for promoting the Midway's Algerian Village. At a preview of the exhibit, he failed to bring musicians for the dance performance. So, he made up his own "Oriental" tune, still popular with school kids even today with lyrics such as, "There's a place in France/where the naked ladies dance/and the dance they do/is called the hoochy-coo." It's found its way into cartoons, movies, and just about everywhere; you've all heard it. There's nothing even remotely "authentic" about it, sorry to say.

Meanwhile, the uncorseted Oriental dancer invited scorn and disdain, eliciting shock and offense from any self-described "decent" member of American society. The *Chicago Tribune* wrote that "the style of movements practiced by these so-called Algerian and other women is something too objectionable for people of refined taste to be of countenance. It is a depraved and immoral exhibition." The *Savannah Times* said, "It is not dancing. It is walking about the stage to alleged music with peculiar swaying and jerking of the body, such as tends to excite the passion." Several dancers adopted the moniker of "Little Egypt" and became famous for their scandalous performances (more on Little Egypt in the next entry).

The exposition's Board of Lady Managers attempted to ban the dance altogether. They called on Anthony Comstock, the head of the New York Society for the Suppression of Vice (what a title!) to investigate the so-called immoral displays. Strangely, his committee singled out the Persian Palace, which featured pseudo-Oriental dancers who actually did wear corsets, calling on them to shut down. They didn't, claiming that the dancing there was "not a bit more indecent than any of the others on the plaisance."

If the shimmying hips and undulating torsos of the dancers weren't enough, the Algerian Village also featured the "torture dance" performed by members of an obscure aesthetic religious sect. After falling into trances induced by drums and incense, performers would pierce their lips and tongue, eat hot coals and live scorpions, and stand barefoot on the edges of razor sharp sword blades. Other dancers would drive ice picks through their eyes, paving the way for many a future sideshow performer. Admission to this macabre spectacle was only twenty-five cents. Needless to say, it was a hit.

Not long after, Coney Island began hawking its own *danse du ventre* and imitators became stock characters in carnivals, circuses, and vaudeville stages from Atlanta to San Francisco. Carnival barkers across the United States lured in audiences by promising them a "cooch show," commonly now known as the "hoochy coochy," performed by American ladies who had likely never seen an actual dancer from Egypt or Algeria or anywhere in the Middle East in their lives. Even Mae West performed the "hooch-ma-cooch" in her vaudeville days before she became famous for her "shimmy-sha-wobble."

In his book, *A Pictorial History of Burlesque*, Bernard Sobel offers up the kind of hard sell that carnival barkers would use to entice casual passers-by to part with their money and have a glimpse at the exotic and maybe even the forbidden:

This way for the Streets of Cairo! One hundred and fifty Oriental beauties! The warmest spectacle on earth! Pre-sen-ting Little Egypt! See her prance, see her wriggle! See her dance the Hootchy Kootchy! Anywhere else but in the ocean breezes of Coney Island she would be consumed by her own fire! Don't rush! Don't crowd! Plenty of seats for all! . . . When she dances, every fiber and every tissue in her entire anatomy shakes like a jar of jelly from your grandmother's Thanksgiving dinner. Now, gentlemen, I don't say that she's hot. But I do say that she is as hot as a red hot stove on the fourth day of July in the hottest county in the state.

As with every fad, this kind of show ran its course and by the end of the first decade of the twentieth century, it was fading, though other movements, such as Salomania (see act II) would keep the interest alive for a while longer. Belly dance found new enthusiasts in the 1940s, in New York nightclubs owned by Middle Eastern immigrants, and would only grow in popularity in the US from there, though today it is miles away from the curious and tantalizing exoticisms of repressed Victorians and their American counterparts.

LITTLE EGYPT AND THE CURSE OF THE SEELEY DINNER
❧ *A little leg and a terrible death* ❧

So, who exactly was the notorious "Little Egypt"? Well, some say that Arab dancer Farida Mazhar was the original Little Egypt, but despite performing on the Boardwalk at Coney Island, and appearing at the Bird Cage Theater in Tombstone, Arizona, in 1881, she lived a bit too normal a life for this book.

In 1896, however, dancer Ashea Wabe—another original "Little Egypt"—found herself at the center of the "Awful Seeley Dinner" scandal. Born Catherine Devine in Canada, she took on the persona of a cheeky dancer from Algeria. She had been hired to perform at a bachelor party for one of P. T. Barnum's grandsons, Clinton Barnum Seeley, at a posh Fifth Avenue venue in New York. A rival promoter snitched on the party, and police raided the event well past midnight. When questioned by the police, she maintained that she thought she had been booked by a group of artists, for "a dance and a pose," which Herbert Seeley probably interpreted to mean that she was to perform nude for a room full of men. Her testimony is equally ambiguous. When police asked her whether partygoers could see her leg through her gauzy skirts, she answered, "Oui, oui, monsieur; but only just my little leg."

"Do you mean your little leg, or a little of your leg?" the police continued.

"Oui, oui, monsieur, just my little leg," she answered. And that was that.

She later testified that her "little Egyptian slave girl" pose "in the altogether" was "proper for ar-r-r-t" (imagine an exaggerated Parisian "r" for this). Only, back then, "in the altogether" was euphemism for nudity. And that was enough for the first Little Egypt to score a contract with Oscar Hammerstein I at the extravagant Olympia Theater on Broadway, reenacting a parody of "Silly's Dinner." The show was wildly successful, and was, in fact, the first American burlesque to parody a current affair. Her name on the billing? Little Egypt. For all this scandal, she is credited by some as being the inventor of the modern strip tease, spurring thousands of imitators on burlesque and vaudeville stages.

The dinner itself, though, was one of those events that would remain scandalous for a long time, and infamous for the seeming curse attached to it. The number of people involved with it who later met with tragedy and violence is astonishing.

Little Egypt herself died under mysterious circumstances in January 1908, according to the *New Orleans Item*, which reported:

> She was found dead in her room under mysterious circumstances. It was clear that she had lain there dead for at least two days. She lay as though the body had been carelessly flung across the bed. Her left hand was tightly clenched. Her mouth, from which blood had poured, was wide open, as though she had died screaming for help. On her throat were livid marks like the imprint of murderers' fingers. No one was able to tell who or what had caused her death.

Another report indicated a more passive demise, in the form of asphyxiation by gas, so the likelihood is that she choked somehow. She was said to have left behind an estate worth some $200,000, an enormous sum for the time.

Her passing was tragic enough, but Little Egypt was not the only performer at the event to meet an untimely end, not by a long shot. The newspaper article continues:

> At North Beach, Long Island, a woman was found apparently dying. She had been shot by a mysterious assassin. She refused to tell his name, and as soon as she was able to move disappeared from view. The woman gave her name as Lottie Mortimer. The name was that of one of the performers at the Seeley dinner, and she was thought to be the same.

And the list of unfortunate guests goes on:

- Herbert Barnum Seeley, who had hosted the banquet, was divorced by his wife, apparently when she found out about it, and eventually he went bankrupt. He was arrested for improper financial dealings, adding insult to injury.
- Seeley's brother-in-law, Archibald Paul Mitchell, also got into financial trouble, and killed himself by lying down on his bed and turning on the gas jets.
- Mrs. Wilson Marshall, P. T. Barnum's favorite granddaughter, died shortly after the dinner and her will was contested, leading to an ugly family dispute.
- Horatio Harper, of publishing fame, was noted as being quite adversarial to the police when they broke up the festivities. The police captain allegedly said, "You've a long lip. It ought to be torn off." Well, sometime later, Harper's favorite horse became agitated with him and lunged forward while he was petting its nose, biting him on the mouth and mangling his upper lip. He nearly died of blood poisoning and was scarred for life.

In addition to all of these unfortunate events, various other performers reported having general bad luck after the party, and there were additional divorces and fallings-out among the guests, all of which led some to suspect that the whole shindig had been terribly cursed. Ultimately, we're not sure exactly what happened to Little Egypt, but she clearly suffered one of the worst fates of all of those at that sinister soiree.

OMENE AND THE SUICIDE CLUB
Coffin dancing and wine in skulls

Like many famous Oriental dancing ladies at the turn of the twentieth century, Omene, known as the "Divine Odalisque," capitalized on the then-current fascination with the "exotic." While not as famous as her contemporaries, such as Little Egypt, Maud Allan, or Mata Hari, she found herself in quite a macabre situation.

She claimed to have been born in Istanbul, Turkey, the daughter of a Circassian woman and a brother of notable Turkish general, Pasha Osman. She claimed that she learned how to dance from her mother—whom she said was "the most famous dancer in Stamboul and Constantinople"—at the tender young age of eight, performing in the harems until she was twelve. Then, she said, an Englishman kidnapped her, brought her to Alexandria in Egypt, and made her his wife. Said Englishman apparently tired of her, and so she found her way to London, where she performed the "Turkish national dance"—the scandalous *danse du ventre*, or "belly dance"—and made a name for herself as an Oriental dancing girl. While in London, she partnered with Yank Hoe, an Italian magician and juggler who performed in yellowface. One of his tricks was placing a potato on her throat and cutting it with a sword. They took their show to New York, but by 1891, she had found fame on her own; his act was just too small potatoes for her. Yes, that joke is not apeeling, but it does get to the root of her issues.

American newspapers reported frequently on Omene's love affairs, and the dancer was soon better known for her tabloid drama than her dancing.

She became involved with the Marquis Edmundo de Olivieri of Hoboken, New Jersey. Yes, apparently there was once a Marquis of Hoboken. But when the love affair went downhill, the Marquis accused Omene of stealing diamond jewelry and a jewel-encrusted snuff box from him. And if that weren't enough, one newspaper reporter was so obsessed with Omene that he committed suicide.

Like many other "Oriental" dancing ladies of her time, she likely performed a kind of proto-striptease, even if she didn't perform in the nude. The *Reading Eagle* in Pennsylvania wrote in 1894 that she began one performance wearing a fez, a face veil, and a long robe. Apparently, she was attended by eunuchs, who helped remove her fez, veil, robe, and sandals, leaving her "entirely free for the dance." Whether these were actual eunuchs or not, we don't know, and that's probably just as well. The reporter for the *Eagle* wrote, "Omene enraptures every spectator on the stage [with] seductive dances of the harem and the wild voluptuous dances of her native land. Her whole appearance is an illustration of grace." This was a surprisingly positive review, given the general opinion of polite society about such things.

She also tried to set herself apart from the plague of Little Egypts and Hoochie-Coochie dancers popping up on every midway, sideshow, and vaudeville stage. She said, "I saw the abortion which the dancers of the Midway presented to the public, and it filled me with heartache and loathing . . . Their dance was but a low-bred copy, designed to excite coarse men." Well, she wasn't wrong.

In 1893, she found herself in an unusual situation, even for a Western European lady posing as a wayward harem girl. Her fame earned her an invitation as the only woman ever to dine with and perform for the members of a mysterious gentleman's organization in Chicago informally known as the Suicide Club. Formally called the Whitechapel Club, it was founded by a group of young, educated, bohemian Chicago newspaper men. At once a press club and a kind of secret society, the founders named their new organization after the London neighborhood where Jack the Ripper hunted for his victims. Charming. They even declared the infamous murderer to be an absentee president. The group called on its members—mostly journalists, but also police officers, preachers, bank presidents, and even magicians, psychics, and convicted murderers—to "laugh in the face of death."

Omene was sworn to secrecy, but of course she didn't pass up an opportunity to speak about what she saw to the *San Francisco Morning Call* several years later. She told the *Morning Call* that what she saw behind the club's closed doors was "so horrible. The whole furniture was coffins." She continued:

> The walls were covered with frightful souvenirs of murdered men, ropes with which the existence of murderers had been terminated. Bloodstained knives adorned the walls . . . It was, in fact, a regular chamber of horrors—far worse indeed than anything I have witnessed before. But I must tell you the worst is yet to come. I had not only to sit down on a coffin but the table was made of coffins also, and the flowers were placed in the heads of the dead men—skulls, I suppose. Yes, skulls; there was nothing else but skulls and bones and coffins. Diablo!

Indeed, the decor included a bloodied shirt from a Native American killed at Wounded Knee, a hangman's noose, a Chinese man's slipper retrieved after he had been hit and killed by a streetcar in San Francisco, and innumerable knives and handguns that had been used in murders. To Omene's horror, she said that she was asked to drink wine from a real human skull. Apparently, the skull goblets had once been in the heads of Chicago's sex workers. The members proposed a toast: *Tears for the living. Cheers for the dead.* The club members then asked her to perform on a stage made out of a coffin, and handed her a skull and bones which she held while she danced. What became known as her "Coffin Dance" only increased the dancer's fame (or infamy) across the United States.

But why was it known as the "Suicide Club," despite its, well, unusual obsession with death? As a gift for her performance, Omene was given an urn. In the urn was a portion of the ashes of Morris Allen Collins, the (former) president of the Whitechapel club who (you guessed it) committed suicide, by shooting himself in the head. He suffered from seizures, and had attempted to kill himself by overdosing on morphine. When the drug didn't work, he resorted to a gun. This might possibly be one of history's most macabre thank-you gifts. She claimed that out of superstition, she carried the vase with her in her dressing case, wherever she traveled.

Like Mata Hari, Maud Allan, and Ashea Wabe, Omene was probably not from the Middle East or South Asia at all, and even reporters at the time knew it. The *Cincinnati Enquirer* snarked, "If the truth were told, it is probable that the only Turkey in Omene is what she has obtained from Thanksgiving dinners." *Bedford's Magazine* in 1891 wrote, "Miss Omene may be, and probably is, from the East, but it is the East of London, down Whitechapel way. A cockney of the cockneys is the fair Circassian." Indeed, two police reports hint at her true identity. She was either Madge Hargreaves or Nadine Osborne, two names which don't exactly conjure up images of the seraglio. Whatever her true origins, she didn't last long in this world. In 1899 she died of cancer, at only about thirty years old. The Suicide Club probably would have approved of her untimely exit.

HENRY CYRIL PAGET, "THE DANCING MARQUESS" (1875–1905)
ᔆᕯᕯ *The wildest folly and extravagance* ᔆᕯᕯ

Henry was quite the flamboyant one. He lived a short but ridiculously extravagant life, squandering a massive family fortune and running up huge debts, while doing nothing of note except being outlandish. *The Complete Peerage*—the compendium of all of the titled folks and aristocracy in those Sceptered Isles, and the last word on British toffery—notes bluntly:

[He] seems only to have existed for the purpose of giving a melancholy and unneeded illustration of the truth that a man with the finest prospects, may, by the wildest folly and extravagance, as Sir Thomas Browne says, 'foully miscarry in the advantage of humanity, play away an uniterable life, and have lived in vain.'

Wow, you can't really put it in a much more insultingly British manner than that! But it was true. Henry was one of a kind, thank goodness. He inherited his title at the tender age of twenty-three, and was clearly completely unsuited to its responsibilities and the wealth that came with it. Whether he had a hoarding disorder or an addiction to shopping, or both, he proceeded over the next few years to blow the modern equivalent of almost half a *billion* pounds of his family's money on jewels, clothing, lavish parties, and having his automobile fitted so that the exhaust was scented with patchouli and Spanish perfume. Really? Patchouli?

He converted the family chapel into a theater, where he performed everything from Shakespeare to pantomimes to slinky improvised dances, which earned him the name "The Dancing Marquess." He was especially fond of cross-dressing and wearing outrageously flamboyant costumes (made at tremendous expense, of course) in which he danced, cavorted, and strutted about the stage. But his antics were not merely confined to the estate's theater. He took his company (that he co-opted and paid lavishly) and its productions on the road and apparently did pretty well; everyone wanted to see the dancing nobleman and his outlandish shows. Regardless of what the troupe was performing, Henry always reserved time at intermission to go out elaborately costumed (one of his outfits was said to have cost at least £100,000) and flit about on stage in what he called his "Butterfly Dance" in the manner of American dancer Loie Fuller (1862–1928), who in her "serpentine dance" swirled yards of silk on long dowels under colored lights of her own invention and was considered Art Nouveau embodied. Imagine what Henry must have done in his own version!

But sometimes he didn't dance at all, at least according to one British lord who saw him perform in Munich:

[He] came between that of a lady with performing pigeons and a company of acrobats. The theatre was darkened. There was a roll on the drums and the curtain went up on Lord Anglesey clad in a white silk tunic, a huge diamond tiara on his head, glittering with necklaces, brooches, bracelets, and rings. He stood there for a few minutes motionless, without any mannequin gestures of display. Then the curtain went down again period . . . The German audience seemed a little disconcerted by the manifestation of British eccentricity.

His personal life was equally odd. He married his cousin, Lilian Florence Maud Chetwynd (how's that for a splendid name?). Some think this was just to keep the family fortune actually in the family (though that didn't work out too well) and for Henry, she really was just another accessory. On their honeymoon in Paris, he bought the entire stock of a jewelry store for her and asked her to wear it all to a race, which embarrassed her. Privately, things were just as bizarre, as her grandson from a later marriage related: "The closest the marriage ever came to consummation was that he would make her pose naked covered top to bottom in jewels and she had to sleep wearing the jewels."

Yet he never showed any interest in her sexually, and she later obtained an annulment on the grounds of non-consummation. This has led some to speculate that he was homosexual, and the fact that his family destroyed his private papers after his death may show that they were trying to hide what would have been a scandal for the time, but it has never been proven. He reveled in camp clothing and extravagance, but defended his enormous wardrobe, once saying, "I may have a hobby for collecting pins and rings, but I never wore more than one of the former and four of the latter at the same time. And if I do use scent, I am not the only living person who does, am I?"

In any case, the Dancing Marquess got himself in financial trouble pretty quickly. He declared bankruptcy in 1904, leading to his possessions being auctioned off, an incredible seventeen thousand lots over forty days. He died of pneumonia only a year later, a few months shy of his thirtieth birth-day. In his short life, his lavishness offended some, but he also earned a good number of admirers who genuinely mourned his young passing. Still, *The Bystander* (a London magazine) echoed the opinions of many when it said, with no pity: "His example will remain one of the strongest arguments against our hereditary system that the most ardent revolutionist would wish for."

8

The Modern Age

The "modern era" is, like the "Middle Ages," a very bad term, because "modern" is always what anyone in any age calls themselves. Whoever happens to be time's latest achievement gets to label themselves as such, so we are "modern," but so were those in the nineteenth century, the eighteenth, and so on. In the arts, the term tends to refer to the time from about 1900 to the present, give or take a decade, but as you'll see from these entries, many living in the "modern" world were actually born before it came about . . . except that their era was just as modern to them at the time. And now this is causing us a headache.

In any case, there was no shortage of weird lives, bizarre fates, and gruesome deaths awaiting those who danced into the twentieth century. In fact, some of these are among the strangest and worst so far. Dancers continued to work as courtesans, but also became notorious spies who met grisly ends, got swept up in political events beyond their control, kept dangerous animals as pets in the big city, and even had their own wardrobes betray them in terrible, if darkly funny, ways.

CAROLINA "LA BELLE" OTERO (1868–1965)
ᶜᵉ⌐ꝺ *The suicide siren* ꝺ⌐ᶻᵛ

Otero was a dancer, actress, and courtesan who seemed to have all of Europe at her feet, almost literally. But it wasn't always that way. Born in northern Spain, she suffered the horrible trauma of being raped at the age of eleven, which left her sterile. Determined to overcome this awful crime, she resolved to make a career as a dancer, adopting the name "La Belle Otero," and styling herself as an Andalusian Romani ("gypsy") dancer. She made her way to Paris in 1889, and found work as a dancer and performer in the musical revue show, the Folies Bergère.

As both a dancer on stage and as a courtesan off of it, she solidified her reputation and her fortune. Her popularity soon made her the most desired woman in Paris, and possibly in all of Europe. Her eventual lovers were numerous and included the most powerful men at the time: King Leopold II of Belgium (who "was not very generous at the start but I taught him how to give. He was an apt student."), King Edward VII of Britain, Tsar Nicholas II of Russia ("he really stank," she said, and "he had the strangest views about sex."), Emperor Wilhelm II of Germany, Prince Albert of Monaco (who apparently had difficulty standing at attention, but she encouraged him, and he eventually "strutted about the room."), King Alexander I of Serbia, King Alfonso XIII of Spain ("I taught him how to relax," she reminisced), Prince Nicholas of Montenegro, Emperor Yoshihito of Japan (who gave her an island in the Pacific after one performance!), the Khedive of Cairo, the Shah of Persia (who she said was a "dirty, smelly old man, and very strange in his desires."), and American businessman William K. Vanderbilt. They lavished jewels, money, and other gifts on her, and she became immensely wealthy. In her prime, she managed to amass a fortune in excess of twenty-five million dollars. Her voluptuous figure was such that a joke circulated saying that her breasts entered the room at least fifteen minutes before she did.

She freely chose her lovers, and also when to leave them, whether they were rich or poor. When she was done, she simply moved on, with little concern for the effects she had on them, which led to tragedy for some of her former companions. Among those unhappy gentlemen she left in her highly charged wake, it is said that:

- The son of her drama coach jumped into the Seine and drowned.
- Two different noblemen shot themselves in the head.
- Two others leapt out windows of high buildings.
- A young art student threw himself under a coach and was crushed to death.
- A teacher hanged himself from the tree in the Bois de Boulogne, the place where he had first laid eyes on her and apparently in his despair, he wanted it to be the last place he would see.

Wow. Apparently, two men also fought a duel over her, so she was obviously in great demand and had a huge effect on those whom she charmed. Despite her adventurous and extravagant life, she squandered her fortune in casinos and lived a meager life in her last years. She died in her nineties in a small flat in Nice, her glamorous decades as the belle of Europe's royalty all but forgotten.

IDA RUBENSTEIN (1883–1960)

ᏧᏌ *Cat got your tongue? Or your curtains.* ᏧᏌ

Rubenstein was a Russian dancer and actress of Jewish descent, an icon of the *fin de siècle*, known for her controversial performances and lifestyle. She came from a wealthy family, who were scandalized by her performances in Paris, since they considered being an actress as being little more than a prostitute. Her brother-in-law actually had her declared insane and committed to an asylum for a time, but she was released and then married her first cousin, who seemed not to care about her activities onstage. This apathy allowed her to go back to her controversial life.

In 1908, she appeared in a staging of Oscar Wilde's play, *Salomé*, performing "The Dance of the Seven Veils," a dance included in the play that is not fully described, but which many inferred involved the removal of clothing, making it a kind of Orientalist striptease (see chapter 8 in act II for more on Salome). Indeed, Rubenstein interpreted it as such, and she incorporated the dance into her other performances, no doubt to the horror of many, as she undressed down to nothing but a bra and a beaded skirt.

Though not properly trained in ballet, she caught the eye of dance impresario Serge Diaghilev (1872–1929). He brought her in to his celebrated new company, the Ballets Russes. Due to her lack of training, she was never going to be a star ballerina, but because of her striking looks, she did quite well in other roles as a mime or even a statue, such as Cleopatra (in 1909) and Ta-Hor in *Schéhérazade* (in 1910). She eventually broke with Diaghilev and later started her own dance company, Les Ballets de Madame Ida Rubinstein, where she often took lead roles that she was not really qualified to dance. But she was generous with her patronage of the arts. She is famous for having commissioned *Boléro* from Ravel—you may have heard of it—and other works from various French composers. Her family's wealth meant that she had the money to poach dancers away from other companies, including the Ballets Russes, and naturally, they weren't too happy about that.

Her private life continued to be both scandalous and completely acceptable in the growing liberalism of Paris. She is said to have had male and female lovers, she posed nude for at least two painters, and she enjoyed keeping exotic animals as pets. She had a pet leopard that she took for walks in the streets of Paris; just imagine trying to do that these days. Apparently, when store owners got wind that she was out and about, they would often close early to prevent her and her feline companion from entering the establishment.

In addition to a fear of being mauled (Rubenstein herself apparently had a fair collection of claw mark scars), they had good reason. She also had a black panther who was said to be inordinately fond of eating people's gloves, hats, and other accessories, as well as climbing up curtains and walls. Just what a specialty Parisian clothing boutique wants! Actually, the kitty was like a regular housecat, only bigger and deadlier. Once, Diaghilev visited her home, and said panther was in a testy mood. For some reason, it didn't like his coat and made a move toward it. Diaghilev jumped up onto a table and cried out in terror, and the cat retreated to a corner, where it crouched and growled. So, just another day at Ida's apparently; she laughed, picked up the animal by its scruff (no easy task), and took it into another room. It was undoubtedly one of the more interesting social calls that Diaghilev ever made!

MAUD ALLAN (1873–1956)
Cult of the clitoris

One of the most famous "Salome dancers" (see chapter 8 in act II) was Canadian-born Californian dancer Maud Allan. Born in 1873 as Beulah Maud Durrant in Toronto, she, her parents, and brother moved to San Francisco in 1879, when she was still quite a young girl. A budding pianist, she left for Berlin to finish her musical studies when she was eighteen, a common destination for artistically inclined young women at the time. Most of these ladies would return to live in the United States, but Maud Allan did not. Ultimately, she would have some very good reasons to want to be away from her family.

San Francisco at the turn of the nineteenth century was particularly wild and woolly, and Maud's brother Theodore was no exception. An aspiring doctor and assistant superintendent of the Sunday school at the San Francisco Emmanuel Baptist Church, he had displayed troubling psychological behavior even as a child. He was rumored to have a dark side, but it turned out to be far more than just that. He and his sister were close and when she left for Berlin, he was bereft. Maybe her departure sent him over the edge?

As a young man, he most likely visited brothels, which wasn't particularly unusual for men at the time who lived in San Francisco, with its famed Barbary Coast district. What was unusual (okay, straight-up disturbing) was that some said that he would bring a pigeon or a chicken with him to the brothel. At a certain point during his visit with a given prostitute (use your imagination) he would slit the bird's throat and let the blood trickle over his body. People and their strange dinner preparation rituals. . . .

Anyway, he must have been a bit of a charmer, because witnesses say that they saw him chatting with two young ladies on separate occasions: twenty-year-old Blanche Lamont and twenty-one-year-old Minnie Williams. A certain Mrs. Caroline Leak saw Durrant and Lamont enter the San Francisco Emmanuel Baptist Church together. Witnesses also say that nine days after Lamont's disappearance, Williams and Durrant argued in front of the church.

Neither woman was ever seen alive again.

When preparing for an Easter Sunday event at the church, one of the ladies opened a china cabinet and the mutilated corpse of Minnie Williams tumbled out. Williams' bloody body had been strangled and hacked to death with a knife that was still buried in one breast. When the police came, they searched the belfry and found the naked body of Blanche Lamont laid out face up, her head wedged between two boards, as if prepared for a medical examination; she had been there for ten days. Talk about a morbid version of an Easter egg hunt!

Theo, as he was known, was immediately accused of the girls' murders. He was tried, amid much media frenzy. More than 3,600 people had to be interviewed for the jury before twelve suitable candidates could be found. William Randolph Hearst's *San Francisco Examiner* called it the trial of the century. Other papers were quick to compare Durrant to Jack the Ripper.

He was found guilty, and hanged at San Quentin Prison on January 7, 1898. During the trial, Theo maintained his innocence and never confessed, believed only by his mother, who, after the execution, calmly ate her lunch next to his dead body.

Beulah, however, was traumatized by the scandal. Wracked with guilt that she could not be there for her younger brother, as well as facing impending poverty—her family's finances had been drained in Theo's legal defense—she began a transformation that would alter the course of her whole life. She changed her name to Maud Allan, distancing herself from the Durrant name and the stigma of her brother's alleged crime, though she continued to believe that he was innocent.

Abandoning the piano, she received a commission to illustrate a two-volume German sex manual for women (as one does), in which she drew detailed images of female genitalia. She also became an artists' model, posing nude, perhaps most famously as a laughing Salome.

When she heard of a new form of dance which required no childhood training in ballet, the twenty-seven-year-old Maud reinvented herself once again. Other than the famous Isadora Duncan (see later in this chapter), this new "barefoot dancing" had little competition and was sweeping Europe by storm; one could even say off its feet. One could. Instead of attending dance classes, she researched ancient poses in libraries and museums and practiced imitating them in front of her mirror at home.

All the while, she was strongly encouraged by her mother, who might have been the twentieth century's first "stage mom." Maud first performed in 1903, but her unsatisfied mother wanted her to be even more famous. She pushed Maud to find a competitive edge over her "rival" Isadora, and Maud found it in the character of Salome, whom she had already embodied. By this time, "exotic" solo dancers were taking over Europe, but Maud was the only one who specifically chose to portray the controversial Biblical princess.

In 1906, Allan made her debut as Salome in Vienna to an audience of about one hundred people. In a costume of beads, pearls, and sheer silks, she appeared without a corset, her midriff and ankles exposed. At the time, she would have been considered practically naked. One witness wrote, "One moment her dancing is hot, barbaric, lawless, the next, grotesque, sinister, repulsive." In London, high society women threw themselves "Maud

Allan" parties, which would, according to the *New York Times,* "be undese-crated by the presence of any man." She finally was receiving the attention and fame that her mother wanted.

She performed at the Palace Theatre in London, which, ironically, was the same theater that Oscar Wilde intended to stage his *Salomé* play, before it was banned by Lord Chamberlain (see chapter 8 in act II for all the unsa-vory details). In her lifetime, she broke all box office records, and gave at least two hundred and fifty performances. Interestingly, when she per-formed her "Oriental" dances, her audiences were nearly ninety percent women. Of course, this set off alarm bells in the repressed minds of the male establishment of the time, who wanted to know what these uppity women were getting up to.

On February 16, 1918, the *Vigilante,* a political magazine looking for a scapegoat in the throes of World War I, published "The Cult of the Clito-ris," an article suggesting that Maud Allan was organizing a group of "perverts" in her touring *Salomé* production. Noel Pemberton Billing, the anti-homosexuality campaigner who owned the publication, claimed that she was also connected to a pro-German secret society determined to destroy Great Britain by "propagating evils which all decent men thought had perished in Sodom and Lesbia." It's always amusing to read the words of those from the past who try to describe something that they hate and can't mention with euphemisms and winks.

It was already rumored that her friendship with the British Prime Minis-ter's wife Margot Asquith was more than just a "friendship." Maud took the bait, and sued for libel, resulting in a sensational court case in which she was also accused of necrophilia, among other things, because, why not? Her brother's crimes were presented as proof that perversion and insanity ran in the family. The jury ultimately ruled in Billings's favor.

Alas, due to this kind of backlash, the Salome craze was short-lived, and so was Maud's career. From the 1920s to 1938, she lived in London with her secretary and lover, Verna Alrich (defiantly proving the rumors right), and later died in Los Angeles.

MATA HARI (1878–1917)
⌘ Couldn't keep her head ⌘

Born Margaretha Geertruida Zelle in 1878 in the city of Leeuwarden, in the Netherlands, the woman we know as Mata Hari grew up rather privileged. Her father, a humble shopkeeper, found financial success in the burgeoning oil industry. With his new wealth, he showered his "Little Princess" with gifts, spoiling her, and perhaps making her crave male attention a bit too much throughout her life. But in 1889, he went bankrupt and abandoned Margaretha and her siblings when he divorced her mother, who died two years later.

Not one to be discouraged, she was soon a precocious young lady with a propensity for seduction. At the age of sixteen, she was discovered messing around with her fifty-one-year-old high school principal. When she was eighteen, she answered a Lonely Hearts advertisement in a Dutch newspaper. Dutch Colonel Army Captain Rudolph MacLeod was looking for a wife. He was twenty years older than her and suffered from rheumatism and diabetes. Like we said, Margaretha probably had daddy issues. Apparently, she told him that she wanted to do "crazy things." They were engaged six days after meeting, and married three months later. Yeah, that's pretty crazy. Then, logically enough, they moved to Malang in eastern Java, in the Dutch East Indies.

Once they got there, Margaretha earned a reputation for eyeing the other Dutch officers, and she certainly found the role of a "traditional" wife stifling. She said she wanted to live like a "butterfly in the sun," presumably flitting about as she willed, not exactly what the age expected of women. She and MacLeod did have two children, but were they his? In any case, because both wife and husband were routinely unfaithful to each other and he was a violent alcoholic, their marriage was a disaster. MacLeod physically abused Margaretha regularly, and blamed her for his not getting promoted. As if that weren't enough, he also kept a regular concubine, a common practice at the time.

Outside the home, Margaretha pursued her "butterfly" life, and knowing what we do about MacLeod, who can blame her? She sought out lessons to learn Gandrung, an Indonesian courtship dance thought to have once been performed in devotion to the goddess of rice. She studied intensively for several months and apparently that was enough training for her to secure a place in a local dance company. Dancing became the chrysalis in which she could make her transformation. In 1897, she chose the stage name that would stay with her for the rest of her life: Mata Hari, meaning "Eye of the Dawn" in the Malay language.

However, tragedy soon befell the disintegrating MacLeod family. In 1899, their son Norman fell ill when he was only two years old. It was rumored at the time that the nanny, exacting revenge for some unknown wrong, poisoned the boy. Some say instead that one of MacLeod's enemies poisoned the children's supper. Others even claim that MacLeod himself poisoned not only Norman, but also their daughter as well, in revenge for Margaretha's philandering. Talk about double standards. It's more likely, however, that the boy contracted congenital syphilis, and he either died of the disease itself or the cure. The barracks doctor probably gave the boy an accidental fatal overdose of mercury, often used to treat the disease in those days before antibiotics. Their daughter survived—the syphilis or the poisoning or both—because she had not yet been weaned.

What remained of the family returned to the Netherlands, and Margaretha, now Mata Hari, plucked up the courage to ask for a divorce. She got it, but didn't win custody of her daughter. To add insult to injury, the vindictive MacLeod took out an advertisement in the local newspapers telling local shops not to give Mata Hari credit. Destitute and alone, she drew on her limited dance and extensive seduction experience and put them to use. In 1903, she sought fame and fortune in Paris.

And there she found it. She capitalized on the Parisian obsession with anything remotely "Oriental" at the time. She also had impeccable timing, having arrived just on the heels of Salomania (see chapter 8 in act II), as well as the recent sensation of barefoot dancing, as performed by Isadora

Duncan and Maud Allan. With her dark eyes and dark hair, many believed her claims to be from the "exotic" Orient, although she changed her backstory frequently. Her two most common fibs were that she was the daughter of a Hindu priest and a European woman, or of a Scottish lord and a Malay woman who died in childbirth. Both were widely believed and disbelieved.

She said that she had learned her "devotional" temple dance as a young girl, often in reverence to the Hindu god Shiva (himself a dancer), and promoted her performances as ritual and spiritual practice. But audiences didn't come to her shows to see Indonesian temple dances. Mata Hari would often strip down to either a flesh-colored bodysuit or to absolutely nothing, defending doing so by claiming that her dances were "purely religious." She did, however, feel particularly shy about her breasts, which she thought were too small, and she frequently left her bejeweled brassiere on while performing, authenticity be damned.

By 1905, she had become a sensation. A Parisian newspaper said Mata Hari was "so feline, extremely feminine, majestically tragic, the thousand curves and movements of her body trembling in a thousand rhythms." Those who came to see her performances were, as you can imagine, hardly interested in whether they were seeing real devotional temple dances. And when she wasn't dancing, she used her charms and beauty to dance into the salons of the upper class as well as into the beds of many wealthy men. She still had a particular affinity for men in military uniform, which would ultimately be her undoing.

As she reached her late thirties, she turned almost completely to working as a courtesan, rather than a dancer. And she fell in love with Vladimir Masloff, a Russian soldier, who had been sent away to fight on the front in World War I. After being gassed by the Germans, he recovered in a hospital in the town of Vittel, in northeastern France. Mata Hari desperately wanted to visit him there, but needed special permission, because it was in the war zone. To get there, she befriended a Frenchman, Georges Ladoux, head of French counter-espionage.

Ladoux wanted Mata Hari to spy for the French because of her neutral Dutch nationality—she could easily travel across European borders—and her acquaintance with a variety of military men. He offered her a handsome sum of money, and she accepted. He sent her to Brussels, to gain access to the German head of occupation in Belgium. But she had to get there via Great Britain. She was arrested as soon as she stepped on British soil. Ladoux vouched for her, and had her sent to Spain.

By the end of 1916, she had made contact with German Major Arnold Kalle, but the intelligence she acquired from him was stale and outdated. The French intercepted a message from Kalle to Berlin referring to agent H-21, now believed to be in reference to Mata Hari. Was she also working for the Germans?

After the Germans launched renewed submarine attacks in February 1917, Mata Hari was arrested at the Elysée Palace hotel in Paris, and offered chocolates to the arresting police officers, wearing only a German helmet; well, she gets an "A" for effort in trying to get out of it. She was interrogated seventeen times while she was held at the Saint-Lazare Prison. When she stood trial at the Palace of Justice, massive crowds gathered outside. She seemed doomed from the start: the prosecution characterized the dancer as a promiscuous and unscrupulous woman. They accused her of being the "greatest woman spy of the century," responsible for sending twenty thousand (or fifty thousand, or one hundred thousand depending on who you ask) allied soldiers to their deaths. Public opinion was firmly against anyone remotely accused of spying for the enemy. She was found guilty and sentenced to death by firing squad. It's likely that Ladoux set Mata Hari up, looking for a scapegoat for the German assault. A woman who had made her living off of seducing military officers seemed the perfect victim. Mata Hari's beauty and wiles were no longer enough to save her from her fate.

She seems to have made peace with her execution, which took place on October 15, 1917. When a soldier approached her with a blindfold, she asked, "Must I wear that?" She was not tied to the stake. When the twelve officers raised their rifles, she blew a kiss to her priest and her lawyer, who had also been her lover. When the shots fired, she collapsed, and an eye witness said, "she lay prone, motionless, with her face turned towards the sky." A non-commissioned officer then approached her body, held his revolver to her head, and delivered a definitive final shot.

Her body was not claimed by any family members, not even her estranged daughter, and so was used for medical study. Her head was removed (!), embalmed, and kept at the Museum of Anatomy in Paris, as part of an exhibit of infamous criminals. When the French Minister of Education threatened to shut down the museum in 2000, curators found that the head had mysteriously disappeared. Apparently, it had gone missing forty-six years earlier, when the museum had changed locations. Not exactly the same as losing your keys. Apparently, no one had noticed in all that time.

As for the Elysée Palace hotel? It became the French headquarters of banking firm HSBC. Employees claim that Mata Hari's ghost still haunts the halls, maybe eternally searching for her lost head?

LIDIA IVANOVA (1903–1924)
ᔕ *Propelled forward . . . or in many directions, actually* ᔕ

Ivanova was a friend and classmate of the legendary choreographer, George Balanchine (1904–1983). The two worked together during the last years of imperial Russia and she performed some of his early works, eventually weathering the Russian Revolution as best they could. Given that the years following the events of said revolution were not great for artists, it became obvious that it would be in their best interest to get out if possible, at least temporarily. In July 1924, Ivanova and several others were due to leave, and were awaiting their visas. However, one day, Ivanova was on a boat with four soldiers in the canal in St. Petersburg, when it was struck by another boat—a ferry—allegedly in an accident. The thing is, the other three (or four, depending on who you believe) passengers were rescued by the ferry and a tugboat that happened along. They all managed to survive, while Ivanova was apparently swept under the boat and into the turning propellers. Ick.

If that was the case, it's no wonder that her body was never found, and it seemed an end that was perhaps a bit too convenient. She was an excellent swimmer, and if she had been knocked off her boat and into the water, could very likely have escaped without much difficulty. None of her friends believed that this tragedy was an accident and there was little attempt at an official investigation, suggesting that someone wanted her out of the way.

She was apparently romantically linked to a communist officer, which made things even more suspicious. She liked to socialize with communist party officials; had she perhaps heard too much and become a liability? Rumors began to spread that the survivors were seen soon after, toasting at a restaurant, and bragging about how they had survived. Further, Balanchine claimed that the permission to leave the country that the dancers were waiting on conveniently arrived the next day, but not hers, of course. He and the others left Russia on July 4, and even though they were summoned to return to the Soviet Union at the end of the summer, they never did. Were they afraid of what had happened to their colleague? Maybe.

So, who might have wanted her dead, and why? Good questions. The whole thing may have been a tragic accident and the survivors merely covered up their incompetence or cowardice in handling the situation. On the other hand, there is a theory that one of the other passengers was a spurned suitor, and saw this boat trip as a way of enacting revenge, knowing that she was planning on leaving the country. But would he really have risked having the boat rammed, unless he also planned to die in some sort of murder-suicide act? A few have suggested that there was something more political afoot, and that she was murdered by the fledgling KGB, but the fact is, we just don't know, and anyone who did is long gone.

ISADORA DUNCAN (1877–1927)
ᵔᵔ Putting her neck on the line ᵔᵔ

Born in San Francisco in 1877, Isadora Duncan is today considered to be the mother of modern American dance. Ever a rebel in her youth, she grew up surrounded by music, art, and an appreciation for radical self-expression . . . a hundred years before Burning Man.

Famous for dancing barefoot while wearing Greek-inspired togas and robes, Isadora was no stranger to misfortune, from childhood to her last days. Her mother, when pregnant with the future dancer, predicted that her daughter would "surely not be normal." Parenting . . . you're doing it wrong.

Isadora was never one to shy away from embellishing her life story (and that's putting it mildly), claiming that her earliest memory was being tossed to safety from the window of a burning building. This may or may not have actually happened, but later, the 1906 earthquake did destroy the San Francisco home in which she was born. She wrote that her life was "always fire and water and sudden fearful death."

Even if not counting Isadora's unusual life, the Duncan family was no stranger to misfortune, particularly her father. After arriving in San Francisco from the East Coast, Joseph Duncan, a boom-and-bust banker, organized a lottery that lost him $225,000. He was also a notorious ladies man, and may also have been a lover of the famed "Spanish dancer" (well, she was actually Irish) Lola Montez. Isadora's aunt described him as "a demon who ruined your mother's life," causing Isadora to imagine him "with horns and a tail." No Father's Day cards for him, then.

Perhaps her aunt was right. After losing thousands of dollars in his lottery, his Pioneer Bank collapsed after he promised to pay his working-class investors a whopping twelve percent interest, but was unable to deliver. He speculated the investments, forging stock certificates and selling them to unsuspecting brokers, sending the bank into $1,240,000 of debt. Duncan closed the bank and went into hiding; it was rumored that he'd go out into the city in woman's clothing to evade the police! "Honestly, constable! My name is . . . Josephine Duncan!" Eventually he was found and charged with forgery and "false swearing." He later died in a shipwreck off the coast of England, along with his third wife (!) and their child.

After the Pioneer Bank scandal, Isadora's mother, Mary Isadora Duncan, divorced Joseph, and moved herself and her four children across the bay to Oakland—still quite lush and bucolic at the time—where they lived in poverty, bouncing from home, to apartment, to walk-up, to flat. Isadora described her itinerant childhood as being "a perpetual state of terror. . . . " Ah, childhood memories. Mary could not earn enough by teaching piano and selling her knitting, so they endured many hardships.

At the age of ten, Isadora dropped out of school, claiming it was a "waste of time when I could be making money." In fact, she caused a ruckus in elementary school by exclaiming that Santa Claus wasn't real (the little hell-raiser!), and that her mother was "too poor" to be the yule-time gift-giver. Instead, she taught dance to neighborhood children to earn money for her family, but had no formal dance training herself. Eschewing the slippers and fleshings (the tights of the time) of ballet, she claimed that her greatest artistic teachers were "Beethoven, Nietzsche, and Wagner," three men not especially known for their terpsichorean prowess.

She tried to make it as a dancer in the United States. However, all dancing other than ballet (and sometimes even ballet) at the time was still synonymous with sex work (see the ballet courtesans' entry in the ballet chapter in act II). But, Isadora imagined dance as Art with a capital "A," not simply something to titillate easily scandalized audiences. She and her family eventually found themselves at the gloomy Windsor Hotel in New York City, which, of course, they could barely afford. They were in their apartment teaching dance to a small group of young girls on Saint Patrick's Day when a hotel guest's match caught the curtains on fire, destroying the entire building in less than an hour. Isadora, her mother, sister, and brother, as well as the young pupils, escaped, but all of Isadora's costumes were lost in the blaze. Isadora had joked only days before that the only thing that could have saved them from the heavy expenses of living in New York would be for the hotel to burn down. Well, that was convenient!

After deciding that her dancing was just too misunderstood in the United States (a true artist is never understood in their own time and place, of course), the Duncans set sail for London, where Isadora performed her Greek-inspired dances in the salons of the wealthy. Fascinated with Russian Bolshevism, she traveled to St. Petersburg to perform, but had a narrow escape; only two days after she left in January 1905, the revolution broke out in St. Petersburg, including the Bloody Sunday massacre of peaceful protestors outside the Winter Palace.

She had several love affairs, which resulted in two children, Dierdre and Patrick. Tragedy then followed Isadora to France. She claimed that she suffered from terrible visions and hallucinations, including one of two rows of child-sized coffins in the snow, and another of great black birds and three unlucky black cats in her studio. Soon after, in April 1913, she left her children with their chauffeur and nanny in a rented hand-crank Renault. When he got out to turn the crank along the banks of the Seine river, the car lurched forward across a wide boulevard and literally drove itself into the water. Dierdre, Patrick, and the nanny drowned.

After a tryst with an Italian sculptor in 1914, she became pregnant again, only to lose the child shortly after his birth. When her tour of the United States turned into a financial disaster, she nearly booked passage on the ill-fated voyage of the RMS Lusitania. Her creditors, however, threatened to seize her trunks and prevent her from leaving the country on any ship, and she could barely afford her more humble voyage on the Dante Alighieri, a much more pleasant-sounding vessel (one wonders if they resisted painting "Abandon all hope, ye who enter here" over the walkway to the ship!).

In 1921, she traveled again to Russia, and though speaking no Russian, convinced poet Sergei Yesenin to marry her; by the way, he spoke no English. Most Russians came to believe that Isadora ruined "the most famous poet in Russia," but his propensity for drunkenness and hallucinations (one not necessarily caused by the other) already afflicted him well before their meeting. Yesenin had tried to commit suicide several times: he threw himself in front of a train, tried to leap from a fifth-floor window, and stabbed himself with a kitchen knife. He eventually met his end in 1925, where he was found hanging from the heating pipes in the ceiling of his St. Petersburg hotel room, a poem penned in his own blood nearby. Hang on, it gets worse . . .

The misfortune that Isadora seemed to leave in her wake finally caught up with her one day in Nice in 1927. She had always had a penchant for flowy garments, and that day she wore a two-yard-long red batik scarf, the "color of heart's blood," she said. As she climbed into the seat of an Amilcar automobile and waved adieu to her friends, the silk fringe tangled in the spokes of the car's wheels, hurtling Isadora from her seat into the street, trapping her head between the body and the tire. Her neck was broken, and she died instantly.

Filmmaker and Isadora's longtime friend Jean Cocteau wrote: "Isadora's end is perfect." He clearly had an odd definition of perfection.

Like many groundbreaking artists, her influence on dance was not always recognized by her contemporary critics. Writer and critic Percival Pollard summed up her strange and tragic life in these rather unflattering words that he wrote in a review of one of her performances: "Let us applaud Miss Duncan as much as we like; let us give solemn ear to all the noble lessons she would teach with her toes; but let us not imagine that she, her pupils, or her theories will live one-half as long as the portrait F. A. von Kaulbach painted of her in Munich in 1902."

Despite these tragedies and her many eccentric behaviors, she is still considered one of the most influential figures in twentieth-century dance, showing a generation of women that they could dance and express themselves without corsets, pointe shoes, or tights.

intermission

We pause and take a breather, while the dancers spin off the hellish stage and back into the dark recesses of history. Obviously, this little march of folly can only shine some much-needed light on a handful of tales and historical accounts—to say nothing of genres and styles—and many of the more prominent dancers, companies, and choreographers were fortunate enough to live lives that don't merit them being included in this book; lucky them!

Unlike the history of music and drama, dance is one Western art that has been very inclusive of women, but as revealed over and over from just these accounts, this was not always a good thing! In fact, fear of women dancing was something that stuck in the craw of controlling male moralists over the centuries. As we will see in the next section, that fear, combined with other societal restrictions and pressures, only ensured that things were continually and especially difficult for female dancers, whether in the throes of superstitious dancing plagues, at the mercy of sleazy ballet patrons, or being compared to the most evil dancer of all time.

In any case, dancing could not be crushed, no matter how hard some authorities tried, and most eventually realized that they had no choice but to live with the fact that quite a lot of folks just want to kick up their heels and celebrate from time to time. As we've seen, this was true across all classes and time periods, from the richest king to the poorest peasant. The urge to move to music seems to be ingrained and comes in an endless variety of styles.

Our performance now shifts away from a straight historical tour and offers you a masquerade of the macabre, a galliard of the gruesome, and a dance of the damned. Return to your seat and join us on a fascinating journey into the realms of dancing mania, where the afflicted had no control over their wild movements. Shiver at how intertwined dancing and death are in medieval allegories about the march of time, or be unnerved at the dark side of the world of ballet, from the works themselves to the shady goings-on behind the scenes. Have a laugh or even a gasp at the anti-dance campaigners and their torturously long tomes. Think twice about dancing in fairy tales and folklore and be chilled to the bone by ghostly dancers and their haunts. Finally sample a smorgasbord of choreoddities to send you chasséing on your way.

Settle back in with a mug of something warm, or a flask of something stronger, and prepare for a second promenade into some very strange territories of the mind, body, and feet.

Magura cave drawings, featuring dancing women and men who are standing at attention and eager to join in. (Wikimedia Commons.)

An ancient Egyptian dancer doing a creative (if uncomfortable-looking) backbend. Pottery fragment, ca. 1292–1186 BCE. (Wikimedia Commons.)

Rhea and the Curetes, protecting baby Zeus from being eaten by his father, Cronus. The goat looks a bit unsure about all of it. (*Manual of Mythology* by Alexander S. Murray. Philadelphia: David McKay, 1895.)

A third-century Roman sarcophagus with scenes of Bacchic revelry at a wedding. A wedding and a funeral? (Creative Commons, Wikimedia Commons.)

The carole-like dance of Mirth and Gladness (and don't they look mirthful?), from a manuscript of the *Roman de la Rose*, Paris, ca. 1380. (Courtesy of the British Library.)

A rabbit playing a pipe and tabor, surely to accompany the Salisbury Hare! From an English Book of Hours, ca. 1320–ca. 1330. (Courtesy of the British Library.)

The horrific execution of György Dózsa, including cannibalism, impalement, and even worse . . . bagpipes! (Wikimedia Commons.)

William Kempe, kicking up his heels in the Nine Days Wonder. (Wikimedia Commons.)

Witches and devils dancing and making merry, getting up to all sorts of mischief. (Creative Commons, courtesy of the Wellcome Collection, London.)

King Louis XIV in *Le Ballet de la nuit* in 1653, looking every bit the Sun King, what with all those suns. (Wikimedia Commons.)

Oliver Cromwell, surrounded by severed heads (including Charles I's) was secretly not so against dancing. (Courtesy of the Rijksmuseum, Amsterdam.)

Marie Thérèse de Subligny, who allegedly took no crap from a musician, but may have given him some. (Courtesy of the Österreichische Nationalbibliothek, Austrian National Library, Vienna.)

"The Carmagnole" by Harry Furniss. 1910. Clearly this revolutionary dance could get way out of hand. (Courtesy of Philip V. Allingham and the Victorian Web, www.victorianweb.org.)

The appalling dangers of crinoline, whether dancing or otherwise, ca. 1860. (Creative Commons, courtesy of the Wellcome Collection, London.)

One of the many "Little Egypt," dancers, World's Columbian Exposition, Chicago, Illinois, 1893. (Library of Congress and Wikimedia Commons.)

The scandalous Omene from a Virginia Brights Cigarettes card, ca. 1888. (Metropolitan Museum of Art and Wikimedia Commons.)

Henry Paget, dressed like the fantastical lead singer of a 1970s glam band, ca. 1900. (Wikimedia Commons.)

Carolina "La Belle" Otero, ca. 1890, who left a pile of broken hearts and corpses in her wake. (Wikimedia Commons.)

The infamous Mata Hari, dressed modestly in a bra, ca. 1910. (Wikimedia Commons.)

Trying to restrain two women possibly afflicted with choreomania. Engraving based on a painting by Breugel. (Wikimedia Commons.)

Gruesome skeletons kick up their heels, with a shawm to get them hopping. From *Danse macabre* by Michael Wolgemut, 1493. (Wikimedia Commons.)

Curing the bite of the tarantula by dancing, eighteenth century. Though, everyone looks strangely happy. (Courtesy of the New York Public Library Digital Collections.)

Marie-Anne Cupis de Camargo, whose unintended public nudity caused quite the stir in late eighteenth-century Paris. (Courtesy of the Bibliothèque nationale de France.)

The Ballet of the Nuns, wherein the spooky sisters are rising from their graves. (Wikimedia Commons.)

Franceska Mann, the ballerina who kicked Nazi butt and died a hero in doing so, late 1930s. (Wikimedia Commons.)

Increase Mather, he of remarkable wig and remarkably ridiculous opinions on dance. (Creative Commons, courtesy of the Wellcome Collection, London.)

A typical pointe shoe that has seen better days, but don't throw it away! (Creative Commons, Wikimedia Commons.)

The angel and Karen from Hans Christian Andersen's rather disturbing *The Red Shoes*. (Wikimedia Commons.)

Fairies in a ring dance, presided over by their sovereigns, who look a bit bored. (Creative Commons, courtesy of the Wellcome Collection, London.)

Anna Pavlova as the Dying Swan, ca. 1908-09. She's still swanning about as a ghost, according to some. (Wikimedia Commons.)

The masquerade costume worn by King Gustav III of Sweden when he was assassinated. Hey, if you've got to go, look good doing it! (Creative Commons, Wikimedia Commons and the Livrustkammaren, Royal Armoury of Sweden.)

Maud Allan as Salome, surveying the severed head of a certain baptist. (Wikimedia Commons.)

act II

A Dark and Weird Dance Miscellany

1

Choreomania: The Dancing Plagues of the Middle Ages and Renaissance

On a warm summer day in July 1518, in the city of Strasbourg (on the border of Germany and France), an elderly woman named Frau Troffea stepped out of her front door, and began to dance in the street. She wasn't celebrating anything, and no music played for her, but she danced furiously throughout the day—to the great distress of her family, who attempted to stop her without success. Only when she was completely exhausted did she finally collapse and sleep for a few hours, before rousing and commencing her crazed toe-tapping again. Bizarrely, over the next few days, many others seem to think that this was a wonderful idea and joined her. While the strange spectacle grew, town residents and authorities became increasingly alarmed, and who wouldn't?

So began an episode of choreomania, the "dancing plague" that occurred at various times in European history during the Middle Ages and Renaissance. Any number of people, from a handful to hundreds, might be afflicted in a given instance. Actually, the plague seemed to be contagious, almost always starting with small numbers and growing. It drove otherwise normal people to dance uncontrollably, some to their deaths, or at least to suffer serious injuries (and probably very sore feet!). Accounts of this odd phenomenon date back to the eleventh century (and there was an unusual legend in ancient Greece, which we'll also examine) and each seems to have started under different circumstances. Some may be nothing more than legends, but the events of others, such as Strasbourg, were well-documented and undoubtedly real.

Medical historians have looked for explanations, ranging from ergot (a fungal poisoning in grain that can cause hallucinations, a sort of medieval acid trip), to civil disobedience (the dancing was frequently lewd and shocked the reserved and religious), to mass hysteria (new dancers joined the mob daily with no explanation). Some form of group hysteria seems to be the most likely cause, brought about by superstitions, pent-up repressions, and difficult times—the area around Strasbourg, for example, had recently suffered crop failures and economic ruin. Germany had an unusually high number of instances, which may be a sign of these tough times, shared beliefs, and cultural biases, or maybe it was just the strong beer.

One of the more intriguing facts about it all is that dancing plagues were often blamed not on demonic possession—which would seem a likely explanation—but rather on saints' curses, especially those of Saint Vitus; the mania actually became known in some areas as "Saint Vitus' Dance." Many believed that in order to appease the angry saint, the afflicted needed to dance out their sins and make a pilgrimage to a shrine dedicated to him—many believed that both Vitus and John the Baptist were saints who granted healing and cures for the afflicted dancers. In certain instances, towns or authorities even provided musicians for the dancers in an effort to help them achieve this purging. That's one way to support the arts! In other cases, the afflicted individuals themselves made the music, often simple tunes with repeating phrases. Some even danced themselves to the shrine of the given saint and then walked away from it later, presumably cured.

It may or may not be significant that the whole strange phenomenon waned in the seventeenth century, as scientific progress began its first tentative steps toward modernity. Well, all right, there were still witch hunts and plenty of religious wars, but manic group dancing gradually became a thing of the past, at least until outdoor music festivals, raves, and flash mobs.

This chapter will look at various accounts of the dancing plague, without trying too hard to explain them; readers can make up their own minds, since scientists and historians are still scratching their heads.

DANCING MANIA IN GREEK MYTH

Before the great medieval mosh madness, there were myths and legends of similar behavior in ancient times. Variations of the details abounded, but one of the more popular was that of the daughters of Proetus, king of Argos and Tiryns. It was said that when his three daughters came of age, they were stricken with madness, either by Dionysus because they wouldn't worship him (or that their father forbade them to worship him), or perhaps by Hera, because they had proclaimed themselves to be more beautiful than her (and you know how vain those Greek gods could be!).

For whatever reason, these young ladies fell into a dancing frenzy, singing manic tunes and tearing at their clothing, but being unable to stop their fleet feet from flying, they danced around southern Greece. Some accounts say that they were also afflicted with a leprosy-like disease at the same time, which made them hideous to look at, while other versions leave this out (and it's just as well). The famed healer and seer Melampus offered to cure them for a third of Proteus' kingdom (well, that's gracious of him), but the greedy old king wouldn't pay such a large price, and so the girls' dancing mania got worse and became contagious. Soon, other women joined them in frenzied flailing about and the whole thing took on the nature of a plague. Seeing that the mania was spreading, the alarmed king finally agreed to Melampus' demands, but the wily old soothsayer now insisted on a part of the kingdom for his brother, Bias, as well.

Proteus gave in and once this was secure, the brothers set about pursuing the ladies. One of the daughters died, but the other two were chased down and collapsed in exhaustion; then they were cured through various mystical means and purifying rites.

This odd story seems quite at home in a collection of mythology, but there are aspects to it that are very similar to medieval stories and can be found in documented cases of dance mania 1,500 years (and more) later, which makes it all the more strange.

ᶜᵉᵒ *Kölbigk, Saxony, 1017–18* Ꮼᵛ

This is one of the earliest examples of the medieval dancing plague and is merely a legend, though maybe it has some small kernel of truth at its core? One account was given by a certain Othbert, who claimed to be one of the afflicted still suffering the effects of his dancing several decades later, which gives one pause to wonder about the truth. In any case, at the same time that this event was alleged to have taken place, a series of real-world disasters did actually befall the region: a disease that killed many, a comet sighted in the sky (always an ominous portent in medieval belief), at least one severe winter, and spring floods that killed many people. It's not hard to see how this kind of suffering would spawn legends about the cause of a bout of manic dancing, and how those who sinned were punished.

Whatever its origins, this tale obviously served as a warning about not behaving inappropriately in certain places at certain times. On Christmas Eve of 1017 (or 1013, 1018, or 1021, accounts vary, take your pick), a group of young people, "twelve young fools" (or eighteen, in different versions) apparently caused a big disturbance in the town of Kölbigk, in Saxony. It was said that several of these locals were motivated to dance in a graveyard; whether because they wanted to be defiant and rebellious, or they were just horrible people, we don't know. They may have just been carolers (as we've seen, early carols were dances). So, off to the local church grounds they processed, to begin their little ball among the dead, ringing in the holiday in their own grotesque manner.

The dance music began with singing, and moved on to pipe and tabor playing. Unfortunately for them, a priest conducting mass in the church of Saint Magnus the Martyr next door heard them and was more than a little annoyed. He ordered them to stop their "ring dance of sin," but they didn't pay any attention to his boring old demands. So, he took the rather forceful action of cursing them for it, calling on God and Saint Magnus, who, it was said, forced these young rebels to dance for a year without stopping. One man, John, saw his sister among the revelers and tried to pull her away, but instead, her arm came off in his hand. If it were less of a horror story, this could be a scene from a Monty Python skit. Presumably, she screamed and bled, but there was nothing to be done. That'll show them! The afflicted partiers couldn't let go of each other's hands or stop moving. They danced and danced, without rest, food, drink, or sleep. They danced non-stop, night and day, regardless of the weather. Incidentally, the lady's arm was apparently preserved in the church as a kind of reminder of the "miracle" that had occurred. Some miracle!

One dancer, Theodericus, later said, "We held hands and lined up in the courtyard of the church for our sinful dance. The leader of the blind fury, Gerlef, struck up, in jest, the fateful song: 'Bobo rode through the green forest. He had the beautiful Merswind with him. Why do we stand? Why don't we go?'" Can you imagine having to sing that over and over for 365 days? After six months, it was said that they were knee deep in the ground, but still couldn't stop. After six more months, they had worn the ground down to their waists.

At the end of the year, the curse was lifted, and they fell down as if dead, but happily for them, they rose again three days later—spot the obvious religious imagery. Actually, some of them died in this magical sleep. But ever after, the survivors couldn't walk properly, instead skipping everywhere they went (which must have been rather embarrassing when buying things at the market or waiting in line for the outhouse, to say nothing of public executions!). They also could never join hands again, probably to ensure that they wouldn't try their little mass-disrupting follies in the future. Most were said to have ended up as paupers and beggars, so that's what uninhibited dancing on Christmas Eve will get you!

ᏋᎧ *Wales, 1188* ᏝᏋ

Giraldus Cambrensis (Gerald of Wales, but that doesn't sound as cool, ca. 1146–ca. 1223) was a royal clerk who wrote a large number of historical texts over his long life. One of his more interesting accounts is that which took place at Saint Almedda's Church in Southern Wales in 1188, where he described dozens of people beginning to sing and dance in the churchyard. This was apparently an annual tradition on the saint's feast day in August, and led to some very strange behaviors:

> The circumstances which occur at every anniversary appear to me remarkable. You may see men or girls, now in the church, now in the churchyard, now in the dance, which is led round the churchyard with a song, on a sudden falling on the ground as in a trance, then jumping up as in a frenzy, and representing with their hands and feet, before the people, whatever work they have unlawfully done on feast days; you may see one man put his hand to the plough, and another, as it were, goad on the oxen, mitigating their sense of labour, by the usual rude song: one man imitating the profession of a shoemaker; another, that of a tanner. Now you may see a girl with a distaff, drawing out the thread, and winding it again on the spindle; another walking, and arranging the threads for the web; another, as it were, throwing the shuttle, and seeming to weave.

After this bizarre activity had gone on for some time, there was, luckily for the afflicted, a solution:

> On being brought into the church, and led up to the altar with their oblations, you will be astonished to see them suddenly awakened, and

coming to themselves. Thus, by the divine mercy, which rejoices in the conversion, not in the death, of sinners, many persons from the conviction of their senses, are on these feast days corrected and mended.

This strange affair may well be true, and would speak to the power of belief and even of mass hysteria, if it really were something that happened every year. There could have been an excitement in anticipating it, leading otherwise normal folks to carry out these weird behaviors so that they could be "cured" at the end of the day.

It's worth noting that Gerald also described a Welshman named Meilyr who had many remarkable abilities, including being able to tell when anyone was lying, because he could see a demon dancing on the liar's tongue. Now that would be a useful skill for interrogations!

Erfurt, 1247

In the Imperial town of Erfurt, it was said that in the year 1237 (or 1247, or 1257, again, versions vary), well over one hundred children (some sources say over a thousand) began furiously dancing and hopping all about the streets, eventually moving as a crowd out of the town gates. When they finally reached the neighboring town of Arnstadt some twelve miles away, they collapsed from exhaustion along the walls and in the streets. They were later found by their distressed parents, who strangely, are not recorded as having tried to do anything to stop the whole spectacle before the children danced their way out of Erfurt. Sadly, they discovered that some of the children had died. Others had afflictions that would remain with them for the rest of their lives, such as tremors or constant fatigue.

This weird legend clearly has some affinity with the Pied Piper story of children dancing out of the town, following the sinister piper, never to be seen again. It may have been one strand of inspiration for the famous folk tale. In the fifteenth century, some chronicles that recalled the incident claimed that it happened on July 15, which is the feast day for Saint Vitus, an obvious attempt to link the children's behavior to the saint often seen as being behind all of this madness, but this was probably just an invention of the time to describe an event that may well have never happened.

⤸ *Maastricht, 1278* ⤸

A few decades later in Maastricht, a far grimmer spectacle unfolded, if the histories of the time are to be believed. Whether filled with irreverence or taken by a dancing plague, it was said that over two hundred people began to dance uncontrollably.

They moved to a bridge over the river Moselle, as their mania consumed them. The quality of bridge construction being what it probably was in those days, there was no way it was going to support that kind of weight, especially when vigorous jumping and prancing were added into the mix. Chroniclers recorded that they danced so lewdly and irreverently that God punished them, but really, it was probably just basic physics, if it happened at all. The bridge gave way and collapsed, and they all fell into the water below and died.

This is another of those early accounts that probably has some origin in truth, but then was wildly embellished later on, tabloid style, in an effort to instill a fear of punishment into those doing things not church-approved, and also simply because a good gruesome story is irresistible.

⤸ *Aachen, Ghent, Metz, and Northern France, 1374–75* ⤸

While the previous accounts have much of legend about them and may be fantastical retellings of smaller events blown out of proportion to make a good story, the events that hit northern Germany and France in the later fourteenth century were very real and well-documented. This was a time when people still remembered the bubonic plague that had ravaged Europe, and for many, the end of the world most certainly was due any day.

So, with a pervasive mindset of fear, superstition, and uncertainty, it's not surprising that wild dancing might be one form of mass hysteria that could hold a crowd in its grip and not let go. Prior to these events, there was a brief mention of a possible instance of dancing mania in London in 1364, where it is said that crowds of people danced for days before falling down in the streets, but the details are mostly missing.

According to records, the next large outbreak began, once again, around July 15 in Aachen, and moved west throughout the summer and autumn months, reaching as far as France and parts of the Netherlands by October. There apparently were a large number of religious pilgrims who had traveled from Hungary to visit various shrines, and in doing so, they seem to have brought a very unpleasant affliction with them. But this one was not blamed on Vitus or John, despite beginning around the former's feast day. It was fairly obvious to those who witnessed it that they were seeing the devil's handiwork. A monk named Peter of Herental was an eyewitness to a portion of the events and described what he saw in detail:

> A strange sect ... came to Aachen ... This was their condition. Both men and women were abused by the devil to such a degree that they danced in their homes, in the churches and in the streets, holding each other's hands and leaping in the air. While they danced they called out the names of demons, such as Friskes and others, but they were unaware of this nor did they pay attention to modesty even though people watched them. At the end of the dance, they felt such pains in the chest, that if their friends did not tie linen clothes tightly around their waists, they cried out like madmen that they were dying.

Some theorize that this mischievous demon's name was the origin of our word "frisky," so just remember that the next time you use it to describe a puppy or a kitten. Fortunately, there was a cure on offer, courtesy of the local priests:

In Liège they were freed of their demons by means of exorcisms . . . Those who were cured said that they seemed to have been dancing in a river of blood, which is why they jumped into the air.

But the folks of Liège had an explanation for why they had been afflicted to begin with. A very scientific explanation:

[They] said that they had been attacked in this way because they were not truly baptized, inasmuch as most of the priests kept concubines.

Wait, what?

For this reason, the populace proposed that they rise against the priests, kill them and take their property, which would have happened had not God provided a remedy through the aforesaid exorcisms. When the people saw this their anger subsided to such an extent that the clergy were held in even greater reverence than before.

Well, isn't that convenient? So, oddly, instead of accusing witches or heretics—the usual scapegoats—these folks (rather bravely, it must be said) blamed priests who had been getting "frisky" with their mistresses for not being able to give them sufficient spiritual armor at birth to begin with. The only solution, naturally, was to murder the priests and loot their houses. Thankfully, said priests were able to show that they did have the mojo after all, and whisked away the demonic compulsion to dance, by the power of suggestion, if nothing else.

If there is any truth to this hostility, it shows that in the aftermath of the plague's devastation, people were a lot less content just to take their religious leaders' word for whatever was happening to them. Since the church had utterly failed to save people from the Black Death, it had lost a lot of moral high ground over the previous few decades. Yet, that simple people were talking openly about killing priests and confiscating their belongings is still pretty astonishing.

This particular outbreak was widespread, "infecting" hundreds of people. Most of them exhibited the same kinds of behavior, such as screaming in pain and claiming they were possessed while dancing wildly and begging God and the saints for relief. They wandered from town to town, and their presence acted like a contagion, spreading the mania wherever they went. Some regained control of themselves after a few weeks, but even among these victims, there were relapses. At one chapel outside the German town of Trier, a large number of afflicted built small huts out of whatever materials they could find, and danced wildly while they hoped for a cure.

Eventually, the mania died down, but it flared up again in 1375–76 and 1381 in the same areas, exactly like an outbreak of a disease. It was all put down to demonic possession, so some towns took actions to forbid anyone from dancing publicly (especially in streets or in churches) in an attempt to keep the contagion under control, a kind of dancing quarantine. These outbreaks were the worst yet recorded, but lucky for you, dear reader, there was more to come.

DEADLY DANCES IN THE FIFTEENTH CENTURY

A small number of incidents are recorded in the century following the Aachen hysteria. In 1418, it was said that a group of people in Strasbourg who had fasted for several days suddenly sprang into action and began to dance furiously, though this event was nothing compared to what was to assail the city exactly one hundred years later (see below).

In 1428, there were reports of a group of women dancing madly in the Water Church in Zurich, an unusual instance of dance mania outside of Western Germany (in 1452, another man did the same). Also in 1428, at the Benedictine Monastery of Saint Agnes at Schaffhausen (also in

Switzerland), sources claim that one monk danced himself to death during the time of—you guessed it—the feast of Saint Vitus in July.

By 1463, the hysteria popped up again in Trier, when a large group of pilgrims came to the shrine of Eberhardsklausen, apparently looking for some relief. It was said that many of them had been suffering from the affliction for months. One Wilhelm von Bernkastel wrote that:

> . . . these dancers jumped about in circles, always, separately, thinking that they could by exertion and body movement drive out the pains they felt in their heart and viscera.

But this didn't work, and they called on John the Baptist for relief, believing him to be responsible. They said that as they danced, they could see his head floating in blood; charming. Perhaps they turned to him because of his unfortunate encounter with the infamous dancer Salome (see the entry on Salome, later in the book). Curiously, many claimed not to be able to see the color red otherwise. Some had broken bones from their self-inflicted abuse, but they kept on dancing because they claimed it offered them temporary relief from their suffering. Sometimes, those with broken bones died of their injuries. According to those who witnessed the horrid spectacle, when the dancers finally collapsed in exhaustion, they could be revived and begin again if wine was poured on their hands as they were lying on the ground, their arms outstretched . . . now there's a marketing idea for the German wine industry!

⸾⸙ *Strasbourg, 1518* ⸙⸾

The Strasbourg incident is the best-documented case of dancing plague from either the medieval or Renaissance eras. There is no question about it being legendary, or even particularly embellished. The bizarre events that unfolded over the summer (once again, right around the time of Saint Vitus' feast) still defy explanation, though many have tried.

As noted, the elderly Frau Troffea stepped out of her house on July 14, one day before Vitus' holiday, apparently after a squabble with her husband, and simply began to dance, "because nothing annoyed her husband more than just dancing." Her behavior was rightly seen as bizarre by their neighbors, but most took no further notice, thinking perhaps that she was simply defying him in some domestic dispute, since he demanded that she cease. But she paid no attention to him, said nothing, and simply continued to dance in silence. After a while, it must have been an eerie spectacle that became increasingly sinister in the minds of those prone to seeing demons in all things and supernatural threats everywhere.

Her dancing became increasingly manic, but no one could get her to stop until she collapsed and slept for a short time. Soon, she was at it again, and continued dancing about for the next several days, attracting a growing and bewildered audience of townspeople. She rested only when she could take no more, but as soon as she could, she was up and at it again. Her feet became bruised and bloodied, but still she continued.

After a few punishing days, some began to suspect that this was not the work of a demon, but rather of Saint Vitus, who was inflicting his wrath upon the poor woman as a message to the city. Someone in authority (the chronicles are a bit vague about it) ordered that she be taken to a shrine for the saint near Saverne in the Vosges region, west of the city. So, off she went, and the citizens breathed a sigh of relief, thinking that a pilgrimage there would appease the angry saint, and all would then be well. Oh, how wrong they were.

Within a few days, more than thirty other city folk had taken up the crazed dancing. Some of them were even more enthusiastic and danced themselves to death in the hot weather. It was clear that Troffea's affliction was not a solitary curse, but rather the beginning of a plague that could potentially be as deadly as any airborne illness. Indeed, as the city and guild leaders debated about what course of action to take, many physicians offered up a naturalistic explanation, blaming overheated blood. But as the behavior spread to more and more people, fear gripped the city; it really did seem to be contagious. Within four weeks of Troffea's first dance, it is recorded that over four hundred people were engaged in the crazed, chaotic capering and could not be compelled to quit.

In order to quell the rising panic, the city officials thought it would be best to simply let those so touched dance it out. One chronicler, Daniel Specklin, records:

> So they reserved the guildhall of the carpenters and the dyers and set up platforms in the horse market and in the grain market and paid [unaffected] people to stay with them and dance with them [to the accompaniment of] fife and drum.

Well, that's one way to employ the musicians' guild! Unfortunately, as the chronicle continues, "all of this helped not at all." In fact, the idea was soon abandoned because it was believed that the instrumentalists were actually making things worse and encouraging the affliction to spread. Sure, blame the musicians. Accordingly, the XXI (the town leadership) stepped up and:

> ... forbade, on pain of a fine of 30 shillings, that anyone, no matter who, should not hold a dance until St. Michael's Day [September 29] in this city or its suburbs, or in its whole jurisdiction. For by doing so they take away the recovery of such persons. The only exception is that if honourable persons wish to dance at weddings or celebrations of first Mass in their houses, they may do so using stringed instruments, but they are on their conscience not to use tambourines or drums.

Oh, those dangerous, sinful percussion instruments! Actually, it did seem that powerfully rhythmic music had a stronger effect on the dancers than softer string music did, so perhaps they were on to something. Drumming seemed to help spread the "infection."

At this point, the city officials realized they were reaching a crisis, and figured that they may as well try divine intervention, sixteenth-century medical diagnoses being what they were. Perhaps Troffea had made a full recovery and this encouraged them; unfortunately, the chronicles don't say what happened to her, but the absence of any mention of her dying may be important. So, it was decreed that the sufferers were also to be trucked off to the shrine of Vitus, according to Specklin:

> They sent many wagons to St. Vitus . . . and others got there on their own. They fell down dancing before his image. So then a priest said Mass over them, and then they were given a little cross and red shoes, on which the sign of the cross had been made in holy oil . . . In St. Vitus' name they were sprinkled with holy water. It helped many and they gave a large contribution. This is why it is called St. Vitus' dance.

The red shoe detail is especially interesting; you'll recall that the sufferers of the 1463 incident claimed not to be able to see the color red, and also asked for pieces of red coral to hang around their necks. Is there some connection in the hard-wiring of the brain between perceiving red and the compulsion to dance? We don't know, but it's a fascinating detail. In folkloric beliefs, red symbolized not only blood, but also fire, anger, passion, and love, as well as potentially signifying various and sundry diabolical things.

The officials were undoubtedly grateful for the apparent cure, but took extra precautions in having extra masses said, and seeing to it that various undesirables were expelled from the city at least for a certain amount of time, all of which was designed to appease the angry saint. Vitus was seen by many as both the cause and the cure for dancing mania; indeed, a common curse of the time was "may Saint Vitus attack you!" So, there was obviously an ingrained belief in the power of said saint to afflict those who wronged him. Legend held that Vitus was a third-century Sicilian who was known for his laying-on-of-hands healing. He was martyred by being boiled alive, and was said to be capable of curing those with limps and trembling limbs. Hence, he was the perfect candidate for being both the source of and the cure for the dancing madness.

Strasbourg's was the last large outbreak of the mania, but there were other, smaller incidents well into the seventeenth century. One writer described a woman in Basel in the 1540s who obsessively danced with city guards and could not be made to stop; she danced until her feet became raw. She wore—wait for it—red-colored clothing. Various writers of the early seventeenth century noted that the dance craze was an annual affliction for some in Germany. It began in various locations in June and often only lasted a short time, while they danced in frenzy at a given shrine to the saint, then fell down and recovered, only to repeat it all again the next year:

> They [the dancers] are convinced that they can never be calmed and relieved if they cannot shake out this disease by dancing at the shrine of the saint, and their success confirms them in this. And truly they are as a rule free of this madness for the rest of the year once they complete this annual dance, which they usually do for the space of three hours.

This very short version of the sickness contrasts strongly with those who danced for days and even killed themselves. It was something they anticipated each year and knew exactly how to "treat" when the compulsion to prance about came over them, like taking a spiritual ibuprofen and getting on with their daily lives. Maybe it was a sign that belief in it was starting to wane?

For whatever reasons, the sickness seems to have disappeared from Germany and surrounding areas by the mid-seventeenth century. This may have been because of improved living conditions, a weakening of superstitious fears and restrictions, or any number of other reasons. But the legends of the mania lived on, and found their way up to the nearby north and into Scandinavian folk tales, which added a decidedly devilish element to them.

CHOREOMANIA, FIDDLING DEVILS,
AND DANCING SKULLS IN SWEDEN

These historical German accounts have some similarity to a set of folk tales that circulated in Sweden, which date back to at least the eighteenth century, but which are probably much older. Variations on the story are found in the regions of Hanebo, Dalarna, and elsewhere. They also have plot elements in common with the "devil comes to the dance" stories that have circulated throughout North America (see the "Fairy Tales and Folklore" chapter).

The Hanebo legend tells of a village named Hårga, where the residents would from time to time enjoy a Saturday night dance that extended into the wee hours. It happened that once, this dance occurred on the night before a major religious holiday, and a stranger appeared, well-dressed and amiable, wanting to join in. He was most welcome, of course, and the revelers joined hands and formed a circle. But something sinister was afoot—get it? One of the young men not dancing noticed that this stranger's feet were not human at all, but were hooves. At that point the man desperately tried to pull his fiancée from the circle, but he was unable to, and ended up pulling off one of her arms instead. Remember (dismember?) Kölbigk? This little bit was almost certainly borrowed from that legend, and changed to a bride-to-be instead of a sister.

The dancers could not stop, and in their frenzy, the stranger led them out of the dancing hall, over hills, and up the side of a mountain, Hårgaberget. None could escape, and their dancing only became more intense. Their diabolical leader left them to their fate on that mountain, where they were unable to stop. Not only did they dance themselves to death, but also their skeletons continued to dance until the bones wore down and nothing but skulls remained, and even these clanked about forever on the mountain top, prancing and jigging as disembodied skulls are wont to do, or not.

Satan must have been busy in leading sinful revelers astray, because the legend of the frenzied dancers is found in other regions of Sweden. A version from Dalarna tells of a group of dancers who met on a mountain top (no need to be led up there!) specifically to dance when they weren't supposed to. Once while engaged in their illicit fun, a stranger arrived with a fiddle under his arm, and offered to play for them. The dancers enthusiastically and foolishly encouraged him, and he began to play. Only, they found that as he played, they couldn't stop. They begged him, but he only increased the tempo of his music, forcing them to dance ever faster. They wore out their shoes. Then they wore down their feet. Then they wore down their legs to their knees, but still the evil fiddler would not relent. Finally, all that was left were their heads, and even on these, the flesh fell off until only their skulls remained, hopping up and down to the devil's tunes.

Now, a certain clergyman came by, having heard about this terrible crime. He recognized the fiddler as the devil and ordered him to cease. The evil one had no choice but to obey and depart, tail between legs, though that tail had been the bow with which he had fiddled. Presumably, there was now a whole pile of skulls resting on the ground.

Another variation on the legend concerns people gathered for a dance at a hall, or a farm, or some similar location. Two travelers (sometimes students, sometimes beggars, sometimes Saami) arrive, asking for lodging for the night, but are turned away, since the barn is already full. The strangers leave, the dance begins, and fun is had by all. Only, they can't stop. They soon discover that nothing they do can make them cease dancing. A few realize that the strangers must have had something to do with this strange curse, and set out to find them. When they eventually do, the travelers tell them that they inserted a slip of paper into the door post of the hall, and that when this is removed, the dancers will be able to stop. The farm folk rush back to the barn—no word on what they did to the strangers, who may have been demons or sorcerers or some such—to find that, yes indeed, there is a paper, on which is written "People will dance here," or similar words. Once that paper is removed, the dancers are able to stop immediately, much to their relief, since several of them were near death. At least they didn't get worn down to their skulls! Such stories played up the fear of "otherness" in strangers and implied that they could be hiding some very dark secrets.

All of these Scandinavian tales serve not only as warnings against the sinfulness of excessive dancing, but are likely informed by legends of Choreomania from the south. Given the prevalence of German accounts of the phenomenon, it's entirely possible that one or more of them made it to the north, by legend or by chronicle, where the story was incorporated into local surroundings in classic urban legend style and then blamed on the devil rather than Saints Vitus or John the Baptist. Or perhaps the dancing plagues really did infect Scandinavia during the Middle Ages as well, and lived on, if only in these strange accounts of a fiddling devil and his ballet of perpetually scampering skulls.

2

Dances for Illness, Evil, and Death

dancing, like music, has been used around the world for thousands of years as a form of therapy, to assist in cures, and to solve problems both physical and psychological.

In the Middle Ages and Renaissance, the allegorical Dance of Death also served as a warning to a terrified continent ravaged by the bubonic plague that their time on earth was limited and that death was common to all, whether peasant or king. Life was but a dance of death toward the inevitable grave.

For those concerned about the supernatural trials and travails of life while on that journey, dancing oneself into a trance has long been believed to be a way to exorcise evil spirits, and the more vigorous the dancing and movements, the greater the chance of success. Presumably the spirit will get uncomfortable with all that moving and want to pass on to some place (or someone) else more peaceful. It's kind of the ghostly equivalent of telling the neighbors to keep the noise down.

Frenzied dancing could also cure the effects of a spider bite, at least as far as those in southern Mediterranean countries were concerned, and a whole genre of music and dance grew up around this curious folk custom.

Dancing to commit mass suicide was one way for the women of an oppressed people in the early nineteenth century to show their conquerors that they had had enough, and their defiance was shocking and oddly inspiring, if horrific.

For those who have died, various cultures have created elaborate and sometimes quite joyous dancing rituals to honor their passing, which at first seems a bit inappropriate, but actually makes a lot of sense, when you read more about them.

And of course, professional dancers could not always stay healthy, so one famous modern ballet company came up with a creative, if extreme, way of dealing with illness. The show must go on, after all.

THE ZAR: GRANTING WISHES TO GENIES

In Arabic-speaking lands, the *jinn* (more commonly known to English speakers as "genies") are believed to be spirits made of smokeless fire that existed even before the Biblical Adam and Eve. The pre-Islamic people of the Arabian Peninsula likely believed in these mischievous, lusty, trouble-making beings before the time of Muhammad, and their folklore was folded into Islamic scripture. Each *jinni* has a name, a personality, and preferred songs, foods, and drinks; just like a petulant teenager. And like those petulant teenagers, the *jinn* can cause quite a bit of trouble.

Humans can anger them by spilling water on the ground; indeed, possession is believed to be more likely around water, such as rivers, wells, springs, or the bathroom . . . wait, what? *Jinn* also like dark, in-between places such as caves, stairwells, and doorways. There's a low-budget horror movie in this, for sure.

The most feared among them is the Moroccan *jinniyya* Aisha Qandisha, who lingers near springs and rivers, seducing young men who happen to be unfortunate enough to pass by. However, despite her preference for men, most *jinn* are far more likely to possess women, particularly in rural areas. In Egypt, Sudan, the Horn of Africa, and the Arabian Peninsula, as well as southern and western Iran, rural and lower-class women have for centuries held ritual gatherings known as *zar* to alleviate themselves of a wide range

of *jinn*-induced ailments, including: stomach aches, infertility, epilepsy, insomnia, anxiety, depression, alcoholism, unemployment, marital problems, death in the family, and even a flat tire, which just seems petty on the *jinn*'s part somehow. But the *jinn* are like that. Intense emotional states such as anger, sadness, and fear, or having a fight with one's husband or even yelling at the kids can invite a *jinni* into a woman's body. In fact, the Arabic word for "crazy"—*majnun*—has the same root as *jinn*. People in these regions believe that the *jinn* are contagious; if you love or hate someone, you can pass your *jinn* to them.

Once the *jinni* has entered your body, there's no getting rid of it; they claim squatter's rights. But you can make the *jinni* happy by having a raucous party with all your female friends, family members, and neighbors, complete with drumming, dancing, drinking, feasting, and animal sacrifice. Oh, and drinking the blood of the animal you've sacrificed, if your *jinni* is into that sort of thing. No men allowed. These *jinn* aren't exactly like the comedic shape-shifter in Disney's *Aladdin*, but they do love a good party. You ain't never had a friend like this.

These parties, called *zar*, can be both public and open to any woman for a small fee, or, if one's husband has the means, private for invited guests only. The village *shaykha*—an older, often unmarried kind of priestess—organizes the ritual, prepares an altar of dried fruits and nuts, and gathers together musicians who specialize in the kind of songs and rhythms known to please them, a *jinni* top forty. She uses incense to purify everyone and everything at the ceremony, including, um, bodily orifices (remember that the *jinn* like dark, damp places). The woman seeking relief from the *jinni* possession, often called the "patient," dresses in her finest gown, jewelry, and wears her best perfume. The *shaykha*, who is a trained singer herself, guides the ensemble of musicians—mostly women, but sometimes men, the only ones allowed to the event—who play a variety of instruments, but mostly hand percussion. They watch the afflicted woman and discern which rhythm will please the *jinni* possessing her. It is believed that the *jinni* in question will demand certain foods. Some female *jinn* love cola, while

male *jinn* prefer whiskey. Of course they do. Probably aged and expensive varieties, too.

The "patient" sways and swings her upper body, rapidly shaking her shoulders, and throwing her head forward and back or in a figure-eight motion in time with the pulsing rhythm. Here, she can make demands otherwise prohibited to her in daily life: smoking, burping, drinking alcohol (which is otherwise forbidden in Islam), wielding weapons, asking for extravagant jewelry or clothing, and, of course, wild dancing. As the ritual continues, the musicians play louder, increasing their tempo with greater intensity. If they get the song right, the patient will dance herself first into a trance, then into exhaustion, after which she often collapses to the floor. This reminds us a little of the effects of choreomania, as seen in the previous chapter, and it definitely has some affinities with the southern Italian tarantella dances, which we'll get to in a bit.

The other women in attendance will comfort and soothe the patient, tending to her every whim. On the last night of the gathering—which can last anywhere from one night to one week—an animal is often sacrificed: poorer women can often only afford pigeons and chickens, while wealthier ones sometimes purchase camels. A man (the only other male present apart from some musicians) slits the animal's throat, collecting its blood in a bowl. And even though Islam forbids it, sometimes the patient will drink the blood from the bowl. The *jinni* has been pleased, at least for now.

Anthropologists and psychologists believe that the *zar* allows poorer women in this part of the world a kind of psychotherapy to cope with their restricted and often repressive lives. Outside the *zar*, a woman must often be dutiful, quiet, and obedient to her family and her husband. But once she is diagnosed with possession, the *zar* gives her a chance to let off steam and be surrounded by other women who are there to support her. And as we mentioned, once a woman has contracted a *jinni*, it never leaves, so there will be many more occasions when this wild dance of pacification will be needed. In fact, those who attend the *zar* believe that if the *jinni*'s desires

are not satisfied, it will cause further problems for the afflicted. In these cultures, you grant the *jinni* wishes, not the other way around.

DANSE MACABRE: A RAVE FROM THE GRAVE

A pope, an emperor, a knight, a merchant, and a peasant. No, it's not the start of a joke. What do they all have in common? None can escape their mortality, of course! From the early fifteenth century, shocking visual reminders of this fact began to appear all over Europe. Rotting corpses, some still in their burial shrouds, or perhaps even decayed all the way down to nothing but bones, arise from the grave and take the hands of the living. No matter what their position in life, these striking creatures grab hold of mortals to escort them to their final destination with a dance. Some of the dead carry weapons, some of them carry the implements that buried them. A few play musical instruments and strike up the tune, often on bony xylophones and other percussion instruments. And so they begin their procession, ushering the living to their inevitable fate . . . so begins the dance of death!

How did this remarkable artistic phenomenon come about? One theory is that it began after the calamities of the fourteenth century. The specter of the Black Death (bubonic plague) still hung like a shadow over Europe, ever since its first devastating spread in the late 1340s. That horrid epidemic, which culled at least one-third of the population of Europe, was followed by smaller outbreaks over the next few decades, and completely upended the social order of the time. As if people weren't well enough aware of it before, their impending mortality became an even bigger issue, and calls for repentance in the face of the angry deity that had sent such a calamity grew ever louder. Add to that the usual dangers of war and famine, and the four horsemen of the Apocalypse became very real in the minds of many. Death could take anyone at any time, no matter their age, gender, background, wealth, or social status.

While there is certainly some truth to this, the problem is that artistic representations of the dance were rare to non-existent in Ireland and Spain, with only a handful in Italy, where the plague hit just as hard, if not harder, than elsewhere. Likewise, the dancing dead were unknown in the lands of Eastern Europe, the home of Orthodox Christianity, as opposed to Roman Catholicism. So, what was really happening? Well, the Franciscan and Dominican orders were enthusiastic supporters of the idea of the death dance and worked it into their preaching missions, especially in France, Germany, and England. They were keen to reach out to the lower classes, and using this startling dance motif was apparently an effective way of doing so.

It became a form of social criticism, a reminder that everyone, regardless of their station in life, needed to be humble and to repent. It was a warning to the corrupt in the church and in secular governments that they were not immune from divine judgement and that their sins would have to be accounted for when they died. By leveling the playing field, the dance of death told everyone, including the majority of those who were illiterate, that an equalizer took them all at the end. This was probably both frightening, yet oddly appealing. This was the "one last dance" taken to extremes.

But why the reanimated corpses? Interestingly, in the post-plague years, another popular image circulated in Europe, both in literature and art: that of three young kings meeting three corpses. In a forest, three carefree young men meet three decomposing dead bodies that repulse them, but startle them even more when they speak, warning: "As you are now, so once were we; as we are now, so shall you be." The young men realize that they have been living their lives dangerously, courting death with no repentance, and they resolve to abandon their sinful ways and become godly. This kind of grotesque imagery likely had some influence on the boogieing bones of a few decades later.

The first known (or at least earliest surviving) visual representation of this deadly dance was made in Paris between 1424 and 1425, carved on a wall of the Innocents' Cloister in the city's largest cemetery; but soon, more followed. The idea of death enticing humanity with a final dance to the grave proved to be irresistible, especially to the lower classes who gazed in wonder and terror at these grisly images, and the motif began to appear more widely. There was something dreadfully egalitarian about it all, a warning to pope, bishop, king, soldier, and peasant alike that their days were numbered. A *Totentanz* (the German name for the dance) from a fifteenth-century book begins with these humbling words placed under an image of a corpse talking to a king:

> Emperor, your sword will not help you
> Sceptre and crown are worthless here
> I have taken you by the hand
> For you must come to my dance

This exhortation was a vivid reminder that those in power were still subject to the greatest power of all.

Later, reformers in the sixteenth century would happily adapt this ghoulish imagery specifically to attack the Catholic Church, with popes, bishops, and monks becoming the prime targets of the dancing corpses, while counter-reformers did the same against their Protestant enemies. And so it continued, up until about 1800, when the imagery began to fall away in the face of the approaching "modern" world and its concerns about social reform, improving quality of life, curing disease, and a host of other things that the dancing dead couldn't stand up against.

So, did people in the Middle Ages actually *dance* a "dance of death?" It's an intriguing idea. There were examples of songs such as the Spanish *Ad mortem festinamus* from about 1400, which warns: "We hurry towards death, let us desist from sin." This is, perhaps surprisingly, a lively, jaunty tune that could easily have been used for dancing. But we don't know if anyone ever donned costumes specifically to put on such a spectacle, though it certainly would have been right at home on the stages of medieval theaters. Actors did take on the role of Death, often squeezing themselves into tight leather outfits and wearing creepy skin-tight masks to give themselves an appropriately bony appearance. Throw in a drum, and the gruesomely-clad actor could easily have danced and led the other players to their fates.

But dancing corpses had the strongest effect in the artistic world. The common people beheld them in all their grisly glory and feared for their own limited time on earth. In the end, they were reminded of their fate with jarring, creepy imagery and a simple yet, all-encompassing phrase: *mors omnibus communis*: "Death is common to all."

THE TARANTELLA:
THE VIGOROUS DANCING CURE FOR A SPIDER BITE

In southern Italy, there was a whole different kind of dancing mania with its own Mediterranean charm . . . or maybe not. The tarantella was a dance often undertaken by those who believed themselves to have been bitten by a wolf spider, the *Lycosa tarantula*—not to be confused with the better known (and hairier) tarantula. This creature, though not as large as its creepy cousin, is found in southern Europe, and especially in Puglia, the "heel" of Italy's boot. Occasionally, some victims claimed they were stung by a scorpion. For the locals, its bite was said to induce a condition known as tarantism (a bitten dancer was called a *tarantata*), with some surprisingly similar symptoms to those grooving to Choreomania up in Germany.

As might be expected, the earliest recorded incidents of spider-bite plagues come from the Middle Ages. The little beast's venom is not especially dangerous, but most believed that the only cure for it was to dance wildly, even manically, often for hours, or even days on end until one's system was purged. To this end, musicians were provided to offer the victim a way to keep moving, just like in the German outbreaks. But in Italy, the dance and music themselves evolved into specific forms that later were always employed to do the trick. As an art form, the tarantella is an integral part of southern Italian folk culture, now characterized by virtuoso tambourine playing and lively tempos to make dancers really kick up their heels, no toxic venom required. From the fifteenth century onward, many composers wrote pieces called tarantellas and the name became known in Western classical music.

An interesting thing about tarantism is that, like the dancing plagues, people believed that it was contagious. As the afflicted danced out their venom, they were sometimes joined by others. Some of these folks claimed that they had previously been bitten by the spider and that being around a new victim somehow reactivated their old wounds, while others were not bitten at all but claimed that just being around one sick dancer compelled them to dance, too. There was definitely an element of mass hysteria at work here, just like in the plagues that struck in Germany. German physician Justus Hecker (1795–1850) wrote: "Entire communities of people would join hands, dance, leap, scream, and shake for hours."

Another similarity was that tarantism generally only happened in the summer months, when the weather was hot and certain saints' feast days were approaching. Like their northern counterparts, the dancers had preferences for certain colors, though here, red was just fine; instead, it was black that made these dancers very unhappy. The victims were mostly working-class people and peasants, and women tended to exhibit symptoms far more than men, often almost exclusively; and those symptoms were definitely real. People had headaches, difficulty breathing, vertigo, aching joints, their skin could change color, their faces could swell, all of which suggested something physiological was going on. Writer and librarian Francesco Cancellieri (1751–1826) made a study of the affliction and noted of the sufferers:

One cries, dances, vomits, trembles, laughs, pales, cries, faints, and one will suffer great pain, and finally after a few days, if unaided, you die. Sweat and antidotes relieve the sick, but the sovereign and the only remedy is Music.

The mania reached its height in the sixteenth and seventeenth centuries, but detailed accounts of later attacks are known. In one from 1728, a spider supposedly bit a young woman, Anna Palazzo, on her elbow while she worked in a local vineyard. She became sick immediately, and was delirious and unconscious by the time she was set down in her bed. But have no fear, help was on the way: the musicians had arrived. They struck up the appropriate tunes on their guitars and tambourines, and sure enough, the young lady eventually responded, launching into a wild dance over the next two days that cured her.

In long-held superstitious belief, many felt that the affliction had nothing to do with the spider's venom, but rather was a kind of spirit possession, thus requiring the frenzied dance to shake it off, as with the *jinn* on the other side of the Mediterranean. But true to the unique nature of the Italian affliction, dancers sometimes made spider-like moves: crawling on the floor, trying to climb walls, jumping about. Essentially, they became the spider in order to exorcise the evil inside them. Maybe they even developed spidey sense.

Some found dancing to be only a temporary relief, and discovered that every June, the mania would come back. As with those who had gone to the shrines of Saint Vitus, these *tarantatas* would make a pilgrimage to the city of Galatina on June 29, the Feast of Saint Paul, and pray and beg for healing and relief from the grip of the spider's evil.

Later, seventeenth-century doctors tried prescribing herbs and medicines as a cure; wine was also prescribed as a treatment—honestly, it's good for most things. But usually they found that music and dancing were still the best remedies. Old folk traditions die hard. Capitalizing on the need, guilds of tarantella musicians sprang up, charged for their services, and made house calls. Summer was obviously their busiest time of the year.

Musicians had long known that if they stopped playing, the afflicted would relapse into their symptoms, and only when the music was struck up again did they recommence dancing, so the musicians had to be in it for the long haul. No wonder they charged high fees for their services.

If the condition was psychosomatic, then the long-held cure dominant in the culture was the one most likely to relieve it. Later anthropologists made a good case that since most of the sufferers were women, the dance was a way for them to act out in otherwise socially unacceptable ways (again like those dancing the *zar*), and that their frenzy actually brought communities and families together to support them. Some also theorized that these wild dances were a survival in another form of ancient frenzied dances to Dionysus or Cybele from Greek and Roman times.

Like so many other curious mass hysterias, tarantism faded as the modern world progressed—though scattered cases were still being reported in the 1950s—and the cultural myths that kept the mania alive became less relevant, until they were no longer needed, or at least no longer remembered. Tarantism was undoubtedly a real affliction, just as choreomania was, but its exact causes are still debated, and probably will be for a long time to come.

THE DANCE OF ZALONGO (1803)

The unthinkable faced an unfortunate group of women, a ragtag group of survivors from Zalongo, a town in Souli in the region of Epirus in northwestern Greece. In 1803, the area was still under the control of the Ottomans, but a resistance movement, the Souliotes, who had been giving the Turks hell for nearly two centuries, had established a quasi-independent region, the Souliote Confederacy, that continued to frustrate their would-be occupiers. This almost-nation received support (both moral and material) from Russia, France, and other European nations eager to see the "sick man of Europe"—the Ottoman Empire—get a little bit sicker. The Ottomans, of course, had been a thorn in the side of Europe since the fourteenth century, with their expansionist ambitions and that odd little desire to rule the world, which stirred up more than a bit of resentment. If the Souliotes could stick it to whichever sultan happened to be sitting on the throne at that moment, so much the better.

But by 1803, Sultan Selim III had had enough (he was eventually deposed and murdered by his own people in 1808, but that's a whole other story). Selim asked the local ruler of the region, one Ali Pasha, to bring the rebels down once and for all. Faced with infighting and betrayal, the Souliotes finally began to crack. The usual treachery and backstabbing and secret deals were made, and in the end Ali Pasha had the upper hand. He agreed to sign a peace treaty with certain rebels that offered them guarantees of safe passage and relocation.

The Souliotes who accepted this deal with the devil were betrayed almost immediately. Ali Pasha ordered the men to be murdered and the women and children taken as slaves. He was ruthless and the order was carried out with no pity. On December 16, the Ottoman forces cornered a group of rebel women with their infants, numbering fifty or so, on a cliff edge in the mountains of Zalongo. Facing an inevitable life of slavery, the Souliote women did what anyone might do in such a dire situation: they danced.

Wait, what? Yes, it's true. They struck up a nationalistic folk song and danced a circle dance, defying the Ottoman forces and showing that they would never sacrifice their freedom, only their lives. Indeed, with some holding infants in their arms, these women danced to the edge of the cliff and threw themselves off, one by one. To the Turks, it must have been completely inexplicable, but they had badly underestimated just how rebellious the Souliotes would be. This grisly dance of death was reminiscent of the mass suicide at Masada in 73/74 CE, when the Hebrew Zealots refused to be taken alive by Roman soldiers. Only this time, there was a bit more festivity in the air.

It was said that so many women danced to their deaths that their bodies formed a kind of macabre cushion, and a few infants cast down by the last women to throw themselves over were actually found alive.

A popular Greek folk song commemorates the event. Its words, in part, declare:

Farewell springs,
Valleys, mountains and hills
Farewell springs

And you, women of Souli
The fish cannot live on the land
Nor the flower on the sand
And the women of Souli
Cannot live without freedom

The women of Souli
Have not only learnt how to survive
They also know how to die
Not to tolerate slavery

This last act of defiance was certainly impressive, though it would be a few more decades until the resistance was finally able to succeed. The remaining Souliotes eventually found themselves in alliance with other resistors, and the Greeks were able to overthrow Ottoman rule and be recognized as an independent nation in 1832. The dancing women would no doubt have been proud and struck up a lively folk dance in celebration.

FUNERAL DANCES: A BALL FOR THE BEREAVED

It would seem that a funeral is a somber affair, a ritual for loved ones to grieve and others to pay their last respects to someone who has passed on, and of course, that is their main function. But many cultures have traditions of celebration at funerals, filled with food, drink, merry-making, and of course, dancing. Two of the best examples come from very different cultures, Ireland and the American South.

The Irish wake is perhaps the best known of all dancing sendoffs. It's a curious blend of solemnity and giddiness, possibly with pre-Christian origins. Feasting, drinking, dancing, drinking, laughing, and drinking are all intertwined with genuine affection for the deceased. The Catholic Church has long had mixed feelings about these affairs, and has often tried—with little success—to curtail drinking at wakes. Technically, a wake began at the time of death and continued until the body was taken for burial, but, of course preparations for a gathering took time, unless the death was expected.

The deceased's loved ones partook in a variety of superstitions. Sometimes, they would leave a window open in the dead person's room so that the soul could escape; it was considered bad luck to stand or even walk between the body and the window. After a few hours, the window was closed to prevent the spirit from returning to the body, which could be yet another plot for a potentially good horror film. Other customs included stopping the clocks at the time of death, covering all the mirrors, and preparing the body for display. The women would then begin keening, a form of vocal lament that was sung over the body, done both for mourning and to keep away evil spirits. Tobacco and pipes were sometimes laid out by the body; the smoke was believed to keep those same spirits at bay.

At some point, the friends and family arrived, viewed the body, paid respects, and then settled in to have a fine old time. As Irish comedian Dave Allen wittily remarked many years ago, "The terrible thing about dying over there [in Ireland] is that you miss your own wake. It's the best day of your life. You've paid for everything and you can't join in." One Irish legend half-seriously claims that the reason the body is kept on public display is that lead poisoning from tankards could induce catatonic states, so heavy drinkers might fall into such a state and be mistaken for being dead. Keeping the body visible allowed for anyone to spot signs of life and prevent the pour soul from being buried alive. The horror movie plots just keep coming.

In any case, the music and dancing then began in celebration of the dead one's life, rather than only mourning their death. Sometimes these gatherings, mixed with alcohol, could get way out of control. There are stories of enthusiastic revelers taking up the body, putting its arms around one or more of the living, and making it dance one last jig around the room to the great amusement of those present (and probably the abject horror of some). Imagine if the person wasn't actually dead after all and revived on the dance floor?

More recently, wakes have evolved into receptions after a funeral, rather than including the participation of the deceased, which means no possibility of dancing corpses, but that's not as much fun.

Across the sea in New Orleans, a different type of funeral dance developed in the nineteenth century. Now known as the "jazz funeral," though that term was for a long time somewhat distasteful to those involved, it was an elegant send-off for a deceased man of African descent, normally a musician. Influenced by beliefs and ideas from West African spirituality, southern American Christianity, and even some voodoo practices, musicians with brass instruments would process to the burial site, playing solemn pieces, such as hymns. After the burial, the band would strike up again, but this time with much more lively music as it processed back.

The parade was divided into two sections, the first and second lines. The first was reserved for friends and family, while the second line was for anyone that wanted to join in. And it was here—post funeral—that the fun began. The second line developed a tradition of lively dancing and the whole thing became a big street celebration of life. The twirling of umbrellas and the waving of handkerchiefs have become signature dance moves from these parades, known as "second lining." Around the turn of the twentieth century, second liners detached themselves from always appearing in funeral processions (though they continued to be a part of them), and became their own unique occurance. No need for someone to die to throw a good party. Eventually, they formed their own clubs and societies and are now considered an important part of the cultural heritage of New Orleans.

Earlier in the nineteenth century, African slaves were given Sundays off from work, when they were permitted to gather in New Orleans' Congo Square. There they set up a market, played music, sang, and danced. These dances blended African movements with more recent introductions from around the Caribbean, particularly Haiti, along with costumes and even faux-voodoo rituals (though the genuine ones were kept secret). As the Civil War loomed, the white establishment tried to suppress these public displays, but they certainly influenced later dances and the big funeral celebrations. The second line itself might have origins in West African circle dances, with the street-bound parade lengthening the circle into a line. The dance movements performed in the second line are certainly similar to those once performed by slaves in Congo Square. As a result, some white communities in the earlier part of the twentieth century viewed second lining as threatening, even sinister, and discouraged it in their neighborhoods. But you can't keep a good party down, and the dancing has survived and thrived as a celebration of freedom and life in the shadow of enslavement and death.

THE DANGEROUS BALLET RUSSES
DE MONTE CARLO HEAD COLD CURE

The Ballet Russes was, despite its name, a company that never performed in Russia, owing to the tumultuous events occurring during the Russian Revolution. Founded by impresario Sergei Diaghilev, the company instead performed in Europe as well as in the Americas from 1909 to 1929, to music commissioned from Ravel, Debussy, Satie, Prokofiev, and many others.

After Diaghilev died it ceased operations, and a second company, the Ballet Russes de Monte Carlo, rose to take its place. Again, despite its name, it toured mainly in the United States, often rigorously.

The dancers were not immune to the stresses of intense touring, and at some point, someone devised an apparently effective, if harsh treatment for illnesses (head colds and such) to better cope with their grueling schedules. Ballerina Ruthanna Boris recalled what one needed to do to get healthy again:

- Lay out several sets of clothes for sleeping.
- Prepare a bed.
- Prepare a very hot, almost intolerable bath.
- While the bath runs, mix hot water, lemon, honey, and strong alcohol in a drink (Jack Daniels was an apparent favorite).
- Get into the bath and drink the drink slowly.
- Exit the bath, wrapped in a towel and don the first set of clothes before drying off.
- When profuse sweating begins, change clothes until it happens again.
- Continue though all sets of clothes.

She noted that at the end of this intense self-treatment, "you're either cured, or you're dead."

3

The Scandalous and Sometimes Awful World of Ballet

ballet is seen in the Western world as an incomparable dance art, the supreme manifestation of a dancer's skill, grace, beauty, and athleticism. It takes its place alongside classical music, opera, and theater as one of the great performance arts, beloved by many, while considered elitist and snooty by others. Still others complain (quite rightfully) about the dreadful toll that being a ballerina takes on one's body and psyche. Until very recently, being a professional ballet dancer had been a short career with many lifelong side effects.

The dance's vast and varied history is the subject of countless books, but we will, of course, focus on some of the more unpleasant aspects of the art, not trying to provide anything like a comprehensive survey. Here, we will encounter dark and disturbing storylines lurking under the grace of the choreography, tales for ballets that are ghostly, haunting, and just plain weird, a controversial ballet that provoked a donnybrook in a most respectable setting, and some truly awful stories about young dancers who perished in appalling ways, taking suffering for their art far too seriously. Finally, we pay tribute to a ballerina who fought back and killed Nazi guards during World War II, in an act of great heroism and sacrifice.

BALLET COURTESANS

French aristocratic women had danced in ballets during the seventeenth century, but their roles were often limited and consisted of graceful movements for show. The court composer Jean-Baptiste Lully (1632–1687) changed all that; he wanted women who could demonstrate great skill and technique, which required hours of practice and dedication, so he did what any artist with a lot of influence would do (or maybe not): he had a law passed that allowed said ladies to be freed from parental or spousal control and obligations. They became directly answerable to the king only and were immune from various prosecutions and legal problems. This brought an undreamed-of amount of freedom to these young women, and those who showed the required skills were eager to be brought into the fold. Social and economic class was no longer a barrier if the talent was there.

So, by the end of the first quarter of the eighteenth century, the Paris Opéra would feature some eighty-seven ballerinas among its stars, a huge change from the previous decades. Women from common backgrounds could now rise to the ranks of the socially important, though often not without a price. Many young women were unable to make their way simply as dancers in professional theaters, even with their elevated status—they were still paid less than men, of course—and so became courtesans and mistresses to high-paying aristocratic clients, which afforded them a life of luxury. Most were able to choose their lovers, which gave them significant political and social power. Many were shrewd businesswomen who set aside money and provided futures for their own children and families, gladly taking money from the very well-off who had far too much of it.

Some of them did very well, having multiple lovers and incomes. One young dancer, Émilie Dupré, entertained at least two dukes, the regent of France, Philippe d'Orleans, and a count, Roche-Aymon, who was also a musketeer and apparently a bit of a trouble maker. On a dare, the count went up to Dupré and kissed her on the cheek, which angered one army colonel, Monsieur Fimarcon, who was also one of the dancer's lovers. This led to a whack on the hand with a cane by one man, and a slap on the cheek with a glove by the other. Of course, that meant they had to duke it out in a duel, right? Even though dueling was forbidden, they agreed to use swords, and Roche-Aymon managed to break Fimarcon's. Roche-Aymon graciously allowed the colonel to retrieve another, but apparently, Fimarcon then wounded Roche-Aymon, who fell into a ditch, and the colonel was obliged to flee from the area, to avoid being prosecuted for dueling. It seems that the two reconciled eventually. It was also noted that Fimarcon at one time lodged with Émilie, and that "he went out every day, dressed as a woman, and went to the Opera, in a box, with little Émilie, who was his mistress. This shows how the laws are observed in this country!" It does, indeed.

Françoise Prévost (1680–1741) was one of the earlier and most astonishing examples of a ballet courtesan. She is remembered for being the first ballerina to have taken on students of her own, inaugurating a chain of masters and apprentices studying her technique. She was famed for her dancing, choreography, and teaching, and was active at the Paris Opéra for nearly thirty years. She carefully cultivated her reputation as a dancer and it was secure, but her life as a courtesan was a very different matter.

Her most famous liaison was with Jean-Jacques de Mesmes, the French ambassador to Malta. This poor fellow apparently wasn't good at much, but he was wealthy and smitten with Prévost. She agreed to be his companion, and her own mother helped to secure the deal. Given that she already had another lover, she informed him of her conditions:

> The bargain that was reached in the end was that he [Mesmes] would take second place. He would be told when to visit and when to fill in when lover number one was absent, and he would also pay the bills incurred at taverns and restaurants.

Well, that's a bit harsh! But Mesmes accepted and eagerly indulged with her when he could. He spent large amounts of money on her, securing a furnished apartment, buying expensive clothing, and keeping her in a lavish lifestyle. They stayed together for years, only she had no intention of being faithful. The child she gave birth to during their relationship was another man's, the Count of Middelbourg, and more than once, poor Mesmes found her in bed with other men.

Eventually things fell apart, and in 1726, she filed a court petition asking him to provide her with six thousand livres a year for life. He protested, saying he had wasted his money on her and was broke in both wealth and in heart. But in the end, the court sided with Prévost and she took his money and set it aside for her children. At her death, she even succeeded in getting herself buried in a chapel—hallowed ground—not something normally permitted for undesirables like entertainers, actors, and dancers.

Her student, Marie-Anne de Cupis de Camargo (1710–1770), also rose to fame and fortune by her skills both on the stage and in the bedroom. Eventually, she and Prévost had a falling out, after discovering that they had slept with the same man, a ballet dancer named Michel Blondy (1675–1739). Further, Camargo was younger, more beautiful, and was now getting all the applause, which naturally aroused jealousy in her mentor. Prévost tried to banish her to the *corps de ballet*—the back row of ensemble dancers who often work as an anonymous moving backdrop for the principle, named, and star performers—but Camargo wouldn't stay there for long; her talent was too great to be ignored.

She is famous for removing the heels from her shoes, creating the first modern-style ballet slippers, and also shortening her skirt to mid-calf length, to show off her leg work and allow greater room to move, a bold and scandalous act at the time that later became the norm. But she didn't just shorten the hemline, oh no. In an effort to increase her desirability, she chose to go commando. So those jumps and leaps and kicks might allow a glimpse, teasing her audience even more. Even Casanova wrote of her: "She was the first woman dancer to jump: before her women dancers did not jump, and the wonderful thing about it is that she doesn't wear drawers." Of course he would say that.

By the age of eighteen, she had been the mistress of the Comte de Mehun, and later took up with Louis, Comte de Clermont, a grandson of no less than Louis XIV. That was quite a score (in more ways than one), and probably set her up for life. She was known for her other daring activities and excesses as well, including an incident that happened at the Opéra's administration on a June afternoon in 1731. At a special private party for patrons, Camargo and other ballerinas danced naked and indulged in various other . . . activities. This wouldn't have meant much, except that the windows were open on a presumably hot summer day and their racy show was easily visible from the street.

As you can imagine, a scandal ensued. Even though King Louis XV thought it was all rather funny, the public was not so amused. The king ultimately had to remove the Opéra director, not so much for hosting the party, but for being stupid enough to get caught doing it. Whatever happened backstage, the dance had to at least give an outward show of respectability.

The story of Marie Sallé (ca. 1707–1756) was altogether different. Another talented Parisian ballerina and choreographer (actually, the first woman to choreograph and perform her own work in the ballet), she was invited to attend a nude dance, quite possibly the same one as Camargo, but she refused, allegedly on moral grounds. Unfortunately for her, this was not an acceptable response, and it led to her being ostracized and even harassed by theater management, among others; some things haven't changed, unfortunately. She decided to leave Paris and go to London, where she obtained patronage from the Duke and Duchess of Devonshire. She had more freedom in England and less pressure to give into sexual advances, while the reasons for her steadfastly resisting male advances slowly began to emerge.

When she did return to Paris and work again, she was also seen frequently in the company of one Manon Grognet, a dancer whom she had met in London. Indeed, Sallé only ever surrounded herself with young women. The French press referred to her as the "Vestal" after the famous Greek virgins who were devoted to the goddess Diana, but it's fairly likely that she was a lesbian and wanted nothing to do with being the mistress to various men, regardless of their wealth. Paradoxically, this refusal to partake in the orgies and escapades rampant behind the stage led to her being more desirable. She was the unattainable one, and of course people want what they can't have.

Unfortunately, this reputation led to rumors spreading about her likely orientation and that was enough to put off many audiences. Despite her success in London, in April 1734, she appeared at Covent Garden wearing a boy's costume, portraying Cupid for a ballet in Handel's opera *Alcina*. Fifty years earlier, theatergoers had delighted in so-called "breeches roles" for women, wherein said actresses dressed like men, but tastes had changed and this was not what the audience wanted to see. They booed her and the press savaged her brazen attempt to step beyond then current standards of womanhood. She never performed in London again and retired in 1740. However, she was true to herself and lived openly with an English woman, Rebecca Wick, in Paris in her last years, leaving Wick everything in her will.

By the nineteenth century, this form of ballerina patronage no longer favored the dancer, as more and more young, poor women sought social advancement through dance. However, the patrons increasingly were wealthy, non-aristocratic men (industrialists, bankers, lawyers, and other unsavory ilk) who could exploit them according to their own wishes with none of the imposed constraints of the nobility. And exploit they did, often treating prized dancers as little more than playthings to be traded around between them. These benefactors paid subscriptions to have access to backstage areas such as the *foyer de la danse*, in theory a rehearsal area, but also a place where these "Adonises-over-forty" (as sarcastically labeled by novelist and playwright Honoré de Balzac) could view the dancers and decide who they liked. This was just as unpleasant and offensive as it sounds, but in the days when their money poured in to keep the ballets going, it was not questioned or widely condemned.

The poorest of the girls with less talent had little to no prospect of social advancement at all, often being used and discarded. Indeed, the popular image of the sylph-like, delicate beauty onstage was frequently in sharp contrast to the realities of impoverished young women, malnourished and sickly, their bodies stressed and broken from rigorous training, and psychologically downtrodden from emotional and sexual abuse. One promising young dancer, Guiseppina Bozzacchi (1853–1870), actually died of fever and smallpox, her malnourished and starving body unable to fight the disease.

The Danish dancer and choreographer August Bournonville (1805–1879) visited Paris in the 1840s and was so appalled by what he saw—poverty, desperation, and prostitution—that he returned to Copenhagen determined to pay all of the dancers a fair living wage, so that they would not have to do anything other than dance to make their living. A hero if there ever was one.

The Austrian ballerina Fanny Elssler (Franziska Elßler, 1810–1884) entered into this ugly environment and prospered on her own terms, like her eighteenth-century predecessors. Perhaps avoiding Paris helped, for she made a name for herself in Vienna before traveling to Naples in 1827. There, she became the mistress of Leopold, Prince of Salerno, and while bearing him an illegitimate child, her reputation did not suffer. She went on to become a star in Berlin, Paris, and even New York in 1840, where she was seen in the company of John Van Buren, son of the eighth United States president Martin van Buren, at a time when he was still in office. One is tempted to think of the scandal a similar situation would cause in the modern world, but on second thought, it would probably hardly raise an eyebrow these days.

THE BALLET OF THE NUNS:
SEDUCTIVE, HAUNTING, AND UNDEAD

With a title like *The Ballet of the Nuns*, who could resist? Especially since it was produced at the height of the Romantic Age, which fairly guaranteed that it would be filled with melodrama, tragedy, and cloistered shenanigans! It was actually a short ballet fitted into the third act of an opera, *Robert le diable*, by composer Giacomo Meyerbeer (1791–1864), which premiered in November 1831.

The dance portion of the story tells how Bertram, Robert le diable's father, goes to an old cloister, Sainte-Rosalie. Once there, he succeeds in summoning the spirits of a certain group of nuns who have died in violation of their vows. His ritual brings them back and they emerge from their graves. Abbess Helena, who presumably died in a less than holy state, tells her undead sisters to dance a waltz, which they do with pleasure; well, they did violate their vows, after all! Apparently, they enjoy their reveries a little too much, and dance with abandon.

Then Robert comes into the scene. The nuns at first hide from him, but eventually show themselves before he can flee. At Bertram's request, the not-so-holy Abbess tries to get Robert to take a talisman—a magic branch—from the hand of a statue of Saint Rosalia, which he does; with this branch, he will be able to win the love of a princess. All this time, the nuns are dancing and enjoying themselves thoroughly, tempting him with their praises of vices like gambling and sex. But all good things must come to end, even a ballet of ghostly naughty nuns. Their graves re-open, the sisters prance back into them, and then the stone slabs covering the tombs move again to cover their dead contents. In the background a choir of demons sings, while Robert attempts to fend them off. Wow.

Hans Christian Andersen, no stranger to bloody dance stories (see his horrific *Red Shoes* story in the "Fairy Tales and Folklore" chapter) saw the opera in Paris in 1833, and noted:

> By the hundred they rise from the graveyard and drift into the cloister. They seem not to touch the earth. Like vaporous images, they glide past one another . . . Suddenly their shrouds fall to the ground. They stand in all their voluptuous nakedness, and there begins a bacchanal like those that took place during their lifetimes.

Despite its obviously controversial content, the scene was a sensation with audiences. The *Revue des Deux-Mondes* described the imagery:

> A crowd of mute shades glides through the arches. All these women cast off their nuns' costume, they shake off the cold powder of the grave; suddenly they throw themselves into the delights of their past life; they dance like bacchantes, they play like lords, they drink like sappers. What a pleasure to see these light women.

No less a composer than Frédéric Chopin was equally effusive in his praise, when he wrote:

> If ever magnificence was seen in the theatre, I doubt that it reached the level of splendour shown in Robert . . . It is a masterpiece . . . Meyerbeer has made himself immortal.

Perhaps appropriately for a ballet about diabolical nuns, the premiere was not without its problems. A trapdoor malfunctioned and didn't close, a gaslight fell (potentially a big danger, as such mishaps could set whole theaters on fire), and a piece of the scenery also fell, narrowly missing ballerina Marie Taglioni, who played the abbess. Such occurrences might have portended disaster to the superstitious, but the ballet and the opera continued and the whole thing was a resounding success. Taglioni, however, had enough after only six performances and left the production early, despite being contracted for twelve. Exactly why remains a mystery; she might have been uncomfortable with the erotic content, or perhaps she felt that the opening night near-misses were indeed a sign of tempting fate. She was replaced by one Louise Fitzjames, who would go on to dance the role of the Abbess more than 230 times, apparently without incident.

The Ballet of the Nuns came at the perfect time when audiences were craving the supernatural and were weary of the rationalism of Enlightenment thinking. Its strange imagery and otherworldly allure were very influential for a generation of works that followed, including the very popular ballet *Giselle*. Speaking of which . . .

GISELLE AND NECROMANCY:
BACK FROM THE DEAD, AND READY TO CHASSÉ

The Ballet of the Nuns foreshadowed a new genre, the *ballet blanc,* or "white ballet," featuring a troupe of female dancers dressed in white and presenting an appearance and movements that were ethereal and even ghostly. The stories that they dance are most often supernatural in nature. Dance historians consider *La Sylphide* (1832) to be the first true *ballet blanc,* a tragic story of a forbidden love between a human and a sylph (spoiler alert: they die at the end).

Giselle was first performed in 1841, with music by French composer Adolphe Adam (1803–1856), and like the saucy nun ballet, it tells a sinister story. Set in Germany during an undefined earlier age, it involves a nobleman named Albrecht who has fallen in love with a peasant girl, Giselle, which immediately tells you that things will end horribly. Sure enough, it all goes wrong very soon. Disguising himself as a peasant, Albrecht woos her, inciting the jealousy of the gamekeeper Hilarion, who also has it bad for the young lady. Hilarion is able to expose Albrecht and the slight little problem that he is already betrothed, causing Giselle to fall into a fit, dancing erratically. Her heart is weak and gives out, and she dies in Albrecht's arms. Hilarion's story is not so hilarious.

The end? No, not at all. That's just Act I! Act II, a proper *ballet blanc,* introduces a full-on ghost story. We are introduced to the Wilis, the ghosts of virgin girls who were jilted and died before their weddings (they are common in Slavic folklore). Their sole purpose in the afterlife is revenge. Led by their queen, Myrtha, they haunt the forests in search of men whom they can kill by forcing them to dance themselves to death. They summon Giselle from her grave, and her ghost joins them. Albrecht and Hilarion both return to the graveyard to pay their respects. Bad idea. Hilarion is cornered by the Wilis and forced to dance until he falls down, exhausted. Then they seize him and throw him into a nearby lake, where he drowns.

Now, they set their eyes on Albrecht; he begs Myrtha for his life, but she is unmoved, interested only in revenge. Giselle is compelled to lure him to her, and they begin to dance. She still loves him and tries to sustain him. He manages to survive until dawn (barely), when the power of the Wilis is broken and they are forced to return to their graves. Giselle must return as well, and Albrecht is left alone.

The ballet was very popular with both audiences and critics, helping to shape the mood and increase the demand in Paris for these kinds of other-worldly productions. It was also staged in England, Russia, Italy, and the United States over the next several years, always to similar acclaim. Who knew that a creepy story about vengeful, man-killing, virginal ghosts would be such a hit?

THE RIOT OF SPRING: STRAVINSKY'S BALLET CAUSES QUITE A PRIMITIVE STIR

The Rite of Spring is probably Stravinsky's most famous work, a ballet that has remained essential to the repertoire since its stormy Paris premiere by the Ballets Russes in 1913. It was controversial from the get-go, ignoring typical ballet themes and going for something far more primal and shocking: a human sacrifice, danced out on stage. The composer explained its origin in his autobiography as coming while he was working on another ballet, *The Firebird*:

> I saw in my imagination a solemn pagan rite: wise elders, seated in a circle, watching a young girl dance herself to death. They were sacrificing her to propitiate the god of spring.

This was heady and controversial stuff, and both Stravinsky's music and Vaslav Nijinsky's choreography were jarring, dissonant, heavy, grounded and unlike anything that ballet audiences were used to hearing or seeing. A far cry from the "Dance of the Sugar Plum Fairy." Nijinsky even dared to have his dancers perform pigeon-toed. While an open rehearsal for fellow artists had gone off without a hitch, the opening night performance at the Théâtre des Champs-Élysées on May 29 was rather more chaotic. The audience was disconcerted, and so naturally, a riot broke out during the first act. One attendee, a journalist named Carl van Vechtan, described the unravelling scene:

> A certain part of the audience was thrilled by what it considered to be a blasphemous attempt to destroy music as an art, and swept away with wrath, began, very soon after the rise of the curtain, to make cat-calls and to offer audible suggestions as to how the performance should proceed.

This collection of provocateurs attended such shows in the hopes of seeing anything that would be out of the ordinary and would upset the upper classes. They more than got their wish on this evening!

> The orchestra played unheard, except occasionally when a slight lull occurred. The young man seated behind me in the box stood up during the course of the ballet to enable himself to see more clearly. The intense excitement under which he was laboring betrayed itself presently when he began to beat rhythmically on top of my head with his fists. My emotion was so great that I did not feel the blows for some time.

Being used as a percussion instrument was the least of what was about to happen. The two factions—rebels and establishment—turned their attentions on each other and the poor orchestra. According to conductor Pierre Montexu, "Everything available was tossed in our direction, but we continued to play on." One is reminded of the heroic Titanic musicians, going down with the ship. It wouldn't have mattered, since the crowd noise was so loud by this time that no one heard the orchestra, anyway. It was the stomping and jerking movements of the dancers dressed in pseudo-ancient Slavic clothing, so unlike the graceful swans and princesses in their tutus, that had the audience all flustered, whether in anarchic approval by the rabble-rousers, or in horror and disgust by the upper crust.

So, with who-knows-what flying about the auditorium, and coming to blows among the audience, the dancers tried bravely to carry on. Stravinsky describes the scene vividly:

> As for the actual performance, I am not in a position to judge, as I left the auditorium at the first bars of the prelude, which had at once evoked derisive laughter. I was disgusted.

Not exactly the words a composer of a new work wants to utter at its premier! He continues:

> These demonstrations, at first isolated, soon became general, provoking counter-demonstrations and very quickly developing into a terrific uproar. During the whole performance I was at Nijinksy's side in the wings. He was standing on a chair, screaming "sixteen, seventeen, eighteen"—they had their own method of counting to keep time. Naturally the poor dancers could hear nothing by reason of the row in the auditorium and the sound of their own dance steps.

The dancers seemed to hold it together in spite of the general chaos, to their credit. Unfortunately, the choreographer was less composed:

> I had to hold Nijinsky by his clothes, for he was furious, and ready to dash on to the stage at any moment and create a scandal. Diaghilev kept ordering the electricians to turn the lights on or off, hoping in that way to put a stop to the noise. That is all I can remember about the first performance.

Eventually, it seems that about forty trouble makers were ejected from the show, possibly with the help of the police. This allowed everyone to settle down and get back to watching the ballet, which continued as if nothing unusual were going on. Maybe it was fitting that so much chaos erupted during a ballet about a primal sacrificial event. In any case, the second act went off far better; the dancers and the beleaguered orchestra received applause and curtain calls at the end of the performance, as if it had been a normal night at the ballet.

Stravinsky recalled having dinner with Diaghilev and Nijinsky afterward, and being satisfied with the performance, if not the reception. The work was given five more performances in Paris and four in London, and while audience reactions were mixed (including some booing and hissing), there were no further riots.

Léonide Massine (1896–1979) choreographed a new version for the Ballets Russes in the 1920s, and no attempts to revive the original were made until the Joffrey Ballet painstakingly reconstructed it in 1987, which might have been just as well, given the mosh pit-like reaction in 1913.

THE NUTCRACKER: AN INAUSPICIOUS PREMIERE, BLOODY WOUNDS, AND A SEVEN-HEADED RAT

The Nutcracker is the most famous of all ballets, a holiday tradition known and loved the world over. Even people who don't like or "get" ballet often enjoy making an annual holiday pilgrimage to see a performance, or at least they pretend they enjoy it because it's what they're "supposed" to do. Performances in major cities are routinely sold out, filled with audiences who might otherwise never set foot in a theater to see a ballet. Its mixture of holiday themes and magic is irresistible to millions, but it might surprise you to learn that at its premier in 1892, it was something of a dud, at least as far as critical reactions were concerned.

Pyotr Ilyich Tchaikovsky (1840–1893) accepted the commission to write a ballet on the story so that he also could show his new opera, *Iolanta,* on a double bill at the same performance. Think about that—a ballet and an opera showing back-to-back—and imagine how well that would go over with modern short attention spans. Both works were shown in St. Petersburg on December 18, 1892. The tsar was in attendance and greatly enjoyed the ballet, but the critics and many in the audience were not so kind. Some thought that the choreography was odd and confusing; one critic said that it was "the most tedious thing I have ever seen." Despite the fact that its opening night sold out, many felt afterward that it was too childish to be a "serious" ballet, and Tchaikovsky's own brother indulged in a nasty bit of nineteenth-century body shaming, calling the ballerina playing the sugar plum fairy, Antoinette Dell'Era, "pudgy" and "corpulent."

Tchaikovsky was used to heavy criticism, but the production itself seemed to have been marred by some bad luck. The original choreographer, Marius Petipa, became ill during production and had to sit it out while his assistant did much of the choreography. The first dancer to take the role of the Nutcracker and Prince, Sergei Legat, would later have a falling out with Russian authorities in 1905 and killed himself by cutting his own throat with a razor, presumably to avoid being taken in.

The charming story itself had darker origins, being based on a tale, "The Nutcracker and the Mouse King," written in 1816 by one Ernst Theodor Wilhelm Hoffmann (1776–1822), who later changed "Wilhelm" to "Amadeus," because he loved Mozart so much. Indeed, he is credited with writing one of the first in-depth reviews of Beethoven's *Fifth Symphony*. It was written, incidentally, before he had even heard it, but had only read the musical score. He wrote many stories of inanimate things coming to life, so one can easily see how his version of the Nutcracker came about.

Hoffmann's tale told not of Clara (the young heroine of most contemporary productions), but of Marie, a girl living in the constraints of a conservative household, who falls asleep and has vivid dreams of a fantastical world where a nutcracker comes to life as a prince. In one of them, the prince fights a grotesque, seven-headed rat king. During the battle, she falls and cuts her arm badly on a glass cabinet. Her dreams are bizarre, even nightmarish, but she prefers them to real life. When her family in the waking world forbids her ever to speak of them again, she protests that she would rather marry the nutcracker than endure their world. The nutcracker then comes to life for real, and the two of them leave for his enchanted world, with all of its strangeness and dangers.

Alexander Dumas, of *Three Musketeers* fame, rewrote this story in 1844 to be a little more family-friendly, and his work was in large part the basis for the ballet. That's where the work remains today, though recently, some dance troupes have added in their own reinterpretations on the classic tale, including returning to some of the original source material. And admit it, we all just want to see that seven-headed rat amid the holiday splendor.

BALLET DANCERS WHO ACCIDENTALLY
DIED ON STAGE OR THEREABOUTS

Ballet is a dangerous profession, no doubt, with dancers at constant risk from injuries as serious as those that might plague any other type of athlete. But ballet has its own particular set of risks, or at least it did back in the bad old days before various fire and safety regulations were imposed on theaters. There is a story of how Taglioni (of dancing dead nun fame) was in Paris for a benefit performance, when two dancers dressed as sylphs became entangled as their flying harnesses twisted up. At first, the audience thought it was amusing, but as the young ladies became increasingly distressed, everyone soon realized that it was no joke. French writer Théophile Gautier noted that the two flailed about "like disorientated toads," not the most flattering description. A stagehand was able to lower himself from above on a rope and free them. Taglioni eventually came out to calm the audience and assure them that no one had been hurt.

But while this incident ended happily, many others did not. Here are a few of the more spectacular and tragic stories of ballerinas that met very unfortunate ends and suffered for their art in ways they never imagined they would.

✑ *Clara Webster (1821–1844)* ✑

Clara had a promising dance future ahead of her. Her father had studied with the great Auguste Vestris (1760–1842), the leading French dancer of the time. Naturally, he ensured that his daughter was given proper ballet instruction. She made her stage debut at about the age of nine at the Theatre Royal in Bath. As a teenager, she danced in London, Liverpool, Dublin, and elsewhere.

Her final performance came when she was featured in the ballet, *Revolt of the Harem*, at the famed Drury Lane Theatre in London. Wearing a flimsy "harem" costume that fed into European's ideas about what such places were like, she accidentally got too close to a gas lamp, and her outfit caught fire. Before a horrified audience, she was badly burned, and died two days later.

In an asinine attempt to make her death into something poetic, rather than horrific, this little epitaph appeared sometime later, turning her appalling demise into something from a Romantic novel:

Lovely butterfly of the passing hour, she attracted the gaze of the gay votaries of fashion and pleasure, and like the doomed moth, fluttering in the flame, consumed her ephemeral existence!

Who knew that obituaries could be so saccharine and flowery?

✑ *Emma Livry (1842–1863)* ✑

Emma was a talented young French ballerina, the illegitimate daughter of a famous ballet dancer and a French diplomat. Thankfully, her background was no real impediment to her success, and she debuted with the Paris Opéra Ballet at the age of sixteen. She was soon taken on as a student by Taglioni, by then a prima ballerina known for her pickiness and jealousy of younger dancers. Livry's career was made.

In 1859, there was a government decree that theaters needed to be made safer, at least as much as could be done in those days, by dipping fabrics and costumes in a chemical bath that left them stiff, ugly, and drained of color, but in theory protected against fire. Ballerinas, including Livry, fought against the measure, believing that their appearance onstage was far more important than silly little things like third-degree burns. She wrote to the director of the Paris Opéra Ballet in 1860, "I insist, sir, on dancing at all first performances of the ballet in my ordinary ballet skirt." Another dancer, Mademoiselle Schlosser, saw nothing wrong with the risk, insisting, "We'll burn but once, but have to suffer those ugly skirts every night."

While such a headstrong independence was admirable, it would ultimately prove fatal. At a rehearsal on November 15 (some accounts say it was two days earlier), 1862, Livry fluffed her untreated skirt too close to a gas lamp as she climbed up on a prop to make her entrance onto the stage. Immediately her costume went up in flames, and she ran about the stage screaming. Other dancers and a fireman were able to put out the flames, wrapping her in a blanket, but she suffered burns on over forty percent of her body (though her face was unscathed). It was said that her corset had melted into the skin over her ribs. Taglioni attempted to treat her burns by rubbing greasepaint on them, mistakenly believing that this would work as a burn ointment, but she probably just made them worse.

Even in her injured state, she was defiant about the use of flame retardants, saying, "they are, as you say, less dangerous, but should I ever return to the stage, I would never think of wearing them—they are so ugly." Alas, her wounds never properly healed, and she lived on in agony for eight more months before dying of blood poisoning from infection. After her death, new safety measures were introduced, including better gas lamp designs, the creation of flame-proof gauze, and wet blankets hanging backstage, all of which were no comfort to the young dancer who was the victim of a freak accident.

Perhaps somewhat ghoulishly, surviving parts of her costume can be seen at the Bibliothèque-Musée de l'Opéra National de Paris.

🙠 *Zelia Gale (1843–1861)* 🙢

The Continental Theater in Philadelphia was the scene of several fire accidents in the later nineteenth century, the first of which was probably the most horrific. Gale, her three sisters (all on tour from England), and probably five other dancers all burned as they prepared for the second act of a ballet version of *The Tempest* on September 14, 1861. Gale was adjusting her costume too close to a gas vent. The *Richmond Dispatch* recorded in great detail:

> She [Zelia] stood upon a settee to reach her dress, and somehow flirted it into a jet of gas, when it was instantly ignited. Before the young lady could recover from her fright her clothing was all ablaze, and her sisters and several of the ballet girls from an adjoining dressing room, rushing up to assist her, were in turn set on fire. About a dozen of these helpless girls were thus burning at once, and the fire ran over their gauze and among their underclothes, making fast to their close leggings or 'tights,' and literally burning to the bone. Their screams were thrilling, and no scene of horrors that the stage ever witnessed may be compared to the terrible picture behind the scenes, where the fire from the burning dresses blazed up to the ceiling and singed the lashes and hair of the affrighted women.

This appalling spectacle only got worse, as a horrified audience took it in:

> Miss Cecilia Gale, writhing and still in flames, darted down the stairs as stated, and was caught by Mr. Bayard, a stage carpenter, who at once tore up the sea cloth, a sheet of canvas used to make waves, and wrapped it around her. He was much burned while doing this. The young lady was removed to the hospital soon afterwards.
>
> Several girls leaped into the street, through the second story windows, and Miss Hannah Gale, already badly burned, fell upon the

pavement, bruising her back and head so that her case is considered hopeless.

Miss Phœbe Norden, of Bristol, Pennsylvania, inhaled the flames and was shockingly burned. She was at the point of death last evening.

Miss Annie Phillips died on Sunday morning.

Miss Anna McBride was burned in the breast, arms and legs, and taken to the Pennsylvania Hospital. She suffered the most excruciating pain during Saturday night; but towards morning her delirium abated, and she died in the arms of Mrs. Wheatley.

A few other dancers also suffered severe injuries.

The audience was told to exit the theater calmly. Like that worked. Several women are reported to have fainted, and the general confusion and panic only made things more difficult. Word quickly spread, and crowds of onlookers, filled with morbid curiosity, gathered near the theater. The *Dispatch* added: "The event has spread gloom and sorrow throughout the city."

⤳ *Mathilde Kschessinska (1872–1971):* *She Didn't Give a Cluck* ⟵

Kschessinska, a ballerina of Polish ancestry, lived and worked in Russia before the rise of communism. She had something of a scandalous reputation, having been mistress to Nicholas II of Russia in the years leading up to his becoming tsar in 1894. Nick was, of course, the last of these Russian Caesars, with the Bolsheviks violently murdering him and his family during the Russian Revolution. Long before that, a number of other scandals had already attached themselves to Kschessinska; after Nicholas married, she simply moved on from him and began affairs with two other members of the Russian aristocracy.

In any case, she was also known for jealously guarding her position and the roles that she received, as pretty much any ballerina of the time would. In one of the more ridiculous examples of one dancer attempting to undermine another, she found herself in conflict with a certain Olga Preobrajenska (1871–1962). In 1906, Preobrajenska was given the lead in the ballet *La Fille Mal Gardée*, a role that Kschessinska wanted. So, she devised a simple plan to undermine her rival. For whatever reason, the production made use of live chickens in coops on stage, as you do. And so Kschessinska committed an act of avian sabotage. As Preobrajenska went out in the first act, Kschessinska opened the coop doors, allowing the chickens to escape and fly and strut about the stage. Of course, the intent was to completely frazzle her rival, create chaos, probably make the audience burst out laughing, and—wait for it—ruffle some feathers. Except that Preobrajenska was a total pro about it, and danced as she always had, ignoring the fustercluck whirling about her. The chickens became de facto members of the ensemble and Kschessinska's attempt at fowl play was thwarted.

Ah well, after the revolution, Kschessinska wisely didn't put all of her eggs in one basket. She married into exiled Russian aristocracy and moved to Paris, where she lived to the ripe old age of ninety-nine, the indecent avian incident long behind her.

ᔪ *Franceska Mann (1917–1943): They Did Nazi that One Coming* ᔪ

The public might think ballerinas are dainty and delicate (although after reading this chapter, maybe your perception has changed a bit), but one Jewish ballet dancer defied the stereotype in her struggle to stay alive during the Holocaust. Before World War II, Franceska Mann lived in Warsaw, where she studied ballet and newly-emerging modern dance forms that were gaining popularity across Europe. In 1939, she entered an international dance competition in Brussels, where she won fourth place against 125 other promising ballerinas. She was considered to be one of the best Polish dancers of her generation. When the war started, she was a regular performer at the Melody Palace nightclub in Warsaw, where she performed under the stage name Lola Horovitz. But she couldn't escape the horrors of the encroaching Nazi threat.

After Germany invaded Poland, she went into hiding in the "Aryan" side of the city, but then was imprisoned in the Warsaw Ghetto. She must have thought she had an escape plan when the Germans announced that any Polish Jews holding visas to or passports from the neutral countries in South America would be able to move there. Somehow, she obtained a visa (she might have forged it), and in 1942, along with hundreds of others, sought refuge at the Hotel Polski. But the South American countries in question refused to recognize the visas or the passports. In 1943, the Jews at Hotel Polski were transferred to the Bergen-Belsen camps, then in October of that year, to Auschwitz.

Franceska's story might have ended there with little fanfare if it weren't for a few surviving eyewitnesses, who told an amazing story. When he was sixteen, David Wisnia had escaped the clutches of death at Auschwitz because of his singing voice. The SS kept him alive so that he could sing for them, and as a "privileged prisoner," they put him to work. On October 23, Wisnia was sorting through clothing at Crematorium 4, looking for money and other valuables that had once belonged to the many victims of the gas chambers. The SS ordered the recent arrivals to strip, ostensibly for "delousing." The prisoners were told that this procedure was necessary before they could continue their journey to Switzerland, which, of course, was a lie. Some refused, terrified of losing their precious travel documents, their only hope of escaping. Franceska was one of them.

At first, she refused to undress, and another eyewitness, Berish Erlich, says that she advocated for the other women. So, the SS called officers Shillinger and Quackernack to force these new arrivals to follow orders. But it appears that Franceska was savvy. As she took off her clothes, Schillinger ogled her body. Another Jewish eyewitness who was part of the group says she took advantage of the attention. Flip Müller recalls that she began performing an all-out strip tease, which enraptured the SS officers. And as she did, she leaned against a concrete pillar, took off her shoe, and "slammed its high heel violently" against Quackernack's head. Other accounts insisted she threw an article of clothing at Schillinger, hitting *him* in the head (some say that he forcibly removed her bra). Either way, she pummeled a Nazi, an act of which we heartily approve. In the chaos that ensued, Franceska grabbed one of the SS officer's pistols and shot Schillinger in the chest, killing him. She also shot another SS officer, who survived with debilitating wounds. We'd play the world's tiniest violin for him, but there isn't a tiny violin tiny enough for Nazis.

Inspired by Franceska's bravery, the other prisoners revolted, attacking the guards as best they could. But they were no match against the SS machine guns. Franceska perished that day—possibly by taking her own life—along with hundreds of other Polish Jews, either by gunfire or the gas chamber. We can't be absolutely sure that it was Mann who killed Shillinger, but descriptions of the woman who shot him match her.

David Wisnia, however, survived. He was at Auschwitz for three years before escaping the even worse conditions at Dachau by hitting an SS soldier in the head with a shovel. As of summer 2017, he is living out the rest of his days in Pennsylvania, where he still sings at his local synagogue and educates younger generations about the horrors of genocide.

4

Astonishing Anti-Dance Books from the Renaissance to the Twentieth Century

In this chapter, we're going to look at some of the many, many screeds that were painstakingly crafted (or not) over the last several centuries to condemn all sorts of bodily movements. You might be tempted to think that, after the Middle Ages and Renaissance, such puritanical hatchet jobs went the way of the dodo—which actually didn't go extinct until the seventeenth century, but never mind. In fact, with the "rebirth" of things in Europe in the fifteenth and sixteenth centuries, the scientific revolution, the Enlightenment, and the Industrial Revolution that followed, those who opposed the kicking up of the proverbial heels dug their own heels farther into the ground than ever before, and refused to budge. The advent of the "modern" world only proved the various authors' points about its sinfulness, as far as they were concerned.

Many of said condemnations were from a religious point of view, but later on, some also tried to use "scientific" arguments to reinforce their positions. Reminiscent of the reefer madness and red scares that gripped the United States in the earlier twentieth century, some of these rants also had unpleasant racial overtones, and certainly they always pushed the idea that women needed to be controlled and kept away from "temptation" for their own good. Feel free to roll your eyes and get angry.

However, the titles of some of the nineteenth- and twentieth-century works, in particular, are just irresistible: *From the Ball-Room to Hell* (sounds like a 1970s B-movie), *Where Satan Sows His Seed* (1960s dime store trash novel, anyone?), *From Dance Hall to White Slavery* (well, that escalated quickly!), and *Balls and Their Consequences* (cue twelve-year-old giggles). One of the best must surely be this succinct tract from 1581: *A Treatise of Daunses, Wherin It Is Shewed, That They Are As It Were Accessories and Dependants (or Thinges Annexed) to Whoredome: Where Also By The Way Is Touched and Proued, That Playes Are Ioyned and Knit Togeather in a Rancke or Rowe with Them*. So, pretty much the entire book is in the title. One has to admire how the anonymous (presumably Puritan) author links dancing to prostitution and then says, "Oh, by the way [literally!], plays are bad, too." It also makes you wonder how these upright authors knew so much about the perils of dancing to write about it.

From the sixteenth to the eighteenth centuries, there were several similar rants in French and German, but the English language ones are especially colorful. We'll look at a few of these disparagements of the dance in this chapter, so settle in and prepare to be amazed by the sheer verbosity, audacity, and frankly, the general stupidity of these point-less ravings. We read through several of them in detail so that you don't have to.

A TREATISE AGAINST DICING, DAUNCING, PLAYES, AND ENTERLUDES
✑੭ by John Northbrooke, Minister, 1577 ੮ੲ

A whole section of this long-winded attack on all things fun is devoted to the evils of dancing, and is written, as was often done in Renaissance instruction manuals, in the form of a dialogue, in this case between the allegorical figures of Youth and Age. Youth is a bit of a smart ass with a chip on his shoulder and thinks he has all the answers, but Age gives not a toss about that and is ready to school him appropriately:

Youth: Why do you speake so much against dauncing, sithe we have
so many examples in the scriptures of those that were godly, and
daunced?

Youth proceeds to list no less than eight biblical examples. However, Age
isn't impressed:

Age: I perceyeve you used to reade the Scriptures, for you have collected out many examples for your purpose, which serve you
nothing at all to maintaine your filthie daunce.

Age proceeds to give an exhaustive list of reasons for how each of Youth's
examples were all actually solemn affairs, in praise of God only, not intended
for merriment, and usually segregated by sex. As for the types of fun dance
that Youth longs for, however:

They stirre up and inflame the hearts of men, which are otherwise
evill inough, even from their beginning: and that thing which is to be
suppressed and kept under with great studie and industrye (as the lust
of the flesh, the lust of the eyes, and the pride of lyfe) the same is
stirred up by the wanton enticements of daunces . . . O deceytfull
daunce! It is the mother of all evill, the sister of all carnall pleasures,
the father of all pryde. [A man] shall perceive that men returne home
from these daunces lesse good than they were, and women also lesse
chaste in their mindes (if not in bodies) than they were before. Therefore, perilles are rather to be avoyded than nourished.

After more excessive verbiage about the illicit mingling of young men and
women, Youth tosses out a particularly good point:

I suppose it is bicause you are aged, and nowe are not able to doe as other
young men and women do, and this maketh you to envy it so much.

Ooh, he played the young rebel card! Clearly a child of the 60s; the 1560s, that is. Of course, Age isn't going to take this kind of back-talk from a horny young Elizabethan whippersnapper eager to mingle with the lasses on the dance floor, and after further pontificating on the authority of the scriptures, he shoots back:

> Your beliefe (that you speake of) is vayne, and grounded upon your owne ignorance; otherwise you would have set your finger upon your mouth.

Damn! Anyway, this goes on for quite a while, and eventually, of course, Age wins out and convinces the boy to adopt his anti-dance position, whereupon Youth declares:

> You have alleged strong authorities agaynste this daucing, whereby I do taste how bitter it is unto me, for I perceive by you, howe full of filthinesse and wickednesse it is.

Well, how convenient! Of course, there was no other possible outcome, being written by a Puritan and all. These kinds of attacks would only increase in the coming decades.

AN ARROW AGAINST THE PROFANE AND PROMISCUOUS DANCING, DRAWN OUT OF THE QUIVER OF THE SCRIPTURE
⌇ *by Increase Mather, 1686* ⌇

What a creative title! New England had its own share of anti-dance sentiment, fueled mostly by the prevalence of Puritan beliefs, the same folks who left England so that they could freely persecute others in strange new lands. As we've seen, Oliver Cromwell, the Puritan who led the

Parliamentarians in the English Civil War and deprived King Charles I of his head in 1649, was at least a little fond of dancing, but his enthusiasm didn't seem to carry over to his fellow believers in the New World. Like those before him, Mather invokes scriptural quotes to justify his invective, but adds a little more of his own shade into the mix:

> What is the difference between a Dancer and a Mad man? There was no other difference, but only this; that the person who is truly Phrentick, is mad all day long; when as the Dancer is only mad an hour in the day perhaps. Lud. Vives tells a pleasant story of certain men, who coming out of Asia into Spain, when they saw the Spaniards dance, they were so affrighted, as to run away, supposing them to be possessed with some Spirit, or mad at least. And truly such affected Levity, and Antick Behavior, when persons skip and fling about like Bedlams, as they say, Dancers are wont to do; is no way becoming the Gravity of a Christian.

Well, his position is pretty clear! After nearly thirty pages of hand-wringing, he concludes with the hope that New England churches can resist the urge to get down:

> And shall Churches in N.E. who have had a Name to be stricter and purer than other Churches [i.e., they're Puritans], suffer such a scandalous evil amongst them? If all that are under Discipline be made sensible of this matter, we shall not be much or long infested with a Choreutical Dæmon.

"Choreutical Dæmon," incidentally, is potentially the best progressive math-metal band name ever. If you end up using it, please give us credit.

FAMILIAR DIALOGUES ON DANCING BETWEEN
A MINISTER AND DANCER
ം൦ *by John Phillips, 1798* ൦ം

Moving forward in time with another American publication, this one employs both the dialogue format and the usual scriptural reasoning against dance, invoking the centuries-old "yes it's in the Bible, but that's not what it *really* means" argument. However, this one goes further in attempting to show that dancing is physically harmful. The dancing master argues that "dancing is conducive to health." In what was surely a well-reasoned argument made after a carefully conducted medical study, Mr. Phillips proclaims in response:

What, artificial dancing, taught by a dancing master? With regard to health, I must beg leave to observe further, that for every single person who has suffered in his health for want of learning to dance, there have been thousands who have lost both health and life together by means of dancing.

Wow, thousands! An alarming number, to be sure. This "health and life together" business is also interesting; can you lose your life before your health? Apparently, dancing can make people drop dead, even in their prime. He follows on with a darker and more outlandish accusation: "To say nothing of the number of abortions caused thereby [by dancing] in adults." The less said about this nonsense, the better.

The dancing master makes a few more objections, such as that teaching children to dance at a young age gives them greater strength of movement and more grace, but the minister will have none of it. He goes on a monologue for the next eleven pages, quoting ancient Greek and Roman churchmen and admonishing parents not to mix "Christ and Belial," or to train them "in the fashionable vices and amusements of the age."

The dancing master says nothing more at the end of all of this condemnation. In fact, he probably just gave up and left halfway through. In any case, the minister is no doubt quite smug and pleased with himself. The pamphlet ends with an appendix of writings by other self-proclaimed authorities in support of Phillips' views, which can be summarized in one short sentence by a certain Chief Justice Hale: "Beware of too much recreation." Clearly, fun kills.

THE NATURE AND TENDENCY OF BALLS, SERIOUSLY AND CANDIDLY CONSIDERED
ᴄᴖᴈ *by Jacob Ide, 1818* ᗈᴖ

Come on, with a title like this, who could resist? This publication is actually two long sermons printed together on the same subject, which might have been unbearable to sit through for anyone with a ribald sense of humor. There's no need to even make jokes about this text or give any kind of context, just read the excerpts. Seriously, just read them. It's like being in sixth grade again!

> Balls are, either *very good* things, or they are *very bad* things. Some, who have but partially considered the subject, may suppose that they are of but little consequence, one way, or the other. But this is a great mistake. Every person, who is acquainted with them, knows, that they most powerfully attract the *attention* of the young . . . But, if they are not right, they must be *very bad* things; for it is a great evil to have the attention of youth *strongly* attracted to wrong objects.

It just keeps going:

> Balls not only awaken great attention, but excite very ardent feelings. So adapted are they to the natural vivacity, and playfulness of youth, that they, at once, call into action all the energies of the soul. Never

can they be more truly said to act *with all their hearts*, than when they are engaged, in these amusements.

And going:

Balls have a great and lasting effect upon the human character. This is a natural consequence of the strong and ardent feelings, which they excite, in youth . . . You, my hearers, have doubtless had the opportunity to notice the lives of some, who were, in youth, very much devoted to Balls, and similar amusements.

And going:

But will not every person of common observation, admit, that Balls have a most powerful tendency to divert the attention of youth from their studies?

And going:

There is, it is believed, no amusement, practiced among us at the present day, that has so powerful a tendency to excite an inordinate love of company, as Balls . . . it is a fact that they are *peculiarly* fascinating to the young. And when once they have become engaged in them, they are in peculiar danger of that love of company, which will lead them into every species of dissipation.

One more?

But it is contended, that Balls are necessary. It is said, that "youth must have amusements, and they may as well amuse themselves, in this way, as in any other" . . . [But] if youth were so educated, as to partake largely of the enjoyments of the former [education, friendships, family], they would seldom thirst after the insipid pleasures of the latter [i.e., Balls].

Okay, we lied:

Now it must be acknowledged, even by the warmest advocates for Balls, that they have, notwithstanding all the plausible things, which are said in favour of them, the *appearance* of evil.

Last one, honest:

In view of what has been said on this subject, we see the wisdom of our Legislature, in prohibiting Balls, and similar amusements, at public houses . . . The view, which we have taken of our subject, teaches us, that the prevalence of Balls in any particular place, is evidence of an alarming degree of stupidity there.

Actually, that final sentence may very well be true, if one is speaking about more than just dances . . .

ANECDOTES FOR GIRLS
ᏪᎦ *by Harvey Newcomb, 1853* ᏪᎦ

This book is a collection of pieces of advice for girls and young women on how to be "proper" ladies and do all of the things that nineteenth-century society expected of them. Much of it is pretty eye-rolling stuff, but the author does have a short chapter on the evils of dancing, and this story in particular makes for a ghoulishly good read, like something from an Edgar Allan Poe story. A common warning at the time was that the over-excitement of a dance could bring about sudden death:

Death in a Ball-room

A student was spending a vacation with a celebrated physician. On a beautiful, but keenly cold evening in January, a young gentleman came into the office, and with a hurried air, inquired for the doctor. As the physician was not to be found, the student was requested to go with the young man, which he did. On the way, the young man informed him that there was a ball at the hotel, which had been interrupted by the sudden illness of one of the belles of the evening.

Things were about to get much worse:

On arriving at the hotel, they were surprised at the rapid filling and driving away of the carriages. The hilarity of the occasion had been suddenly exchanged for mute terror. Hurrying through the crowd, they entered the ball-room. It was spacious and brilliantly lighted, but deserted of its occupants, save a horror-stricken group in the center. On a sofa, which had been drawn from the side of the room, sat a young lady, in a stooping posture, as though in the act of rising, with one hand stretched out to take that of her partner, who was to have led her to the dance.

Cue full-on gothic horror and dramatic music:

With the smile upon her lip, and eyes beaming with excitement, death had seized her. The smile of joy was now transformed to a hideous grin. The beaming eye now seemed but a glazed mass, protruding from the socket. The carmine added to give brilliancy to her complexion, now contrasted strangely with the sallow hue her skin assumed, while the gorgeous trappings, in which fashion had decked her, seemed but a mocking of the habiliments of the grave. The pale mother, as she knelt beside her child, groaned out, "Not here! Not here! Let her die at home!"

The author insisted that this was a true tale and a grim warning to all those ladies who wanted to partake of dancing pleasures on a cold winter's night. The men, of course, could dance all night and never feel the ill effects. Sure.

THE ABOMINATIONS OF MODERN SOCIETY
ᢗᢏᢒ *by Thomas De Witt Talmage, 1873* ᡦ᠍ᢣ

Tommy was quite an expert on abominations, apparently, with such splendid chapter titles as "The Power of Clothes," "Leprous Newspapers," "Flask, Bottle, and Demijohn," and "House of Blackness and Darkness." It's pretty much a given that dance wasn't high on his list of approved pastimes, but quite surprisingly, he was a strong advocate for equal employment opportunities for women:

> My judgment in the matter is, that a woman has a right to do anything that she can do well. There should be no department of merchandise, mechanism, art, or science barred to her. If Miss Hosmer has genius for sculpture, give her a chisel. If Rosa Bonheur has a fondness for delineating animals, let her make "The Horse Fair." If Miss Mitchell will study astronomy, let her mount the starry ladder. If Lydia will be a merchant, let her sell purple. If Lucretia Mott will preach the Gospel, let her thrill with her womanly eloquence the Quaker meeting house.

This forward-looking attitude didn't extend to dancing, of course.

> The tread of this wild, intoxicating, heated midnight dance, jars all the moral hearthstones of the city. The physical ruin is evident. What will become of those who work all day and dance all night? A few years will turn them out nervous, exhausted imbeciles. Those who have

given up their midnights to spiced wines, and hot suppers, and ride home through winter's cold, unwrapped from the elements, will at last be recorded suicides.

So dancing is a form of slow suicide? Got it. He then revels in some prose worthy of the best gothic novelists of the age: "There is but a short step from the ballroom to the grave-yard." Sounds like the opening line of an Edgar Allan Poe story. And it keeps going:

There are consumptions and neuralgias close on the track. Amid that glittering maze of ball-room splendours, diseases stand right and left, and balance and chain. A sepulchral breath floats up amid the perfume, and the froth of death's lip bubbles up in the champagne.

If we're still looking for band names, "Sepulchral Breath" is a candidate for the best metal band name ever. And as if suspect bubbly alcohol wasn't bad enough, families who indulge in ballroom dances together will come to nothing but ruin:

The father will, after a while, go down into lower dissipations. The son will be tossed about in society, a nonentity. The daughter will elope with a French dancing master [apparently a common enough occurrence that he felt the need to mention it!]. The mother, still trying to stay in the glitter, and by every art attempting to keep the colour in her cheek, and the wrinkles off her brow, attempting, without any success, all the arts of the belle—an old flirt, a poor, miserable butterfly without any wings.

Oh, the terrible fates of those who indulge in frivolous dancing!

SAVE THE GIRLS
🕰 by Mason Long, 1882 🕰

A pretty straight-forward title for a change! Long's screed is, well, long, and has only one chapter on dancing (thank goodness!), but he is quite sure that the main danger of public dancing balls is that scoundrels await the unsuspecting young ladies, to lure them into lives of sin and much worse. After a lengthy story about a young lady seduced by a gambler at a dance and left to die at the age of seventeen (and the author assures us that that every last detail of his account is true), he continues with a more general observation:

> It is a well known fact that in our cities and large towns the ball room is the recruiting office for prostitution. Balls are given every night, and many thoughtless young women are induced to attend, "just for fun."

Ah, "fun." We all know what that really means. Wait, do we?

> They are mostly those in the humbler walks of life, the daughters of small tradesmen, of mechanics, of clerks, of laborers. Not one in a hundred of the girls who consent to attend these balls preserves her purity.

That's an oddly specific statistic. One wonders about his sample size.

> They meet the most desperate characters, the professional criminals, the gamblers, the murderers, the lowest debauchees. They are thrown into the company of vile women, who picture to them the ease and luxury of a harlot's life, and offer them all manner of temptations to abandon the paths of virtue. They meet with men who tell them all kinds of plausible stories, and work their ruin by various means, not seldom by violence or the use of drugs. The columns of the New York newspapers contain many sad stories of the girls who have been

dragged to their ruin by attending the dances at the Buckingham and Cremorne Gardens in that city. It is a shame and a disgrace that the authorities allow such dens of iniquity to remain in existence: and yet society wonders at the increase of prostitution!

Now, it's not to say that such things didn't happen, of course, because they undoubtedly did. Nineteenth-century society often being what it was, life for the lower classes could be pretty miserable. There's a reason why Dickens and his contemporaries on both sides of the Atlantic spoke up so forcefully about the need for reforms. One suspects, though, that there is a fair amount of exaggeration going on to make the author's point (the whole "not one in a hundred" thing). Whether communist menaces in Hollywood or Satanists in suburbia, nothing attracts audiences like a good hysteria, and Long clearly knew how to milk it for all it was worth.

WHERE SATAN SOWS HIS SEED
⁓ *by Milan Bertrand Williams, 1896* ⤳

Ah, that's more like it! A book title that gets right to the heart of the matter, or the field, or maybe something a bit more suggestive? No, this upstanding "evangelist" (by his own proclamation on the book's title page) would never stoop to cheap innuendo. But he would take the time to rant against the ills of his era, specifically gambling with cards, alcohol, the theater, and of course, dancing. In fact, Bertie sharpens his claws and devotes half of the book to the sins of moving one's body to music, so it obviously was a bone of contention with him.

Even the innocent square dance was no longer immune to the energies of hot-blooded youth, as he described to his horror, when visiting a Fourth of July picnic:

It was a square dance that was in progress, and when I watched for a few moments, I saw a young man grasp his partner by the waist for the swing and swing her with such gusto that HER FEET WERE POINTED ALMOST DIRECTLY AT MY HEAD. I made up my mind to include hereafter, the square dance, as well as the round, in my strictures.

Well, one must draw the line at feet in the air. No more square dancing for you, young people!

He proceeds with page after page of various clerical condemnations, until coming to a rather unusual statement by a certain "Dr. Brookes of St. Louis." He quotes the good doctor at length, who announces:

It is evening, and the hour is late; there is the delicious and unconscious intoxication of music and motion in the blood; there is the strange, confusing sense of being individually unobserved among so many, while yet the natural "noble shame" which guards the purity of man and woman alone together is absent, such is the occasion, and still, hour after hour, it whirls its giddy kaleidoscope around, BRINGING HEARTS SO NEAR that they almost beat against each other, mixing the warm mutual breaths, darting the fine personal electricity across between the meeting fingers, flushing the face and lighting the eyes with a quick language . . .

Dr. Brookes quickly regains his composure and goes on a rant about impropriety, but one might think that he enjoyed writing this passage a little too much, seeing as it sounds more like something from a bodice-ripper than a moralizing editorial. Our good Bertie seems to have a bit of a fixation on such descriptions as well, describing the scandalously revealing ball gowns of the time:

The dress cut so low that every breath caused the breast of the wearer to be apparent, and heave like a little billow, a description peculiarly Byronic. If you, my girl, can stand such things, and escape with health, both of body and mind, you must have a constitution of iron . . . for it is enough to make a man catch cold to look at you. But he doesn't take cold; his blood runs fierce and hot. Do you think a man can mingle in such a throng, gazing on your half concealed charms, far worse than the form in all its nudity: – can hold you in his arms, press that palpitating bosom against his own, twine and intertwine his limbs with yours, and feel no passion. What could such a man be made of?— what, indeed, but putty, basswood or marble?

"Palpitating bosom?" Yes, the good evangelist is clearly a little over-eager in his descriptions! Young men in the presence of such heaving cleavage will have no choice but to run to their closest brothel for relief after an evening of dancing. This is unavoidable, he says: "society cannot put down the brothel, for it remains a physical necessity for men." Once again, he reveals more about himself perhaps, than he intends.

But the men thus tempted are not spared his wrath, as he expresses in some colorful language, bemoaning the fate of a young lady:

> . . . that she comes to the arms of a man who is a moral leper, who has been common with womankind; and receives in exchange for her virgin purity a *blasé* rake, or a worn-out *roué*, whose name is as common on the lips of the *demimonde* as to the devotee of fashionable society.

Okay, but might there be at least some occasions when dancing would be acceptable. He offers this bit of wisdom:

> Well, possibly, though I would not advise it. A young man might dance with his grandmother, if she was not rheumatic, and no harm come of it; or even with his mother or sister. A man might dance with his wife, and under certain restrictions and limitations, it might prove a

healthful amusement. But who ever heard of a man dancing with his wife, save as a matter of conventional form?

He goes, it may be, with his wife, dances with her once or twice to take the curse off, then turns her over to the arms of others that he may enjoy the pleasure with other men's wives. A man would no more think of going to a ball and DANCING ALL NIGHT WITH HIS WIFE, than he would of going out and sawing and splitting wood all night in the moonlight.

Well, that's an odd comparison! But at least he's considerate of grannie's rheumatism.

THE SOCIAL DANCE
ᕯ *by Dr. R. A. Adams, 1921* ᕯ

We'll finish up with one more. Adams bills himself as an "Author, Editor, Lecturer on Higher Eugenics . . ." Wait, what? Also, he's apparently an authority on "Sex Hygiene Prophylactics, and Social Economics." If that wasn't enough, this Kansas quack has written many esteemed books, including: *Exalted Manhood* (again, cue twelve-year-old giggles), *Fighting the Ragtime Devil* (some ugly racist undertones in that one), *Syphilis—The Black Plague* (what is it with all of these things sounding like metal bands and their album titles?), and, wait for it, *The Negro Girl* (the less said about this, the better).

While some barely concealed racism infects this booklet's drivel, it also purports to use science and medical opinion in addition to appeals to religion, to make its points. Adams begins his diatribe with this:

Visit the dancing woman the day "after the ball is over;" hear her weak voice, and look into her listless eyes; note her general lassitude, observe that she has scarcely any life left in her, and you will get some idea of the physical effect of the dance. The most reliable statistics show not only that most habitual dancers die young, but that they suffer more from nervous diseases, and that women dancers have more operations, more diseases common to women as the result of the excessive exercise of the dance.

There are many, many cases where young women have broken down in school and at home because they had danced their strength away. There are many other cases in which they have become hopeless invalids as the result of the same folly.

This was a common argument over and over during the nineteenth and twentieth centuries, with all sorts of "studies" claiming to back up their silly claims. But as the historian R. W. Southern once commented, "Everything conspires to support a hypothesis we desire to believe" (some of the wisest words ever written), so take such scare-mongering with a grain of salt.

Adams has a particular beef with what he calls "animal dances" and early on links these with the dances of "primitive" people. Like his use of "Eugenics" didn't already paint him as a bigot. He is appalled that such dances, which are in imitation of animal mating, are common. His diatribe is amusing to peruse at length:

> It is a sad reflection on the people of this Nation that they should run out of dance steps and dance names and come down to the level of the brutes whose sexual actions they imitate in what are **called animal dances**.

It's just great that he felt the need to bold those words; cue dramatic music! His outrage continues unabated:

> It is well known that these animal dances are imitations of the animals in their sex relations and sex exercise, and that they are intended to arouse sexual desire and result in sex satisfaction.

Ah, now we get to the heart of it! He must have been trying to use the word "sex" as many times as possible, too. For the edification of his dear readers, he expounds on some of these sinful pseudo-mating rituals in more detail:

> "The Chanticleer Dance" imitates the actions of the rooster when he is strutting about the hen and making known his desire to cohabit with her. The "Boll Weevil Wiggle" and the "Texas Tommy Wiggle" are danced in close personal contact intended to arouse sex feeling. The "Grizzly Bear" encourages the closest and most violent physical contact for the same purpose. The "Bunny Hug" is danced in imitation of the sex relation between male and female rabbits. The "Turkey Trot," "Fox Trot," "Horse Trot," "Fish Walk," "Dog Walk," "Tiger Dance" and the "Buzzard Lope," are all imitative of the lower animals in their sex life, sex desire, sex excitement, and sex satisfaction; and these things are in the minds of the dancers who understand the meaning of the animal dances.

The implication is clear. These animal dances harken back to those dances of "primitive" (you guessed it: non-white) peoples who are sex-obsessed, and are unbecoming of respectable, repressed white folks in 1920s Kansas. To drive the point home, he finishes up with a list of current popular dances, all equally detestable:

> "Hoochee Choochee," "Shimmie," "Jazarimbo," "Cheek-to-Cheek," "Lip-to-Lip," "Camel Walk," "Shuffle," "Tickle Toe," and the "Toddle," are representative of the acme of vulgarity and indecency. Thus is apparent the utter immorality of the social dance.

That many of these dances had their origins in ragtime and jazz—music of African American origins—says all that needs to be said.

And so we close the silliness, ignorance and sheer stupidity of these ravings. Dance didn't disappear because of them; the fact that these dusty tomes were essentially forgotten until we decided to delve into some of them and bring their foolish content to light in this book (you're welcome, by the way) proves that. Actually, if anything, dancing probably flourished all the more in the face of such stern (yet oddly amusing) opposition!

5

Superstitions and Bad Luck

Performing artists have no shortage of quirky superstitious beliefs: musicians have any number of silly behaviors and fears that they cling to to ward off unfortunate events, and the theater is legendary for its massive collection of bizarre rituals, aimed at appeasing the forces of bad luck that seem especially interested in plaguing actors and their lot; you've probably heard of never mentioning "the Scottish Play" by name, for example.

Then it should come as no surprise, that in the dance world, a goodly number of superstitious beliefs have grown up over the centuries. Some of these are completely individualistic. Dancers may have any number of private actions that they use to improve their luck, while other beliefs are more widespread. In this chapter, we look at some of those beliefs that haunt dancers and force them to do irrational things, all in the name of ensuring a smooth (or smoother) performance.

Why do we indulge these idiosyncrasies? What compels us to seek out behaviors that we hope will create positive outcomes for us, even though there is absolutely no rational connection between what we do and what happens? Well, it's probably a by-product of evolution, a way of tricking ourselves into feeling that we have more control over the environment than we actually do. Our more primitive ancestors were beset by the forces of a hostile world, where death could come quickly and suddenly, so any actions they took to improve their own odds—however unlikely—were probably pounced on and repeated over generations, especially if, by some fluke, they actually seemed to help once in a while.

Since we seem to love occupying ourselves with activities where things can constantly go wrong, it's only natural that we would try to at least even the odds a bit. Studies have shown that having things like a good luck charm when going on stage can actually increase one's confidence and contribute to a better performance. It's probably purely psychological, but hey, whatever works!

So, just what does a dancer have to worry about to ensure that everything goes off without a hitch? Oh, plenty . . .

WHATEVER YOU DO, DON'T THROW AWAY YOUR SHOES!

Shoes are obviously very important to certain types of dancers: ballet shoes are essential for those amazing feats (see what we did there?), and of course, tap dancers would look and sound pretty silly without the appropriate quality footwear. One old superstition states that ballet dancers should never throw away their pointe shoes. Of course, it's fine to purchase new ones, but it's considered bad luck to discard the older ones. It may have to do with respecting tradition, or perhaps honoring the work that one has done before; to discard said shoes would be insulting to all of the hours of hard work that went into improving as a dancer while wearing them.

Of course, this could lead to problems down the line of running out of storage space, or being faced with the horror of opening a closet door, only to be buried under an avalanche of old and probably not-so-clean shoes spilling into one's hallway. Maybe there's a good luck charm to prevent this? In any case, there's probably yet another cheap horror film to be made from this concept.

THE OLD "BREAK A LEG" WISH . . . FOR DANCERS?

You may know that theatrical folks don't wish one another "good luck" before a show, but often say, "break a leg," instead. This curious custom has had many explanations, from the idea that an excited crowd would stomp their feet and potentially break the legs of their chairs, to the theory that "breaking a leg" referred to a kind of bow to an audience in the sixteenth and seventeenth centuries; in other words, do a performance worthy of receiving cheers so that you can bow in thanks.

Despite the horrors associated with such a sentiment, many dancers hold to the same superstition, and cheerfully wish one another many broken limbs before taking the stage. No one seems to mind that this is essentially wishing a possibly career-ending fate on a given dancer, and it has been a part of Western performances for at least as long as it has been in theater.

One superstition a bit more specific to ballet dancers is a belief that it is extremely bad luck to walk over a dancer's legs if she or he is seated on the floor. This is a common enough position for them to take backstage, but under no circumstances should anyone cross over them, or the dancer(s) so trodden over may very well break one of their legs for real. If one is careless, or just plain dumb enough to do this, in addition to enduring the verbal assault that follows from the panicked dancer, one must walk backwards over said pair of legs again to undo any potential curse that may have been inflicted, no doubt accompanied by evil stares and a sense of overwhelming shame. Basically, just watch where you step, okay?

DANCING ON MAKEUP MAKES UP
FOR BAD THINGS HAPPENING

It's inevitable that things will go wrong backstage. In the chaos of a production, amid the hustle and bustle, things will get dropped, broken, misplaced, and otherwise suffer indignant fates. For dancers, their stage makeup is obviously a very important item; no one wants to go out on stage with circles under their eyes and frizzy hair. Given this, it's obviously a minor catastrophe if one drops and splatters makeup powder backstage, not only because of the loss of said makeup and the money spent on it (have you seen the price of stage makeup lately?), but also—no surprise—it's seen as a bad omen for the coming show. In a world where every little action can tempt evil supernatural forces to engage in a bit of cross-dimensional nose-tweaking, safeguards have to be in place.

Happily, there is one in this case. If said makeup goes "splat," the only remedy to avoid disaster is for the clumsy dancer to dance on the spilled makeup itself. This will apparently appease the offended forces and dispel any plans they had in store for the unfortunate bungling ballerina. Of course, it also makes for messy feet and/or shoes, but that's a small price to pay to forestall certain doom. And given that dancers are never supposed to throw away their old shoes, they are also condemned to keep their make-up-stained footwear to their eternal shame. Maybe next time, they'll be more careful.

ENDLESS PREPARATION RITUALS

As you might imagine, these are as individual as the dancers who rely on them for peace of mind. They offer some psychological comfort, and might actually improve a dancer's performance. So people adhere to them and swear by them. In no particular order, here are some of them:

One of the more common acts is to kiss the floor before taking the stage. This is mostly harmless, unless one is worried about the endless parade of germs that have made their homes on a place constantly trodden with sweaty feet, not to mention splinters. No less important, but equally unhygienic, some dancers kiss their shoes pre-show, presumably before putting them on, though doing so while actually wearing them might make for some funny and awkward moments to help relieve nerves.

Many dancers have rituals about getting ready: specific orders for putting on make-up, fixing their hair, and getting dressed that cannot be changed, at least not if disaster is to be averted. Some even insist that the same person help them get dressed before each performance. There are no hard and fast rules about a specific order of things to do, and it certainly isn't universal, but individual dancers often take such preparations very seriously, and become very distressed if the routine is broken for any reason. Some put on their shoes left first and then right; others reverse the order. Some dancers have spoken of putting a coin in one shoe or the other, though this would seem to be very irritating once out on stage! Others tell of doing certain stretches only before going on, and in very a specific order. Another common belief is that one must be the last dancer to exit a dressing room before going on, and they will hang around while everyone else leaves to make sure that they are. Of course, if everyone believes this about themselves, no one will ever leave the room!

Some dancers say that they make up songs or poems, or recite prayers to various "dancing gods," all in the hopes of receiving the blessings of whatever fates might be out there to bestow them. Some keep special lucky charms (or other keepsakes) in their bags or on their person, to ensure a trouble-free performance.

All of these little rituals are a part of the psychology of what goes into a great performance, however silly some of them may seem to outsiders.

A SURPLUS OF SILLY SUPERSTITIONS

Selling the very first ticket of a performance to an elderly person is seen as good luck; if the sale is to someone young, the show probably won't survive. This may have to do with the idea that the older person symbolizes a long life for the production.

There are dancers who say they must walk the perimeter of the stage a certain number of times before each performance, presumably clockwise, because to go in the opposite direction would be tantamount in some older beliefs to summoning a demon, inviting disaster, which is exactly what an already jittery dance company doesn't need.

Some dancers and directors consider it very bad luck for anyone who is not a part of the production to see the dancers in full costume before the show begins, rather like a bride before a wedding. If it happens, it not only ruins the surprise, but potentially jinxes the performance.

A good, if odd, thing to say to a ballerina is that you hope she trips on the hem of her dress backstage, presumably before going on. This apparently has its origins in English ballet and includes an overlay of belief in fairies. It was long held that the fey folk enjoy making people trip; it amuses them. Either they are a bit sadistic or they clearly don't have enough to do. But rather than get mad, the tripee should instead kiss the hem of her dress. A kiss given is a way of flattering the little folk and joining in their game, and they will bless her with a fine performance in response.

The declaration of *merde* (French for "shit") before going on, in place of wishing good luck, is not confined only to actors; dancers are fond of it as well. One theory suggests that, in older times, live animals were sometimes used on stage and would occasionally leave behind certain odiferous gifts. Yelling "merde" was a way of warning one's colleagues and cast mates to watch their steps. So, it became a way of performers showing that they were looking out for each other. And of course, avoiding stepping in it would certainly improve the overall performance. Alternatively, it may have been said in the hope that a lot of wealthy people would be arriving for the show in horse-drawn carriages, ensuring a large audience and a lot of . . . well, you know.

Some dancers have admitted (bravely) that they wear the same pair of tights, or the same shirt, or other clothing, to every rehearsal in the week before a show . . . and never wash them. Apparently, this last part is key to the whole thing working, and would completely undo all of the magical good they are creating if something as diabolical as laundry detergent were to interfere. Some dancers even extend this into the performances themselves. The effect of this prolonged alavation on their fellow dancers probably varies from troupe to troupe, but it can't be all that good for camaraderie. Other dancers who have followed this strict practice have admitted that if they do have a bad show despite this sensible precaution, they will often change everything: new clothes, new preparation rituals, and so on, for the remainder of the run, as a way of appeasing the forces at work (anti-bathing fairies?) and resetting things.

This next one is more of a theatrical superstition, though dancers have noted it as well: never open an umbrella on stage. This is said to date back to 1868, when an orchestra leader named Bob Williams bid adieu to his colleagues for the weekend, and opened an umbrella inside before heading out into rainy weather. While this might seem to be a sensible precaution, not long after, he was on a boat that was pulling away from a dock. He was again saying farewell to friends, when an engine exploded and killed him instantly. Of course, the only logical explanation for this was that he had opened an umbrella in a theater, and so the superstition stuck. Not that many ballet dancers need to worry about umbrellas in their shows, but a production of *Singin' in the Rain* might run into a few problems. Fortunately, the curse can be averted as long as the umbrella is opened pointing downward.

Finally, as in music and drama, a bad dress rehearsal means that a good performance will follow, because the performers have gotten all of the problems out of their proverbial systems, and surely nothing but good things will follow for every live show from then on. If only . . .

6

*Fairy Tales and Folklore:
Where the Dancing Is Deadly*

a countless number of popular tales around the world include dancing in one form or another, and very often these are innocuous incidents, such as a big celebration at the end of a good story, a wedding, a party, and so on. But then, there are those tales and legends that invoke the darker, creepier side of getting down. With dancing always being a controversial topic among the authorities, it's understandable that some stories would give concrete examples of just how bad it really is, as a warning to the young ones not to be too tempted.

Here, we look at a few selected yarns about dancing as a punishment for evil behavior, as an illicit pleasure that is forbidden, and something that can invoke the wee folk, or much worse, the devil himself, as well as a creepy modern urban legend about a super-creepy dancer that sent one man running into the night in terror. The moral is clear: before stepping into a pair of dancing shoes or out onto that dance floor, think twice; a very grisly fate could be in store for you.

THE ORIGINAL, HEATED ENDING TO *SNOW WHITE*

Snow White is, of course, one of the most beloved fairy tales of modern times. Most often remembered is the 1937 Disney film, *Snow White and the Seven Dwarfs*, with its charming songs and lovable dwarfs, an instant classic that is still treasured by children and adults alike. We all know the story of how the queen, the wicked stepmother who is horribly jealous of the beautiful young Snow White outshining her, plots to put an end to her enemy by disguising herself as an old woman and giving the girl a poisoned apple, which sends her into a magical death-sleep. Of course, the handsome prince arrives, kisses her awake, and the day is saved. The queen falls off a cliff, by the way. Everyone sings and celebrates, and they all lived happily ever after. Or so you thought.

As you might imagine, the original recorded by the Grimm brothers is rather more, well, grim. First appearing in their works in 1812, the queen is actually Snow White's own mother, but just as jealous of her daughter's beauty. She plots to kill young Snow no fewer than four times, but fails each time, thanks to the help of those dwarfs, who are a bit less friendly and sing-songy in the original tale.

The young lady is indeed revived and engaged to the prince, but the queen is still out and about and doing evil things, as wicked queens are wont to do. When she asks the mirror who is the fairest, the mirror truthfully tells her that she no longer is, and that a new younger queen now outshines her. She's not especially happy about this; okay, she's furious. Nevertheless, Snow and the young prince decide to do the magnanimous thing and invite mom to the wedding; except, they're not really planning on being so gracious. The mother goes, out of nosiness and anger as much as anything, but once there, well, let's just read the original ending:

> Still, her jealousy drove her to go to the wedding and see the young queen. When she arrived she saw that it was Snow-White. Then they put a pair of iron shoes into the fire until they glowed, and she [the

mother] had to put them on and dance in them. Her feet were terribly burned, and she could not stop until she had danced herself to death.

Well, that's a new spin on the first wedding dance! No word on what she actually danced or why she couldn't stop (presumably due to some kind of magic), but we can only hope it was a jig or a polka, or something equally lively to go with all the smoke and the burning flesh. A later English version of the story from 1823 took out this brutal ending and had the older queen dying on the spot of her own envy, which is poetic justice, but not nearly as much fun. Still, one can see how it would be hard to feel sympathy for young Snow the sadist, and how this might have been more than a bit disturbing for young children, so later versions of the tale dropped this gruesome dance of death. There's a gritty, R-rated movie remake in this, if anyone is interested.

HANS CHRISTIAN ANDERSEN'S AWFUL *RED SHOES*

Not to be outdone by Snow White's tap-dance torture, Hans Christian Andersen devised an even more unsettling story about shoes, dancing, and death: *The Red Shoes*, which first appeared in 1845. This charming tale gives us the story of the peasant girl, Karen, who is adopted by a wealthy elderly woman. Karen convinces the woman to buy her a pair of fancy red shoes, which she then wears to church, a completely inappropriate place for them. Nevertheless, she wears them to church again, prompting an old soldier who sees them to exclaim: "Dear me, what pretty dancing shoes!" Well, you know this isn't going to end well. These words seem to act like a curse, because Karen is then compelled to start dancing; she has to be forced into her coach, because she can't stop, and inadvertently kicks the old woman in the process.

They get the shoes off and put them away, but Karen is still obsessed with them. The old woman grows ill, and Karen must attend to her, but one day, she opts instead to go to a ball, wearing—you guessed it—the red shoes. After she arrives, the shoes predictably proceed to take on a life of their own, and she is forced to dance as they wish. Once again, she meets the old soldier and once again, he says, "Dear me, what pretty dancing shoes!" He's a man of few words, apparently.

Now she really wants to be rid of them, but they have grown together with her feet and cannot be taken off; gross. She can't stop dancing, day or night, inside or outside, in all kinds of weather. Finally, in a graveyard, she meets an angel holding a sword, to whom she pleads for help. Instead of comforting words, though, the angel says to her:

> "Dance you shall," said he, "dance in your red shoes till you are pale and cold, till your skin shrivels up and you are a skeleton! Dance you shall, from door to door, and where proud and wicked children live you shall knock, so that they may hear you and fear you! Dance you shall, dance—!"

Well, great. She dances her way to an executioner's house on a lonely moor, and begs that instead of cutting off her head, he instead chop off her feet. He does so, but that's not the end of it. The shoes, with her severed feet still in them, dance merrily away, presumably spraying blood everywhere, like something out of a torture porn film. The executioner makes wooden feet and crutches for her, and she now wants to go to church to prove that she has returned to piety, but each time she tries, the red shoes, still inhabited by her severed feet, appear before her, dancing and blocking her way.

Eventually she takes a job in a parsonage, but fears going to church and prays for help. The same angel appears again, this time holding roses instead of a sword. He brings the church to her, and she is so filled with peace that she dies and her soul flies to heaven, where no one will ever speak of the red shoes.

That's all lovely, we suppose, but presumably at the end of the story, there is still a pair of red shoes out there, filled with two slowly decaying severed feet, happily dancing around Denmark? Maybe they're hanging out with the dancing skulls in Sweden. Andersen must have had a hang-up about dancing. In his original story, *The Little Mermaid*, when the mermaid gets her legs from a bargain with a witch, not only does it feel like she's walking on knives with every step, but also the prince whose heart she tries to win is entranced with her dancing, so asks her to dance quite often. The prince ends up marrying someone else, which according to the mermaid's bargain dooms her to death: she dissolves into sea foam. She didn't even get to *wave* goodbye . . .

THE TWELVE DANCING PRINCESSES: DECEPTION AND EXECUTION

Not content to leave things at white-hot dancing shoes, charred flesh, and a hideous demise for a jealous old woman, the Grimms were at it again, with another tale of dancing and death, in this case, execution. Once upon a time, there was a king with twelve daughters; there's no queen in this story, either she died in childbirth or had simply had enough.

Anyway, the king, being a typical understanding father, locked all twelve in a large room each night, presumably to preserve their innocence. The problem was, each morning, he would notice that their shoes were worn out. Now obviously, something was amiss, so the king, being ever wise, trusting, and kind, decided to make an offer to any gentleman who could solve the mystery: he could choose whichever daughter he wanted to be his wife, and would inherit the kingdom after the king's death. And of course, the young lady in question would have absolutely no say in this, because fairy tales.

There was one snag, though: if said man was unable to solve the mystery in three days, he would have his head cut off. The first to try was a prince. He was given a room adjacent to theirs, so he could spy on them, but each night he fell asleep and couldn't figure it out. According to the tale, "his head was chopped off without mercy. Many others came to try this risky venture, but they too all lost their lives." Apparently, the king was also a serial killer in his spare time.

Eventually, an old soldier took up the challenge. However, he had help. An old woman had given him a cloak of invisibility and warned him not to drink the wine that the daughters would offer him each night—aha!

So, he accepted the task, pretended to drink the wine the ladies offered him, and equally pretended to be asleep when they checked on him. It turned out that the wine was drugged, so apparently, the daughters didn't give a damn about sending men to their deaths, either. After investigating their bedchamber, he discovered a hidden trap door under one of the beds. The twelve sisters climbed down into it, and moments later, so did the soldier. He secretly followed them into a magical underground world, through groves of trees with silver, gold, and diamond leaves, and took a twig from each, as proof. Finally, the young ladies came to a large body of water, where twelve princes waited with boats. They sailed across the water to a castle, where the daughters would dance into the wee hours with their beaus, which was why their new shoes were worn out every night; hidden under his cloak, the soldier saw it all. He repeated his spying for the next two nights, just to be sure.

When he was called to tell the king what was happening, the smug princesses were shocked that he knew and revealed their secret. They were forced to confess, and the soldier took the oldest daughter as his wife, along with the promise to inherit the kingdom. Obviously, this can't have been a very happy marriage, given that she would happily have sent him to his death to keep her secret.

Some accounts say that the princesses were then cursed for as many nights as they had spent dancing with the princes. Other versions say that it was the princes who were cursed for the same amount of time, but the actual curse itself is not described; maybe something to do with dancing themselves to exhaustion? Sometimes, the princes are actually demons and the entrance to their world is sealed forever.

In another charming version, there are only six daughters, but five of them deny everything when their dancing secret is found out; only the youngest confesses, so the king orders that the older sisters be beheaded.

Regardless of the version, this king really doesn't sound like a decent fellow at all. He probably couldn't dance, anyway.

IRELAND'S DANCING FAIRIES AND DANCING DEAD

Ireland has an enormous body of fairy lore, and many tales warn of the dangers of interacting with such enchanted folk. Fairy food and drink, fairy music, and fairy gatherings all present potentially fatal pitfalls for unwary mortals, and once ensnared in their clutches, doomed mortals can be fated to spend all eternity with them, which is not nearly as enchanting as it sounds.

One story reminds its audience that November is a particularly perilous period; the veils between worlds are thin then and careless folk can be drawn into things that they should not see or do. Throughout November, the dead leave their graves and dance on moonlit hills with the fairies—the only time they are permitted to do so—before they must crawl back into their graves and endure another year in the cold, dark earth. Each year, they wait for the time "when they all spring up again in their shrouds and rush out into the moonlight with mad laughter."

Once, a young woman of Inishark (a small island off the west coast of Ireland) was coming home at the hour of the dead, and sat down to rest. A young, pale man approached her and told her to wait a while, for soon she would see the most beautiful dancing she had ever beheld, up on a nearby hill.

"Why are you so sad and deathly pale?" she asked.

"Look at me," he answered, "you know me, do you not?"

"Yes, now I do. You are Brien who was drowned last year while out fishing. Why are you here?"

"Look at the hill and you will understand."

Then she saw a huge gathering of the dead dancing to the sweetest music she had ever heard. There was everyone she remembered from life and many more.

"You must run for your life," Brien said, "for if the fairies invite you to dance now, you will never leave them."

As they talked, a group of fairies encircled her and began to dance. She fainted and woke up the next morning in her own bed. But her face was deathly pale, and those around her knew that she had been afflicted with fairy-stroke. A doctor tried to save her, but it was too late, and when the moon rose that night, she died and went to join the others in the eternal annual dance.

WHEN THE DEVIL CAME TO THE DANCE

A curious urban legend is found scattered across North America, stretching from Mexico all the way up to Quebec and several places in between. There are numerous variations, but they usually involve some kind of gathering, often illicit, or at least railed against by the local priest or other clergy. The celebrants ignore these rants and go about their business of happily sinning with drink and dance, when a handsome stranger appears at the door, dressed all in red, white, or black. He strides right in and is a wonder to behold. He may or may not dance with one or more young ladies, but at some point, he is unmasked.

A baby (a baby at a dance?), pure and not yet touched by the evils of the world, recognizes him for who he is and begins crying. This tips her mother off, who fetches some holy water (holy water at a dance?) and sprinkles it about. Furious, the devil rakes his claws into her back and flees; she apparently makes a full recovery by the next day. In some cases, his feet are on fire and the hall burns down; it is unhallowed and no businesses that attempt to operate on the premises after the building is rebuilt ever thrive.

A Mexican version of the tale has a priest warning parents not to let their daughter go to a certain dance, but she sneaks away from them and goes anyway. The same devil arrives, dances with her, and is found out, but instead of fleeing alone, he drags her soul with him back to hell.

One of the better versions of the tale is one said to have happened in the California city of Fresno several decades ago. The dashing man in white asks a certain young woman to dance with him, and she happily agrees. At some point, she looks down, however, and notices that his feet resemble those of a chicken. Okay, how did she not see this from across the room when he walked in? The music stops, people gasp in shock at Mr. Pedi-poultry, and he just smiles and disappears.

Many of these stories have in common their origins in a strong religious background, and they are obviously meant as teaching fables for those thinking about straying from doctrine and doing things that they shouldn't do. Dancing has always been a favorite target in such legends, because it represents a clear gateway into perceived sins. Similar stories can be found all the way back in sixteenth-century Germany, when the devil showed up to dance, and got so into it that he and his partner literally disappeared. So, these little tales were meant to be cautionary, of the "don't dance or the devil will get you" variety. But the guy with the chicken feet? Well, that's another whole mystery entirely . . .

THE MYSTERY MAN WITH A
WALTZ AND A TERRIFYING GRIN

This recent (and decidedly creepy) urban legend appeared online a few years ago. Now, given that the internet is a cesspool of fiction, fake news, and nonsense, one always has to view such tales with a pretty jaundiced eye, but this particular account is just strange enough to be true. It doesn't involve ghosts or monsters, just a very odd individual behaving very oddly.

As retold by the young man who experienced it, he used to enjoy taking nighttime walks in his neighborhood—well, that was his first mistake. Nevertheless, he explained that he always felt safe, given police patrols and the general quality of the area, and on one occasion found himself walking near a park between 1:00 and 2:00 a.m. After turning down one street to head back home, he saw a figure in the distance. This mystery fellow appeared to be a tall, normal man in a suit, except that he was dancing, specifically taking waltz-like steps. With each square movement of the waltz, he would advance forward, so that he was progressing up the sidewalk by dancing.

This in and of itself was strange enough, and, assuming that he was drunk or otherwise chemically enhanced, the narrator decided to move to the side of the pavement and let him go about his dancing business. But as the figure got closer, the young man could see that there was something odd and very unsettling about this waltzing intruder. His head was slightly tilted back, his eyes were wide as they stared off into the distance, and he had a comically wide smile on his face.

Now, this would be more than enough to scare the life out of most of us, and the story-teller decided to get out of the way immediately, crossing quickly to the other side of the street, but without making a scene and running. Once he reached other side, he looked back and saw that the stranger had also stopped and was now facing him from directly opposite his new location, still grinning, still looking off into the distance.

Our creeped-out pedestrian began to walk away, keeping an eye on the dancing ghoul, who didn't move. After a short time, the narrator directed his attention forward again, turning back shortly afterward to see if the smiling man was still there. He was, only now he was on the same side of the street, crouched down. Then he stood up and began to make an exaggerated prance toward the young man, as if tip-toeing. Of course, most of us would be scared out of our minds by now, and our story-teller was, but couldn't find the means to move, much less run away. The smiling man stopped, less than ten feet away and didn't come any closer, but still smiled that horrid smile and stared off into space. Then, he simply turned and waltzed away into the night.

Except, that he didn't. Our storyteller once again watched as he disappeared, only to realize shortly after that now the dancing demon had reappeared and was running full-out, straight toward him. That was enough to break the fear-spell, and the narrator high-tailed it out of there, making his way to a busier intersection, where some late-night traffic could be found. He managed to get home safely, not encountering the weird waltzer again. Needless to say, he decided not to take nighttime walks any more.

After this story appeared, other reports of seeing the smiling dancer began to show up, including one from as far away as Belgium, thus giving the incident a proper urban legend status. But the original poster insists that it's a true story, and that the man looked completely out of his mind. There's no knowing what he might have done if he had caught up to the narrator, but offering waltz lessons is unlikely.

7

Dancing On Your Grave: Ghosts and Haunted Venues

belief in ghosts and the afterlife is older than civilization. Virtually every culture has myths and legends about the dead returning, whether to take revenge on the living, or perhaps because they are being punished for something they did wrong during life. Or even worse, they might just be condemned to repeat an act eternally, such as the event that brought about their untimely deaths. A violent demise in particular can often lead to a haunting; tragedy and ghosthood are common bedfellows.

Every type of structure and natural setting in the world has been claimed to be haunted, from forests to graveyards to creepy old houses, and concert halls are no different. In fact, given the untold millions who have crammed into them over the centuries, resulting in random deaths here and there, it makes perfect sense that at least some ghosts would want to revisit these sites of music, drama, dance, and other performance arts that they were so attached to in life.

In this chapter, we'll look at a haunted tomb and several theaters where dancers and others around them are said to stalk the corridors and manifest on stages, creeping out the living and inviting viewers to join them in a postmortem pas de deux.

ANTOINETTE "TEENIE" SHERPETOSKY
AT THE WOODLAND CEMETERY

Born in 1894, Teenie was originally from Lithuania, but her family emigrated to the United States at some point, and she was known to be living in Chicago by 1910. She showed a great talent for ballet and would go on to be a renowned dancer, working and touring with the Imperial Ballet of Moscow and other companies to much acclaim.

Unlike those dancers we mentioned above who died tragically young, Teenie lived to a fairly decent age, retiring with her husband to the small town of Ironton, Ohio. She grew restless there, however, having been used to traveling far and wide and reveling in the cultural life of big cities. In 1963, the two took a trip back to Chicago for a long stay, perhaps to alleviate her boredom with Middle America. At some point either on the way there or back, they were involved in an automobile accident, and she died of her injuries.

Her body was brought back home and laid to rest at the town's Woodland Cemetery, which should have been the end of things, but even in death, Teenie was restless, and her body was given no peace. She had been buried wearing some expensive jewelry, including a brooch said to have been given to her by the Russian tsar. While his fate was certainly grimmer than hers, she suffered an equally indignant lack of respect for her remains. Thieves broke into the mausoleum where she was interred and smashed their way into her coffin to steal all of her jewels. When some of the rings would not budge, they simply broke off the corpse's fingers to get at them. Charming. As if that weren't enough, two portraits of her on the outside of the mausoleum were damaged by local juvenile delinquents shooting BBs at them.

This would be enough to rouse any spirit from beyond, and that's exactly what locals say has happened. Though she doesn't seem to be an angry or vengeful ghost, many have reported seeing a ballerina dancing around her grave, especially at midnight, supposedly now keeping watch over her body. Whether this is true or not, the violations seemed to have stopped after those early criminal incidents, which means that her spirit may have done a good job of scaring the pants off of any future would-be vandals. Apparently, local ghost-hunting groups like to lead walks to her grave on some nights, in the hopes of catching a glimpse of the ballerina from beyond putting on her spectral show, maybe as a warning to leave her in peace?

AMARGOSA OPERA HOUSE AND HOTEL, DEATH VALLEY, CALIFORNIA

Marta Becket had a crazy idea. A ballerina, artist, and actor based in New York, she had been told by a fortune teller that she would be making a big move and a big change to her life. Becket would relocate to a very rural location, the fortune teller claimed, and would ultimately do her best work there. In 1967, while taking a vacation after a tour, she and her husband stopped in Death Valley Junction to have a tire repaired. She was entranced by an old building that once housed a theater. Feeling that the building was speaking to her, and that this was what the fortune teller had meant, she inquired about renting the property, and soon set about repairing it to host public performances. She spent several years painting the theater walls to cover them with beautiful images of historic and fairy tale-style people who were her "audience" on those days when few people showed up. Word spread about the theater and though Becket passed away in January 2017, people still flock to see ballet performed by the dedicated souls committed to preserving her legacy.

Part of the old building was converted into a hotel to encourage tourism, and it's there that things start to get interesting, because like any old building, the place is apparently haunted as all get out. A portion of the building has not been renovated and of course, looks like something out of a horror film, so naturally, all manner of creepy sounds and ghostly phenomena are said to have been experienced there; the usual creaks and footsteps and the feeling of presences unknown. The area was once part of a dormitory for men working in nearby mines in the 1920s, and deaths in those mines could naturally lead to restless spirits haunting the dorms.

In room twenty-four, guests have said they have heard the sounds of a young girl crying late at night. A girl was said to have drowned in a bathtub nearby in 1967.

Room thirty-two of the hotel seems to conceal an especially unpleasant presence and may be connected to the story that someone was hanged there back in the mining days. Suicide or murder?

Room nine is probably the most unsettling, as guests have claimed that while sleeping, they have felt their legs and feet being held down to the bed. Others have heard the door knob turning, and the always-lovely sound of a giggling child in the hall outside, only to see nothing when they open the door. Is a ghostly boy or girl playing pranks on unsuspecting guests?

The theater itself has had a few spectral incursions, including that of Tom Willet, who acted as a stage manager from 1983 onward, and who died in 2005. Several people have claimed to see him sitting in one of the seats, watching new productions, apparently still keeping an eye on things after his death. The theater also seems to have a resident ghost cat, who has been disrupting things (running across the stage, getting tangled up underfoot) in true feline fashion for decades. As long as there are no ghost cat hairballs on stage to clean up, no one seems to mind.

Throughout the building, there have been numerous reports claiming that the dead are particularly restless: shadows seen dancing on the stage, footsteps with no bodies attached to them, mysterious scents (lilacs are especially common), showers tuning themselves on and off . . . all of which seem to show that Marta Becket's renovations brought a lot more than just an old theater back to life.

THE LYCEUM THEATRES IN CREWE AND LONDON: A BALLERINA, A MONK, AND MORE!

The Lyceum Theatre in Crewe (Cheshire, England) sits on the site of a former Catholic church, which included a graveyard, so you know where this is going. It was later converted into a theater in the 1880s. In 1910 it was destroyed by a fire and then rebuilt, and still stands today as an attraction for lovers of drama and other live-stage delights.

Befitting of a site that has been both a church with a cemetery *and* has burned down, there are several different ghosts who seem to mosey about the place at various times; some consider it to be one of the most haunted buildings in the region. Among the more colorful: the ghost of a restless penitent monk; perhaps he feels like his mission in life was not fully completed? Some say that he also haunts the adjacent Three Lamps pub, so maybe he's at least finding some meaning there, with different kinds of "spirits."

Others have reported seeing a woman wearing period all-white embroidered clothing, who dances as if enjoying an otherworldly ball. Her appearance is usually accompanied by a drop in temperature and the smell of strong perfume, though she has apparently not been seen much since the late 1980s.

Not to be outdone in the dancing department is the ghost of a tragic ballerina, said to have hanged herself in a dressing room for unknown reasons, though some believe that she and the woman in white are the same person. She and the ghost of an actor who never made it big have allegedly been seen often, the latter often wandering around . . . maybe looking for a job? He is said to have been murdered by a jealous rival.

Once, this pair manifested in front of an entire acting company, who confirmed that they saw them standing at the rear of a box seat, watching the performance and apparently pleased by it. At other times, the ballerina has been seen dancing on stage.

These sightings were frequent enough that in 1969, the theater requested an exorcism, which was duly performed and in theory, should have quieted things down. Except that it didn't. The ghostly manifestations showed no signs of stopping, and while not menacing, they certainly seemed to reveal that the dead in the Lyceum had no intention of being told what to do.

In an effort to up the creepy factor, the Lyceum in London has had its own share of ghost stories, but none so charming and ghastly as that of a woman who is seen from time to time sitting in the stalls watching the performance. Nothing especially unusual about that, even for a ghost . . . except that she is reported to be holding a severed head in her lap and stroking it. Couldn't she at least have left that at the coat check? Various theories say that the woman is Madame Tussaud—of wax museum fame—holding one of her creations, or perhaps the head is that of Henry Courtenay, a Cavalier executed by Oliver Cromwell during the English Civil War. One couple who saw the terrifying sight said that the head resembled someone in a family portrait that hung in the theater. Regardless, it's probably best to let the ushers deal with this one.

THE PALACE THEATRE, LONDON:
ANNA PAVLOVA AND OTHERS

This venerable theater is believed to be haunted by a multitude of ghosts, including at least two dancers. Built in the late 1880s and opening in 1891, it was intended for use as a showcase for the operettas of Gilbert and Sullivan and other light works. It also became known in the twentieth century for its musicals and dance shows. For whatever reasons—probably built over burial grounds; it's almost always about being built over burial grounds—the theater has become something of a hot bed for ghostly activity.

Its most famous resident is the ghost of Anna Pavlova (1881–1931), a prima ballerina with both the Ballets Russes and the Imperial Russian

Ballet. Anna toured the world and was a sensation in her day. As she neared her fiftieth birthday, her work had taken its toll on her body, and she contracted pneumonia. While touring in The Hague, she was told that she needed an operation to recover, but after she would never dance again. She refused, saying, "If I can't dance then I'd rather be dead." She got her wish, and died of pleurisy. She was cremated and interred in London. The day after her death, the show went on as usual, but her part was left unperformed. Instead, a spotlight traveled across the stage in place of where she would have danced, a creative and touching tribute.

For reasons known perhaps only to Anna, her restless spirit seems to have taken up residence at the Palace Theatre. There have been many reports over the years of a dancer on stage resembling her. Curiously, these often describe her as being only visible from the waist up, as if she is dancing on a floor lower than the stage. Sure enough, the modern stage is higher than the one that would have been in place during her life. Paranormal investigators have described these kinds of hauntings as playbacks, rather like a video recording of something that happened long past. There have been similar sightings of Roman soldiers in York, for example, only visible from the knees up, walking along an old street long since buried by the centuries. Is this merely a spectral movie, replaying a long-finished performance from decades past?

In life, Pavlova was apparently quite superstitious; she wanted to enter theaters by alternate entrances, to avoid any bad luck that might have been left behind, and she didn't even like looking at images of herself on show posters. Perhaps she willed an image of herself into this place to continue her performances for eternity?

Another dancer is said to haunt the theater, though less is known about her. She is believed to be the ghost of a young woman who, for some reason, hanged herself near the back stairs of the theater. Those who have seen her have said that they have the feeling she is lost and can't find her way. Perhaps she has condemned herself never to leave the place that was the cause of her sorrow.

There are other spirits on hand, in particular two rather testy managers who just can't leave well enough alone. The first, Ivor Novello (d. 1951) has been spotted watching rehearsal, just as he would have done in life. Maybe no one told him that it's time to move on? The second, Charles Morton (d. 1904?) is more aggressive and unsettling. He apparently has no qualms whatsoever about touching people and even harassing them. Witnesses have reported feeling ghostly hands on their shoulders that were not exactly comforting, and one employee insisted that in addition to this invasion of her space, her headphones were ripped off of her head in a violent and threatening manner. Apparently, one needs to request paranormal hazard pay to work at the Palace.

In honor of the various ghosts wandering around the place, the theater leaves two seats in the balcony unsold, so that they can sit down and enjoy the current production. If more than two of them want to take in the same show? Well, they'll have to work that out amongst themselves.

RESURRECTION MARY

This is more of an urban legend, but it dovetails nicely into a ghost story with a definite (sort of) origin in Chicago in the mid-1930s. It also has far more witnesses than a standard bit of folklore might normally have. Back in those days, drivers who found themselves motoring along one Archer Avenue next to Resurrection Cemetery began to report that a young woman wearing a white dress would appear by the side of the road and attempt— and sometimes succeed—to jump onto the running boards of their vehicles (these were wide platforms outside of early car doors that helped one to step up into the automobile). She would then vanish as suddenly as she had appeared.

The accounts morphed into longer and more complex tales soon after. Various men would claim that they had met a young woman at the nearby O Henry Ballroom, whom they would dance with, but who was cold to the touch. They would offer to drive her home and she would always direct them to go down Archer toward the cemetery. There, she would either vanish from the car, or get out of the car and then vanish. This story is a variation on the common "vanishing hitchhiker" trope found in urban legends all around America and the world, so one would be tempted not to put too much stock in it, except that there are several well-reported incidents that make this case stranger and perhaps a touch more believable.

In attempting to determine the identity of the lady, a fairly standard story arose: that she was dancing with her gentleman friend at the O Henry one night in the early 1930s, that they had a quarrel about something, and that she left, preferring to walk home rather than be in his company any longer. As she got to Archer Avenue, she was struck by a car and left to die. Her parents then buried her in Resurrection Cemetery, the body dressed in her white dress and dancing shoes. This seems a logical enough origin (and again, a fairly common one in urban legends), but is there any truth to it?

Some have suggested that the ghost is that of Mary Bregovy, who is buried in the cemetery, but she was killed in an automobile accident downtown in 1934 and thrown through the windshield, a very different (but just as tragic) tale than for our ghost. Further, this Mary had short brown hair, unlike the ghost who is said to be blonde.

Another candidate is Mary Miskowski, who was killed in 1930 while on her way to a costume party. This may be a more likely choice, but the evidence is unclear.

One witness, Jerry Palus, met the ghost at the dance hall in 1939, and the story played out just as we have seen: they danced, she was cold to the touch, he offered her a ride home, she gave him directions that went by the cemetery, and she got out of his car there, telling him that where she was going, he couldn't follow; and then she vanished. Unnerved, he decided to follow up the next day, and went to the address she had given him the night before, only to discover her family there, who told him that she had died some years before.

It seems that Palus didn't publicize his story for a long time (probably due to fear of ridicule), and eventually, he forgot the location of the house that might have shed some real light on the mystery. But he maintained until his death in 1992 that he was telling the truth.

Other reputable witnesses have had similar encounters: cab drivers, clergy, and especially other motorists, who have called the police saying that they accidentally struck someone near the cemetery, only to discover that no one was there. Others have described seeing her in the middle of the road and watching in disbelief as she passes right through their cars. Mary has even been seen in a nearby nightclub and a lounge, pulling the same "give me a ride home" trick. She seems to have expanded her circle of potential dance dates.

In 1976, one driver reported that he saw a girl in a white dress inside the cemetery, grasping at the bars at the entrance. Assuming that she had been accidentally locked in, he went to the local police station, and they sent out an officer to investigate. The officer, of course, found nothing, but was shocked to see that two of the bars appeared to have been pulled apart and scorched by high heat. The cemetery staff insisted that this was due to a truck backing into the bars, and workers subsequently attempting to bend them back into shape using a blowtorch. This seems a reasonable explanation, but several who viewed the bars said they saw what appeared to be finger and small hand prints impressed into the metal, which simply could not have been there if anyone mortal was attempting to bend bars in high heat. Eventually, the cemetery had the bars removed to discourage the curious from stopping by and gawking.

So, while there is much about this strange story that has more than a whiff of urban legend, many of the witnesses are far more credible than the usual "friend of a friend" who retells a standard suspicious yarn and insists that it's true. Many firmly believe that the ghost of a young woman haunts the nearby ballrooms and nightclubs, willing to dance with men who take an interest in her and always trying to get home, but never getting past her final resting place in the appropriately-named Resurrection Cemetery.

8

A Diversity of Dancing Disturbances

and so, as the grand finale beckons, we'll leave you with a few tantalizing tales of other oddities, from an almost very nasty way to make an exit to cringe-worthy stories of extreme cosmetic enhancement involving molten makeup and needles in awful places, and then on to the intrigue of masked dances, where identities were hidden and forbidden activities could take place in defiance of polite society. Or at least the authorities claimed. We'll end with the story of a dancer who simply wanted a man's severed head on a plate after her performance. But was that legend simply used as a cheap excuse to condemn dancing of all kinds throughout Western history? In any case, it inspired a movement that shook up polite society at the turn of the twentieth century, to say the least.

NEAR-DEATH BY PIANO: A GRAND WAY TO GO

Teresa Hill, a young erotic dancer at the famous Condor Club in San Francisco, found herself in a horrifying situation one morning in November 1983. She was nude (part of the profession), lying on a piano hoisted up to the ceiling of the club, and next to her (or on top of her, depending on which version you read) was the body of her then-boyfriend, one "Jimmy the Beard," the club bouncer. Hill yelled for help and was discovered by a janitor at about 7:00 a.m. The poor young lady had no idea how she had gotten up there, much less why her beau had died next to her, crushed to death (he was still clothed, by the way). But she was trapped and understandably upset.

It turned out that the piano was part of the shows (and had long been used by famed dancer Carol Doda), and could be raised up to the ceiling and lowered back down. Hill had apparently been so drunk that she didn't even realize what was happening (or where she even was) when it started to rise. She and her boyfriend had decided to have sex on the piano after-hours, but for her it was all a blur. During their romp, one of them seems to have accidentally bumped the switch on the piano hoist and wasn't paying attention as the whole thing slowly began to rise. As it neared the ceiling, he must have realized what was happening and managed to stop the piano's ascent by rolling off of her and kicking the switch to the "off" position. But for him it was too late.

"If I were to speculate on the cause of death, it would be asphyxiation as a result of being crushed," the detective ruminated, which is, you know, what happens when you're pressed between a ceiling and a freaking piano. His being larger than Hill saved her life, as his muscular body left a few inches for her to move.

The motor had burned out and the fire department had to destroy the mechanism to free her; Hill was later treated for minor injuries. Perhaps on a more sinister note, there was broken glass and spatters of blood at various points in the club, though she had a cut on her hand, so this was probably just from an unnoticed injury. In any case, that was not the best way to begin a career in exotic dancing!

FALSE EYELASH DISASTERS
AND OTHER MAKEUP MISHAPS

Dancers have always relied on stage makeup as an essential part of their performances. The need for performers to make their eyes pop, cheekbones thrust, and lips pout goes way back to Greco-Roman and even ancient Egyptian times, not only for those dancing, but for actors and others onstage, too. As you might imagine, the various substances used to achieve these desired effects were not exactly the safest. Lead-based face paints date back to at least classical Greek times, and were popular right through the nineteenth century, both with performers and in everyday use. The Greek actor Thespis (sixth century BCE) was said to have painted his face with both white lead and wine lees (the dead yeast at the bottom of a vat; with luck, we won't see that beauty trend making a comeback any time soon). Later actors used masks, making face paint unnecessary; probably just as well, given the effects of lead over time. The Romans, for example, also used lead in pipes and drinking vessels, subjecting themselves to slow poisoning and madness, and thus making the crazy behaviors of emperors like Caligula and Nero a bit more understandable.

Lead caused damage to the skin (rotting it away, actually), eventually requiring even more makeup to hide its dreadful toll. Other side effects for anyone wearing these gruesome concoctions for too long included: abdominal pain, miscarriage, loss of memory, paralysis, and death. But both the upper classes and the artists who entertained them needed to look their best, so damn the consequences. Less wealthy performers in Elizabethan times and later used materials such as soot, flour, and chalk on their faces, which were readily available and far less toxic. Of course, sweating from a vigorous dance or monologue could cause these to run pretty easily, making a mess all over one's face and leading the performer to resemble a member of a Norwegian black metal band.

Dancers today still dread putting on fake eyelashes, but the falsies from the local drugstore are a vast improvement over the what dancers used to wear. An especially unsafe technique for dancers and actors developed in the nineteenth century. It was known as beading the eyelashes, which is about as uncomfortable as it sounds. It basically involved putting a small bead of some given coloring on the tip of each lash, so that the eyes and lashes stood out more when seen on stage. One way of doing this was to melt a portion of said black cosmetic in a small frying pan, using a candle or other heating device. Ned Wayburn, a dancer and choreographer in New York whose students included Fred Astaire—among many others—describes the process. After the coloring is melted:

> Take up some of this molten cosmetique on the flat end of your orange-wood stick and apply it with a deft stroke to the upper lashes, painting each one separately and without clotting, so that a little bead hangs to the tip of each upper lash. Use care not to drop any of the black on your make-up.

And, you know, maybe also use care not to drop molten makeup *in your eye*! Acclaimed choreographer Martha Graham was still using this method as late as the 1950s, as seen in the documentary *A Dancer's World*, but thankfully, it had mostly fallen out of fashion by then.

If poison make-up and molten eyelashes weren't hazardous enough, dancers also faced a lack of fire codes and safety procedures in theaters. You can see where this is going. In one example, Joan Bergere, a performer with the Cole Brothers / Clyde Beatty Circus, was using what would seem to be a harmless candle to heat up her eyelash bead goop before a show in 1937. But, as bad luck would have it, the voluminous ballet tutu she was wearing came into contact with the flame and caught fire. Before it could be put out, she suffered first-degree burns. Of course, fire marshals were supposed to regulate what kinds of open flame could be used (if any) backstage, but there was simply no way to police this kind of activity fully.

For those dancers and other performers wealthy enough to opt for something more permanent in imitation of their social betters, there was this gruesome solution, described in a Scottish newspaper from 1899:

> An ordinary fine needle is threaded with a long hair, generally taken from the head of the person to be operated upon. The lower border of

the eyelid is then thoroughly cleaned, and in order that the process may be as painless as possible rubbed with a solution of cocaine.

Needles and cocaine, this is already sounding very suspicious . . .

The operator then by a few skilful touches runs his needle through the extreme edges of the eyelid between the epidermis and the lower border of the cartilage of the tragus. The needle passes in and out along the edge of the lid leaving its hair thread in loops of carefully graduated length.

A needle through the eyelid? No, no, no, just . . . no.

When this has been done another length of hair is sewed through the lid until finally there are a dozen or more loops projecting. By this time the effect of the cocaine has been lost, and the operator is obliged to desist, and put off further "sewing of hair" for another sitting.

Yeah, because you wouldn't want any more needles puncturing through your eyelid unless you were completely high.

The next step in the process is cutting off and trimming the ends of the loops, and the result is a fine, thick, long set of eyelashes. It is the finishing touch, that is to come, that makes them look like nature's own. When they are at first cut they stick out in the most singular fashion, giving the person operated upon the most uncanny look.

It's a shame there are no photos of this step in the process; it probably looked disturbing! The lashes were then curled and the eyes bandaged for a day or so. Lasting beauty was achieved, apparently, but through a rather terrible ordeal.

THE DARK, VIOLENT, AND SCANDALOUS
HISTORY OF THE MASQUERADE BALL

The act of wearing masks while dancing has, as we've seen, a long history in Western culture, going back at least to the Greeks and their pantomimes. During the Middle Ages, mummers stomped their stuff in animal masks, while the manuscript to the fourteenth-century satire, the *Roman de Fauvel*, shows a group of musicians and dancers making loud noises, dancing wantonly, and baring their butts in the streets while the story's anti-hero celebrates his wedding night. These sorts of activities suggest an inversion of the accepted order. This mayhem was actually allowed by the church during the Christmas holidays, but at other times, it was far less acceptable.

The masquerade ball proper probably has origins in the royal courts of the fifteenth century, and soon these affairs became associated with the time of Carnival at Lent, which in Venice, led to people fashioning amazing costumes and masks. Tourists can still buy versions of these in gift shops and they are something of a symbol for the watery city. This social art form had its first heyday in the seventeenth and eighteenth centuries, and such gatherings caused considerable controversy for both religious and secular authorities because masking meant the hiding of one's identity, which made these events perfect for intrigue, criminal behavior, adultery, and other assorted sins.

In 1716-17, the Spanish government was so concerned, that King Felipe V issued an edict titled "Prohibition of balls with masks, and the penalty for transgressors." Given that many were hosting dances wherein the attendees wore masks, as if at a Carnival celebration:

> . . . in which many people disguised in various costumes mingle together, from which innumerable offences against the divine majesty and the most serious improprieties have ensued, because these bayles [balls] are not suited to the temperament and modesty of the Spanish nation; I order that no person, citizen, resident, dweller, or inhabitant in this court of whatever station, rank, or class may have or admit into

his home, under the pretext of Carnival or of a formal social gathering, any people for the purpose of amusing themselves by dancing with masks or without them.

Wow, that's pretty harsh! He also imposed a fine and additional penalties, based on the offender's rank. This same edict was reissued in 1745 as part of a crackdown on crime, and ordered that masks not be worn at all, even at Carnival. Not long after, however, there seems to have been a change of heart, and government-sanctioned masquerade balls began to take place.

Anti-masquerade sentiment continued in certain circles, especially among those who believed in more strictly controlling people's fun. England for example, had a love/hate relationship with masked gatherings. As an island nation still proud of its relative isolation, many saw the whole thing as an insidious foreign plot to undermine all that was good and English. In 1718, one journalist complained that such dances were brought in from "hot Countries (notorious for Lewdness)," while novelist Henry Fielding (1707–1754) wrote that "bad Habits are infectious by Example, as the Plague itself by Contact," implying that the masquerade was an evil contagion. Fielding wrote a satirical poem, "The Masquerade," in 1728, describing the colorful array (let's be honest, probably a bit exaggerated) of costumed characters that one might see in a night's revelry:

So here, in one Confusion hurl'd,
Seem all the Nations of the World:
Cardinals, Quakers, Judges dance;
Grim Turks are coy, and Nuns advance.
Grave Churchmen here, at Hazard play;
Cinque-Ace ten Pound—done, Quater-tray.
Known Prudes there, Libertines we find,
Who masque the Face, t'unmasque the Mind.
Here, Running Footmen guzzle Tea;
There, Milkmaids Flasks of Burgundy.

But there was another side to it all, beyond the fun of seeing faux-Quakers kicking up their heels, coy Turks trotting, and pseudo-nuns indulging in bad habits:

> I saw two Shepherdesses dr-nk,
> And heard a Friar call'd a P-nk.
> Lost in Amazement, as I stood,
> A Lady in a Velvet Hood,
> (Her Mein St James's seem'd t'explain,
> But her Assurance—Drury-Lane,
> Not Hercules was ever bolder,)
> Came up and slapp'd me on the Shoulder.

In those days, a "punk" was a slang word for "whore," hence why the word is partially blocked out. These lines refer to masquerade balls being the perfect places to arrange visits with courtesans and prostitutes. Fielding goes on to describe how the Master of Revels, John James Heidegger (1666–1749) was to blame for putting on these suspect spectacles with royal approval:

> So, for's Ugliness more fell,
> Critical Apparatus
> Was H—d—g–r toss'd out of Hell.
> And, in Return, by *Satan* made,
> First Minister of's Masquerade.

You might have guessed that Satan had nothing to do with Heidegger's position; it was actually King George II who had given him the title, so this was a pretty bold attack on the monarch. Fielding was one of several English writers to include masquerades in their poems and novels as a means of social commentary and to teach moral lessons.

In Portugal, anti-masquerade campaigners even used the tragedy of the Lisbon earthquake in 1755, which devastated the city, as a sign of divine wrath against all manner of earthly sins. Near the top of that list, of course, were the vice-ridden masquerade balls that defied holy authority.

Whatever the opinion of costumed dances, by either humans or gods, such affairs could indeed be the scenes of much crime and skullduggery. In the case of Gustav III, King of Sweden (1746–1792), one masked dance was fatal. Gustav was something of an enlightened despot, consolidating royal power and curtailing press freedom, while at the same time lavishly supporting the arts, initiating social reforms, curtailing torture and executions, and legalizing the presence of Catholicism and Judaism in Sweden. He was also a strong supporter of Louis XVI, and encouraged a counter-revolutionary uprising to restore the French monarch to his throne. Needless to say, with this many contradictory positions, he made a lot of enemies, and one fateful night at a masquerade ball held at Stockholm's Royal Opera House on March 16, 1792, he met his end. Well, almost.

The king had been warned in a letter to postpone the event, given the rumors of assassins plotting their deadly task:

> They [his would-be murderers] are mighty upset to see this not happening at the last masquerade but they rejoice at the tidings of seeing that there will be a new one today. Bandits do not like lanterns; there is nothing more serviceable for an assassination than darkness and disguise.

He gave the missive no heed, having seen such threats before. But this warning was right. The chance to use masks as a way to infiltrate the ball undetected was an almost perfect cover. The conspirators found the king, who, despite his mask, wore the royal regalia on his costume. After greeting the king, one Jacob Johan Anckarström, a military commander, moved behind him, drew a pistol, and shot him in the back. Anckarström was soon arrested and he confessed. He was executed a little over a month later in a terrible manner: he was thrown into irons and flogged in public, had his right hand cut off, then his head, and then his remains were quartered. So much for Gustav's new leniency on capital punishment.

The king survived the initial shot and lived for thirteen more days, before succumbing to an infection from the wound. Curiously, a few years before, in 1786, a fortune teller named Ulrica Arfvidsson (1734–1801) had warned him to beware of a man in a mask. Though she said this man also would have a sword, her prediction was remembered at the time of the assassination. She was later questioned and offered to help in the investigation. The composer Giuseppe Verdi (1813–1901) composed an opera, *Gustavo III*, based on the story, but the censors didn't like the idea of a monarch being murdered on stage, so after several revisions and title changes, it became known as *Un ballo in maschera*, and was set in Boston in the eighteenth century; murder in the New World was apparently just dandy with said censors.

Speaking of Boston, the city outlawed masquerade balls in 1809 for the very reason that they were seen as lewd and open invitations to vice, prostitution, and general immorality. While Puritanism had run its course in the city and the region, some old habits die hard. As late as 1849, the law was renewed with even more force. After a tangled legal word salad in the first half, it lays down some severe penalties:

> Any person who shall get up and set on foot, or cause to be published, or otherwise aid in getting up and promoting any masked ball, or other public assembly, at which the company wears masks, or other disguises, and to which admission is obtained upon payment of money, or the delivery of any valuable thing, or by any ticket or voucher obtained for money, or any valuable thing, shall be punished by a fine not exceeding five hundred dollars; and for repetition of the offence, by imprisonment in the common jail or house of correction, not exceeding one year.

This law, incidentally, was not repealed until 1963, perhaps appropriately enough, on April Fool's Day.

SALOME: HISTORY'S MOST WICKED DANCER?

Salome is the infamous dancer known around the world as the one who asked that John the Baptist's head be brought to her on a silver platter; she is, for many, a symbol of temptation and evil. But what is the real story? Did she demand a man's head? Did she even exist?

In the Gospels of both Mark and Matthew, she is never named. Josephus' *Jewish Antiquities* identifies her as the daughter of Herodias, but never mentions her dancing or being involved in John's death. Josephus' brief biography of her is unremarkable, only saying that she eventually married the king of Armenia and had three children; not exactly the devilish temptress of later accounts. In any case, there is a lot of confusion about her actual age and if this marriage was even possible, or if stories were confusing two different girls, and so on. Further, some scholars say, the idea of a Jewish girl dancing solo in front of men—even a princess whose family had adopted some Greek customs—would have been unthinkable and simply wouldn't have happened.

The story that eventually emerged is well-known: when King Herod throws himself a birthday party, complete with a banquet for his high officials, Salome dances. Her age is not mentioned, and some have suggested that she was still quite young. Her dance so "pleased" King Herod that he told the girl, "Ask me for anything you want, and I'll give it to you." The girl consulted with her mother, who held a grudge against a certain prophet known for blessing people whilst holding them under water. Her mother then said, "Ask for the head of John the Baptist." And the dutiful Salome turned to the king and made her request. Poor Herod, who had given his oath that he would truly give her anything she requested, up to half his kingdom, complied. He didn't want to break his promise to the girl in front of his esteemed guests. So, John was beheaded in prison, and his head presented to Salome and her mother on a silver charger.

If this story is mostly mythic, where might such a grisly account of a wicked dancer and her mother have come from? Well, there was a popular

Roman story about a consul named Lucius Flamininus (died 170 BCE), who in 184 BCE, was expelled from Rome for having a prisoner executed to impress his young male lover, one Phillipus the Carthaginian. The youth had never seen gladiators die, or any men for that matter. Lucius, eager to please his companion, ordered a condemned Celtic man to be brought forth and ran him through with his sword, which delighted his lover very much; it might have been time for some relationship counseling.

This tale circulated and morphed, and in some versions, the young lover was a woman, possibly to make the story more respectable to conservative audiences. In fact, an early report from the senator Cato the Elder (234–149 BCE) specifically stated that Lucius' lover was a woman; Cato was the one who actually expelled Lucius, so he would have known, but he also accused Lucius of being a pedophile, so there was that connection. Later, Seneca (4 BCE–65 CE), who unsuccessfully navigated being in the service of Nero (the mad emperor ordered him to commit suicide, after all), retold a version where a young mistress seduced Lucius by dancing, and he was so enamored that he offered her the head of a man who had offended her. This is starting to sound very familiar . . .

A Christianized version that put the horror of John's death squarely on two Jewish women became the official version as the first century wore on. These writers successfully absolved the Romans of guilt in the whole affair, just as they had with Pontius Pilate washing his hands of the crucifixion of Jesus, placing the blame instead on the Jews. This was useful when going out to preach to Romans; it was a new spin on a tale they already knew and didn't portray them in a bad light. The fact that John's murderers were also women and at least one of them was a dancer only made it more useful as a morality tale.

Interest in Salome as a figure of wickedness only really came into its own in the fourth century, not coincidentally at the same time that there was a growing cult of veneration for John. Salome was identified with the lineage of Eve and the increasingly common idea that women continued to be the downfall of men, just as Eve had been. The fact that Salome was a

dancer allowed overly pious writers to conflate her with the pagan practices that they abhorred: Dionysian rites, Bacchanals, and other such lustful and sin-filled celebrations. Saint Ambrose (ca. 340–397) expressed
these early opinions clearly in his rather suspiciously titled work, *Concerning Virgins*:

> There ought then to be the joy of the mind, conscious of right, not
> excited by unrestrained feasts, or nuptial concerts, for in such modesty
> is not safe, and temptation may be suspected where excessive dancing
> accompanies festivities. I desire that the virgins of God should be far
> from this. For as a certain teacher of this world has said: "No one
> dances when sober unless he is mad." Now if, according to the wisdom
> of this world, either drunkenness or madness is the cause of dancing,
> what a warning is given to us amongst the instances mentioned in the
> Divine Scriptures, where John, the forerunner of Christ, being
> beheaded at the wish of a dancer, is an instance that the allurements of
> dancing did more harm than the madness of sacrilegious anger.

Cue hundreds of years of gnarly paintings of beautiful women holding trays
with the heads of dead bearded men. From about the year 1000 onward,
religious images of Salome abounded, often showing her as being very acrobatic; one reason for this may have been the rising popularity of minstrels
and tumblers in court entertainments, something that many grumpy
church elders didn't like. By bringing out art associating such funambulists
with the most evil dancer in history, the church was making a not-very-sub-
tle statement of its opinion about these new entertainments and where they
would lead. Also, you kids keep the noise down and get off my lawn.

By the twelfth and thirteenth centuries, Salome's reputation as a lustful
woman who not only had desired John but also demanded his death after
he rejected her was firmly established, and no one would hear otherwise.
Artwork began to portray her dancing as more sensual and seductive, rather
than merely gymnastic.

Of course, sinful Salome had to meet an appropriate end, and a particularly creative and grisly death was circulated in Europe well into the Middle Ages and beyond. The Italian chronicler Jacobus da Varagine (ca. 1230–1298) wrote in his *Golden Legend* (a collection of saint's biographies in 1260) that Salome once needed to cross a frozen river and it was then that God took his revenge. She broke through the ice and fell in, so that only her head was exposed:

> This made her dance and wriggle about with all the lower parts of her body, not on land, but in the water. Her wicked head was glazed with ice, and at length severed from her body by the sharp edges, not of iron, but of frozen water. Thus in the very ice she displayed the dance of death, and furnished a spectacle to all who beheld it, which brought to mind what she had done.

This kind of poetic justice was very popular in medieval stories, where the punishment fit the crime. Salome was not only forced to "dance" to try to free herself, she failed and eventually lost her head in the struggle. Further, her death happened in a river, the very same place that John would have baptized those who repented. Other versions of her death involved her dancing with demons, who ended up dragging her down to hell. She was sometimes lumped in with witches and other supposed followers of Satan and called their queen or even labeled as a fairy, showing how different legends and myths could cross-pollinate in the minds of creative believers.

Her popularity as an object of scorn waned somewhat after the Renaissance, but she was never forgotten. In the nineteenth century, she would once again become an object of fascination, dread, fear, and outrage. Salome's sensual presence in drama, opera, and popular fascination would raise more than a few eyebrows and provoke quite a bit of righteous indignation, as she was reclaimed as a symbol of women's independence and a warning to the men who crossed her. No doubt the church fathers would have been horrified.

SALOMANIA: OPERA, THEATER, STRIPTEASES, PARTIES, AND WAX HEADS ON PLATES

While Salome has been dancing through time since her casual mention in the New Testament, much to the chagrin of certain medieval men, she scandalized no one as much as she did the late Victorians and citizens of "proper" *fin-de-siècle* society.

By the mid-nineteenth century, French writers had already transformed Salome into a seductress, and audiences were hungry for more. In 1850, Gustave Flaubert had written about his encounter with the Egyptian dancing girl Kutchek Hanem (See the "Little Egypt" entry), who was the inspiration for the hero of his novel *Salammbô*. In 1877 he wrote "Herodias," a short story about Salome, which of course goes into detail about her dance:

> Opening wide her legs, without bending her knees, she bowed so low that her chin brushed the floor; and the nomads accustomed to abstinence, the Roman soldiers skilled in debauchery, the avaricious publicans, the old priests soured with controversy, all with flaring nostrils shivered with lust.

Gustave (apparently Gustaves had a thing for Salome) Moreau painted several incarnations of the dancer, which when put on exhibit in Paris, attracted over half a million spectators. By the end of the nineteenth century, nearly every poet or painter from England to Poland had interpreted her in some way; by 1912, at least 2,700 poems had been written about her. Stephane Mallarmé's Symbolist and lyrical drama *Hérodiade* (1869) also made a lasting impression on Wilde's own interpretation of the tale. Notably, however, Mallarmé's dancer refuses to give into her desires, while Wilde's is, well, a bit more wild and wily. Indeed, most of the earlier dramatic retellings of the story show Herodias as the villain with Salome playing the role of her dutiful and innocent pawn.

If that were not enough, her story became even more twisted when Oscar Wilde (1854–1900) got a hold of it in 1892. Rehearsals for Wilde's *Salomé* were well underway in London, featuring the tantalizing actress Sarah Bernhardt, until the Lord Chamberlain's licensor of plays reviewed the work. He banned the play, citing that it was illegal to depict Biblical characters on stage. So, Wilde and his crew picked up and moved to Paris, where it premiered in February 1896 at the at the Théâtre de L'Œuvre. The original version was in French, after all, translated by Wilde's lover Lord Alfred Douglas. And the French, with their more liberal attitudes toward sexuality and their already existing obsession with Salome, were happy to welcome this Wilde production to Paris.

Never one to shy away from controversy, Wilde elaborated on the girl's story, making her into a perverse temptress. In his play, Salome is obsessed with John the Baptist, referred to as Jokanaan. She is "amorous of his body" and implores him to let her kiss his mouth at least a dozen times. Jokanaan curses the girl, calling her a "Daughter of Babylon" and a "Daughter of Sodom," but this only stokes her desires further. King Herod, of course, is also enamored of the girl, and it is for this reason that he asks her to dance for him. It is in her dancing that the story deviates from its Biblical roots and becomes a lasting archetype of the *femme fatale*.

Earlier depictions of Salome's dance (such as those from the Middle Ages and Renaissance) show her doing acrobatic movements such as somersaults and backbends. But Wilde's vision of Salome's dance was far more suggestive, not for how he describes the dance, but for what he doesn't say. He conveniently left out the details. Her famous dance is noted in the play only as, "Salome dances the dance of the seven veils." No stage direction. No choreography notes. Not even "Dance of the Seven Veils" in title capital letters. It's likely that Wilde drew his inspiration from the myth of the Sumerian goddess Inanna, who shed her seven articles of clothing while passing through the seven gates of the Underworld, leaving her naked and powerless when she arrives. All of which, of course, must mean that she performs a striptease, right? Of course it does.

The king is so pleased by Salome's dance, that he promises her anything she desires. The dancing girl demands not riches or titles, but the head of the ill-fated prophet. And when Salome finally gets John's head on a platter, she gives a dramatic monologue, promising to finally kiss the now-dead man's mouth, and "bite it with my teeth as one bites a ripe fruit." There's no accounting for taste, is there?

And like many temptresses of the late nineteenth century, she is killed, Herod's soldiers crushing her beneath their shields. Death is a common punishment for sexually liberated fictional women of the late nineteenth and early twentieth century. In another example, Zobeide, the main character of the Ballets Russes' Orientalist ballet *Schéhérazade*, meets a similar fate for lusting after the Golden Slave.

Some have argued that both Salome and Zobeide reflected men's fears that lustful and powerful women might eventually cut off their "heads." Make of that double meaning what you will. Indeed, for a generation of women chafing against their corsets, fighting for the right to divorce, own property, and vote, cutting off a man's "head" may well have piqued their curiosity and fed their obsession with the idea of the "exotic" dancing girl, particularly one from the "forbidden" Middle East. For them, Salome became a symbol of feminine power, a beacon of both chaste virginity and bodily liberation. Scholars have argued that her Jewishness also fed into the anti-Semitic attitudes that circulated at the time.

As so often happens with powerful women, Salome's stage appearances were frequently thwarted by powerful, rich men. Composer Richard Strauss (1864–1949) adapted the Wilde play in 1905 into an equally, if not more, scandalous opera. When it was scheduled to be performed in Italy, the Pope attempted to ban it, only to acquiesce at the last minute. When it came to Berlin, Kaiser Wilhelm insisted on placing a Star of Bethlehem in the set's night sky, as though that would mollify the production's lasciviousness. In 1907, the Metropolitan Opera in New York performed Strauss' *Salome* only once before its financial backers—J. P. Morgan (at the urging of his daughter) and W. K. Vanderbilt to name a few—prevented it from playing again.

They were so offended and outraged by the Dance of the Seven Veils and the decapitated head that they considered it to be too vulgar for such a vaulted institution as the opera. So, the character of Salome headed to vaudeville (viewed as a much more lowbrow form of entertainment), where she was copied many times before the craze died out only two years later.

Regardless of the popularity of the play, *Salomé*'s debut in Paris kicked off a short-lived, but influential obsession with the dancing girl, now known as Salomania. American dancer Maud Allan (see chapter 8 in act I) became the most popular Salome dancer, with her melodramatic and scantily-clad interpretation, complete with a realistic head of John the Baptist (see the photo in the insert). The "Salome" skit in Frolich Ziegfeld's first production, *The Follies of 1907*, at the New York Theatre, was the show's most successful act. So much so, that Mademoiselle Dazié, who played Salome, opened a school for Salomes on the theater's roof, where every morning, she would spend two hours teaching aspiring dancing girls how to undulate and wiggle. By October 1908, there were twenty-four Salomes performing in New York alone, blazing the trail for the great striptease stars only a few decades later.

Somewhat ironically, it was mostly women who protested and railed against this plague of Salomes taking over the Eastern United States. Julia Ward Howe (who wrote "The Battle Hymn of the Republic") wrote that Oriental dancing was "simply horrid, no touch of grace about it, only the most deforming movement of the whole abdominal and lumbar region." Actress Marie Cahill called on President Theodore Roosevelt to denounce the "Salome Craze," which she said was "an excuse for the most vulgar exhibition that this country has ever been called on to tolerate."

A *New York Times* writer joked that Salomania had been breaking out amongst chorus girls at the New Amsterdam Theater, and that at the moment she displayed symptoms of the "disease" that she be immediately "enveloped in a fur coat—the most efficacious safeguard known against the Salome dance—and hurriedly isolated." American newspapers capitalized on the Salome obsession with sensational headlines: "Now the Daring

Salome Dance Rages through the World Like an Epidemic," in *The Sun* in Baltimore, and "The Salome Pestilence," in the *New York Times.*

Meanwhile in Europe, upper-class women held "Salome Parties" in which they would dress up in pearls, jewels, and silks. They would hire photographers, so that they could be immortalized in their costumes on the new-fangled medium of film. They would also produce their own all-female theatricals to imitate Maud Allan's version of the dangerous dancing dame. These women would enact their own Salome fantasies, holding silver platters, complete with wax heads. Though these were popular affairs, we don't have an actual headcount for attendance . . . see what we did there?

Ultimately, the British censors didn't get over their revulsion of Salome's dance until decades later. The first public performance of Wilde's *Salomé* in Great Britain wasn't until 1931; private showings for discriminating audiences had, of course, been going on for decades.

Ironically, the Hebrew root of Salome's name simply means "peace."

the grand reverence

and so the ball comes to a close and the well-to-do say their goodnights and head off home (hopefully without catching their clothes on fire or getting hit by automobiles). Or, if you prefer, the ballet dancers take their curtain call, having survived another performance (also without going up in flames), or seeing the audience erupt into a riot. The choreomaniacs have slipped into exhausted slumber (for now), the tarantatas have excised the venom from their systems, the dancing duels are resolved (without bloodshed, we hope), the fairies will soon emerge to dance in the moonlight and tempt unwary mortals into their realm, and the skulls of the damned are forever bouncing around on a mountaintop somewhere in Scandinavia . . . actually, dancing seems really odd when you look at it like this!

The urge to move in rhythm to some kind of beat seems to be as human as the urges to eat, laugh, make music, and procreate; suffice to say it's pretty powerful and comes in so many varieties all over the planet that one simply can't take them all in. This little book has opened a window into the realm of the bizarre, but many more stories undoubtedly remain to be told, especially from other parts of the earth. The world of dance is as endlessly fascinating, unusual, funny, and horrific as anything we might imagine, as these strange stories have shown. People will continue to dance, and strange stories will continue to accumulate, because wherever humans are, weirdness seems to follow.

We'll leave you with the words of Voltaire, that great philosopher and polymath, who had this to say about the pleasures of movement and reading, which makes it a perfect summary of our book: "Let us read and let us dance; these two amusements will never do any harm to the world."

If only he'd known . . .

Suggestions for Further Reading

So, where to go from here? Dance is, of course, an art that must be seen, whether live or on video, but there is also a lot of enjoyment in reading more about it: its history, its structures, theory, and so on. Here is a small list that will help you continue your journey into the fascinating world of dancing and all of the joys and horrors that go with it:

ONLINE RESOURCES

There are thousands and thousands of dance sites, blogs, and pages on every dance topic that you can imagine (and some that you can't . . . we've seen them). Here is just a very tiny selection of recommended sites to explore further.

Dance. A site with a simple name is just that: a collection of articles about what's going on in the world of dance, all dance, any dance. (www.dance.com)

Gaynor Minden. The website for the famous pointe shoe company, but it has so much more. Poke around a bit on the menu at the top (especially the "Balletopedia" tab) and you'll find a number of resources for ballet and modern dance history. A great place to browse and learn more about all kinds of things. (www.dancer.com)

Contemporary Dance. If you're interested in modern dance, this is the site for you! History, theory, essays, a global directory of schools and companies . . . the list is seemingly endless. Spend an hour or ten browsing here and learn everything you ever wanted to know and more. (www.contemporary-dance.org)

As always, Wikipedia can be a good point of entry, as long as one bears in mind that the information can be inaccurate or out of date. Individual pages often have good bibliography suggestions (books and other sites), so it can be used as a place to spring lightly into other, more verifiable pages, articles, and books.

BOOKS

These selections will provide you with many days and months of fascinating reading, looking behind the scenes to reveal the thrill of dancing victories and the agony of the feet:

Mindy Aloff, *Dance Anecdotes: Stories from the Worlds of Ballet, Broadway, the Ballroom, and Modern Dance* (Oxford: Oxford University Press, 2006). An excellent collection of stories of all kinds, from the serious to the gruesome to the ridiculous. Filled with primary sources from Ancient Greece to the modern world.

Elizabeth Wayland Barber, *The Dancing Goddesses: Folklore, Archeology, and the Origins of European Dance* (New York: W.W. Norton, 2013). A fascinating read that looks at the history of dance and folklore as intertwined subjects (particularly in Eastern Europe), and traces the origins of these customs back to Greek and Roman times.

Jennifer Homans, *Apollo's Angels: A History of Ballet* (New York: Random House, 2010). A one-volume history of ballet that will set the standard for years to come. Lengthy, but well worth delving into if you want a readable and comprehensive study.

Deirdre Kelly, *Ballerina: Sex, Scandal, and Suffering behind the Symbol of Perfection* (Vancouver, Greystone Books, 2012). As the title states, a history of the troubled lives of some of the most celebrated ballerinas from the seventeenth to the nineteenth centuries.

Abigail Keyes, *The Salimpour School of Belly Dance Compendium, Volume 1* (Berkeley, CA: Salimpour School, 2014). Don't let the unwieldy name fool you. The first third of this book outlines the life of Sicilian-American belly dance innovator Jamila Salimpour, and the second gives a comprehensive and readable overview of belly dance—including the stories of Little Egypt and Salome—both in the Middle East and North America.

Mark Knowles, *The Wicked Waltz and Other Scandalous Dances: Outrage at Couple Dancing in the 19th and Early 20th Centuries* (Jefferson, NC: McFarland, 2009). A splendid tour of the scandal of—gasp—partner dancing in the early days of the waltz and its cousins. The condemnations came fast and furious, but the waltz would not go away!

Parmenia Migel, *The Ballerinas* (New York: Da Capo Press, 1972). A simple title which is exactly that: a survey in short biographies of some of the major dancers from the time of Louis XIV up through the beginning of the twentieth century.

John Waller, *A Time to Dance, a Time to Die: The Extraordinary Story of the Dancing Plague of 1518* (Cambridge, UK: Icon Books, 2008). This is an excellent introduction to the great Strasbourg dancing plague, as well as bits and pieces about the plagues that came before it. The book goes into much fascinating detail, but is a quick, exciting read.

acknowledgments

This third tiptoe through the history of the bizarre, amusing, and troubling in the history of the arts has been a new experience, with Tim joining forces with Abigail to produce a hybrid monster the likes of which neither of them could have imagined. Reading and editing each other's contributions was both thrilling and mildly disturbing.

Thanks are due to Caroline Russomanno, who (lindy?) hopped aboard as editor to oversee the weirdness, and to Skyhorse for continuing to subject the reading public to these unsettling, if oddly charming, studies of everything that went wrong in artistic circles over the centuries. Thanks also to Maryann Karinch, Tim's wonderful agent, who continues to believe that these quirky projects deserve a home.

Also, Abby and Tim fully acknowledge that the task of keeping their little house tigers occupied so they can actually get writing and editing done (to say nothing of brainstorming new and increasingly bad jokes) is an ongoing process.

about the authors

TIM RAYBORN doesn't dance. Well, he's given it a go on several occasions, in styles ranging from English country dance, to ceilidh, to salsa, to Balkan line dance, to Victorian ballroom styles, but ultimately, it's probably better for him and everyone else if he just sticks to writing and making music. You're welcome. Still, he has a great love for historical dance music (especially medieval, Renaissance, and various folk genres) and the art of dance in general, inextricably intertwined as it is with music and drama.

Tim has a PhD from the University of Leeds in England, the topic of which (medieval studies) has nothing to do with dancing, but it does allow him to exert an authoritative air on some subjects; or not. He has been lucky enough to perform early music and traditional music all over the world: the United States and Canada, much of Europe, and Australia, as well as in amazing places like Marrakech and Istanbul, though he never did much dancing in said locations, and it's probably just as well. These days, he writes, cooks, makes music, enjoys good wines, and tries to avoid being distracted by cats, which is a losing battle.

For more information, and a bit more humor, visit: www.timrayborn.com.

ABIGAIL KEYES does dance. A lot. She specializes in Middle Eastern dance styles, and is something of an esteemed scholar of Middle Eastern history, culture, and language, having studied all of these at Princeton University. In her previous life, she also worked as a writer and analyst for the

United States government, which didn't involve dancing. She could tell you what she did, but then she'd have to kill you.

Abigail also has an MA in Dance from Mills College in Oakland, CA, and so knows a good deal more about the topic than Tim. She actually *has* danced and taught dance workshops all over the world: North America, South America, Australia, Europe, and Japan. She is a dance instructor for the Salimpour School in Berkeley, CA, a professional writer, happily consumes Tim's cooking, also enjoys good wines, and discovers daily that everything is covered in cat hair.

For more information of all kinds, visit: www.akeyesdance.com.